*Rigging
Period Ship Models*

RIGGING
PERIOD SHIP MODELS

LENNARTH PETERSSON

Acknowledgements

It is my intention to limit this book to the classification of the rigging of *Melampus* and no mention is made of the numerous alternative aspects of square rig to be found during the eighteenth century; this work describes the rigging of a specific period and one specific model. I hope the perspective drawings will help towards an understanding of the use of standing and running rigging for modellers and for all with an interest in square rig.

I would like to thank Captain Olof Pipping; my good friend Vernon Gidman; Mr Alan King, curator of the Bristol Industrial Museum; my family and parents for patience and support; and Julian Mannering, editor at Seaforth Publishing, for help and advice. Beyond that, I take all the blame.

Copyright © Lennarth Petersson 2000
This edition published in Great Britain in 2011 by
Seaforth Publishing,
Pen & Sword Books Ltd,
47 Church Street,
Barnsley S70 2AS

Reprinted 2014, 2016, 2018, 2021, 2023, 2025

www.seaforthpublishing.com

First published in 2000 by Chatham Publishing

British Library Cataloguing in Publication Data
A catalogue record for this book is available from the British Library

ISBN 978 1 84832 102 1

All rights reserved. No part of this book may be reproduced, transmitted, downloaded, decompiled or reverse engineered in any form or by any means, electronic or mechanical including photocopying, recording or by any information storage and retrieval system, without permission from the Publisher in writing. NO AI TRAINING: Without in any way limiting the Author's and Publisher's exclusive rights under copyright, any use of this publication to "train" generative artificial intelligence (AI) technologies to generate text is expressly prohibited. The Author and Publisher reserve all rights to license uses of this work for generative AI training and development of machine learning language models.

The right of Lennarth Petersson to be identified as the author of this work has been asserted by him in accordance with the Copyright, Designs and Patents Act 1988.

The Publisher's authorised representative in the EU for product safety is Authorised Rep Compliance Ltd., Ground Floor, 71 Lower Baggot Street, Dublin D02 P593, Ireland. www.arccompliance.com

Contents

Introduction	1
Fore Channels & Dead-Eyes	2
Main Channels & Ratlines	3
Mizzen Channels	4
Fore Shrouds	5
Main & Mizzen Shrouds	6
Fore Topmast Shrouds	7
Mizzen Backstays	8
Main Backstays	9
Fore Backstays & Shrouds	10
Fore Backstay, Topmast & Topgallant Shrouds	11
Stays (overall view)	12
Mizzen Stay	13
Main Stay & Preventer Stay	14
Fore Stay & Preventer Stay	15
Mizzen Topmast Stay & Topgallant Stay	16
Main Topmast Stay, Preventer Stay, Topgallant and Royal Stay	17
Fore Topmast & Preventer Stay	18
Jibstay, Fore Topgallant, Flying Jib & Royal Stay	19
Bobstay, Bowsprit Shrouds	20
Jibstay & Martingale Stays	21
Cross Jack Truss Pendant	22
Cross Jack Sling	23
Cross Jack Lift	24
Spanker Boom Sheet & Guy Pendants	25
Boom Topping Lift	26
Vangs	27
Peak Halliard	28
Throat Halliard	29
Mizzen Tyes: Topsail, Topgallant & Royal Yard	30
Mizzen Lifts: Topsail & Topgallant	31
Cross Jack Braces	32
Mizzen Topsail & Topgallant Braces	33
Fore & Main Sling	34
Fore & Main Jeers	35
Truss Pendants & Nave Line	36
Main Lift	37
Fore Lift	38
Main Topsail Yard Tye & Halliard	39
Fore Topsail Yard Tye & Halliard	40
Fore Topgallant/Royal Tye & Halliard	41
Fore Topsail, Topgallant & Royal Lifts	42
Main & Main Topsail Braces	43
Fore & Fore Topsail Braces	44
Fore & Main Topgallant Braces	45
Fore & Main Royal Braces	46
Spritsail & Spritsail Topsail Braces	47
Fore Sheet, Tack & Clueline	48
Fore Topsail Sheet & Clueline	49
Fore Topgallant & Royal Sheet, Fore Topgallant Clueline	50
Main Sheet, Clueline & Tack	51
Main Topsail Sheet	52
Main Topsail Lift (Topgallant & Royal Lifts)	53
Main Topsail Clueline	54
Main Topgallant Sheet & Clueline, Main Royal Sheet	55
Mizzen Topsail Sheet & Clueline	56
Mizzen Topgallant Sheet & Clueline, Mizzen Royal Sheet	57
Jibboom & Flying Jibboom Guys	58
Spritsail Sling, Spritsail Yard & Spritsail Topsail Yard Halliards	59
Royal Stay	60
Fore Topgallant Stay & Bumpkin Shrouds	61
Jib Outhaul	62
Flying Jib Outhaul	63
Spritsail Lift, Spritsail Topsail Clueline & Sheet	64
Spritsail Clueline & Sheet Spritsail Topsail Lift	65
Fore Topsail Reef Tackle	66
Main Topsail Reef Tackle	67
Mizzen Topsail Reef Tackle	68
Spritsail Buntlines	69
Fore Course Buntlines & Leechlines	70
Fore Topsail Buntlines	71
Main Course Buntlines & Leechlines	72
Main Topsail Buntlines	73
Mizzen Topsail Buntlines	74
Fore Course & Topsail Bowlines	75
Fore Topgallant Bowlines	76
Main Course & Topsail Bowlines	77
Main Topgallant Bowlines	78
Mizzen Topsail & Topgallant Bowlines	79
Mizzen Mast Square Sails	80
Spanker	81
Mainmast Square Sails	82
Fore Mast Square Sails	83
Yard Tackle & Tricing Lines	84
Yards	85
Main Yard with Stunsail Boom & Stunsail Boom Irons	86
Fore Staysail	87
Main Staysail	88
Mizzen Staysail	89
Fore Topmast Staysail Stay	90
Fore Topmast Staysail	91
Fore Topmast Staysail	92
Main Topmast Staysail	93
Mizzen Topmast Staysail	94
Main Topgallant Staysail	95
Jib	96
Flying Jib	97
Belaying plans	98
Cross-section	102
External Hull	104
Square Sails	106
All Fore and Aft Sails	107
Studding Sails	108
Quarter Deck	111
The Bow	112
The Stern	113
Waist & Forecastle	114
Index	116

Introduction

I SET OUT TO CREATE this series of detailed drawings because, as a modelmaker, I needed the answers to a number of questions relating to the intricacies of square rig. I could find no publication which allowed me to study a ship's rigging in the way that one can, for example, in front of a model in a museum. And even then, of course, the sheer complexity is confusing and difficult to grasp. Most modelling books, while dealing extensively with hull construction, often approach rigging in a rather cursory fashion. The genesis of this book was, therefore, the desire to fill that gap. I decided to study and depict each item of a ship's rigging on its own, isolated on a page, so that the reader might understand where a particular sheet or halliard, for example, leads and how it functions.

One of the pleasures of researching and putting together all these drawings was the realisation of how logical and functional the rigging of a square-rigged ship is. This really should not have come as a surprise. Sailors are nothing if not practical, and the apparently complicated confection of ropes and tackles is, in fact, a wonderfully simple and ordered creation with no unnecessary or redundant parts. My intention in the book is to show this simplicity and, at the same time, draw to the reader's attention the basic principles by which square-rig functions; throughout the centuries, square-rigged ships have followed the same principles when it has come to catching the wind.

Though these principles have remained the same I felt it important, both for the sake of accuracy and for the benefit of modellers, to draw from a contemporary model, and I decided on an English frigate which should have retained most of its original rigging. By going to a three-dimensional source I hoped to be able to depict the intricate details in the clearest possible manner, and by choosing a contemporary model create a scheme which was authentic. With the help of the publisher I found a suitable model, with much of its original rigging intact, in the Bristol Industrial Museum. It is a beautiful model of the *Melampus*, a 36-gun, 18-pounder frigate. It was donated to the museum in 1844 and while it has received the attention of restorers over the years its rigging is considered a reliable representation. I photographed and sketched the model from every angle and the results of the exercise were the source for the drawings in this book.

Melampus seemed a suitable choice not just because of her authenticity but also because of her relatively small size and her long and quite distinguished career. All modelmakers, I'm sure, feel happier working on the model of a prototype which distinguished herself and *Melampus* had a long career during one of the most turbulent periods of the Royal Navy's history.

She is one of four models of ships which were built by the Bristol yard of James Martin Hillhouse and is assumed to have been commissioned by the builders. The ship herself was launched in 1785 and was one of the biggest frigates of her day. She was one of the first of a new generation of 18-pounder frigates and carried 36 guns rather than the 38 of similarly sized vessels and, subsequently, had more space on her gundeck and performed well at sea. Her reputation spread soon enough and she was coveted as a command by, among others, Prince William Henry – later William IV

During her thirty years of service in the Royal Navy she took part in a number of actions. In 1794, for instance, she was with the *Arethusa* and two other frigates in Warren's action against Desgarceaux's squadron, which ended in the capture of three French frigates. Under the command of Sir Richard Strachan, *Melampus*, along with four other frigates, chased a French convoy into Carteret Bay where every ship bar one was destroyed by the ships' boats. Three years later, in 1798, under the command of Captain Moore, she was involved in the interception of the Brest fleet off Ireland and captured the *Bellone*, a 44-gun frigate. Two days later she took another frigate, the *Resolue* 36. She was later, in 1807, to experience the fall-out of the *Leopard-Chesapeake* action when two-hundred of her water-casks were burnt by the enraged inhabitants of Norfolk, Virginia. In 1811 she captured the slaver *Fortune* and brought her back to Plymouth, and, finally, in 1815, she was sold off to the Dutch navy. Despite being thirty years old, she continued to serve for another decade.

I hope this book will make the task of rigging easier for modelmakers at all levels. Certainly, researching and drawing out the illustrations answered a lot of questions for me. There are other works which any modelmaker needs to refer to and which have been stalwart guides for me. Foremost are James Lee's *The Masting and Rigging of English Ships of War 1625-1860*, and C N Longridge's *The Anatomy of Nelson's Ships*. Any modeller's book shelf also requires *The Ashley Book of Knots*.

Finally, the journal *Seaways* and *The Nautical Research Journal*, from Nautical Research Guild in the US, have been useful guides for me.

LENNARTH PETERSSON
Habo, Sweden, 2000

Fore Channels & Dead-Eyes

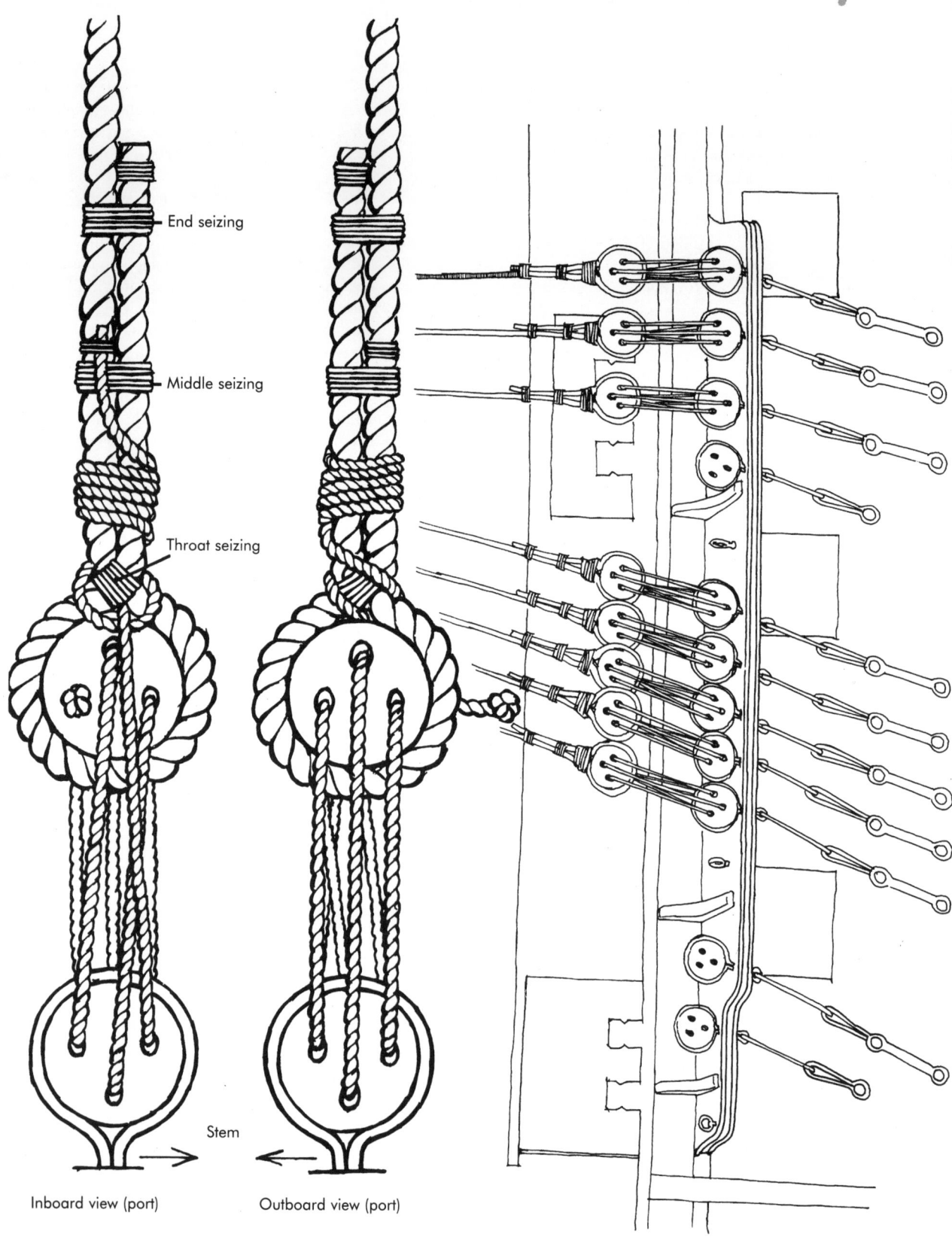

Inboard view (port)

Outboard view (port)

End seizing

Middle seizing

Throat seizing

Stem

2

Main Channels & Ratlines

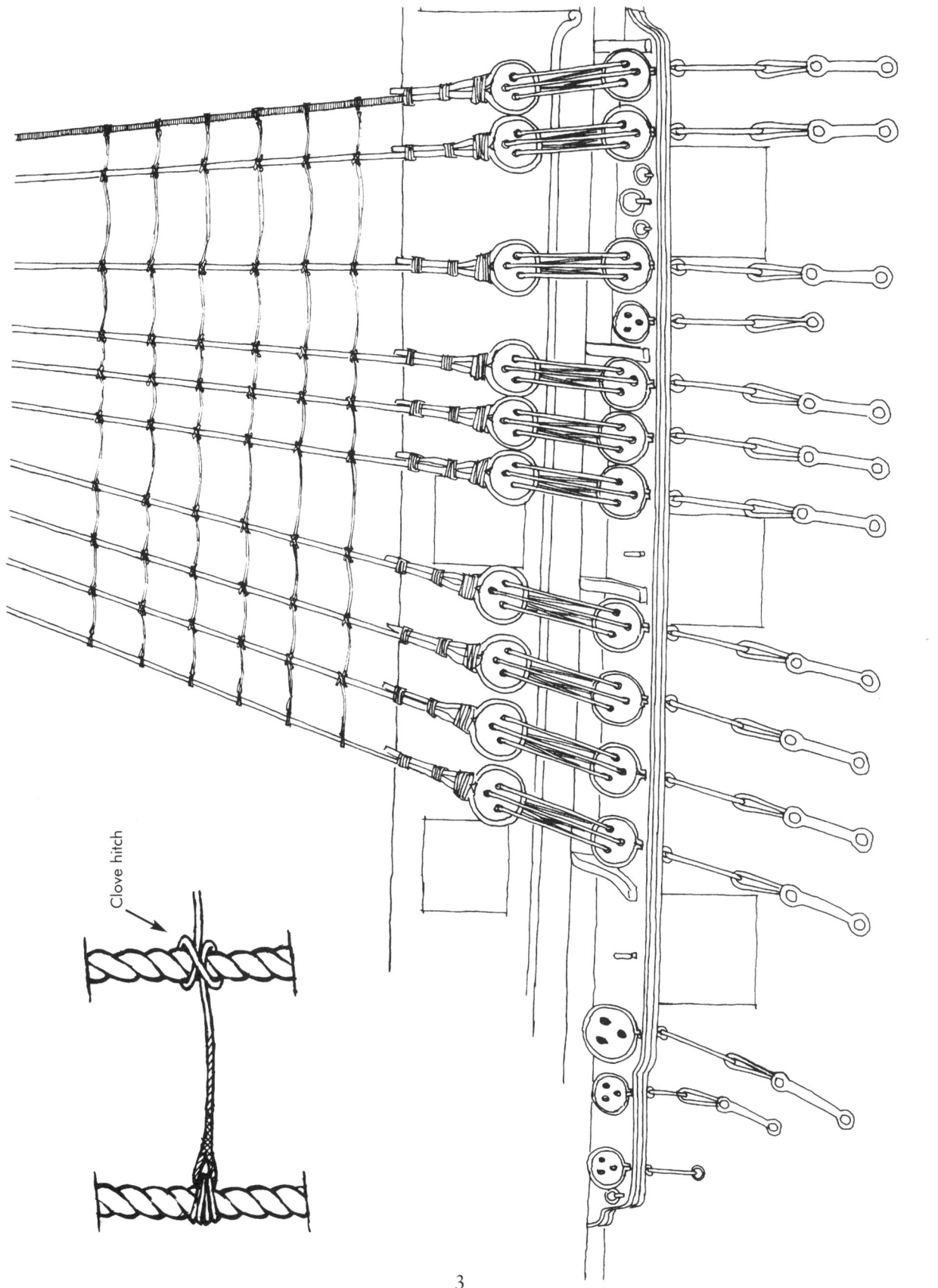

Mizzen Channels

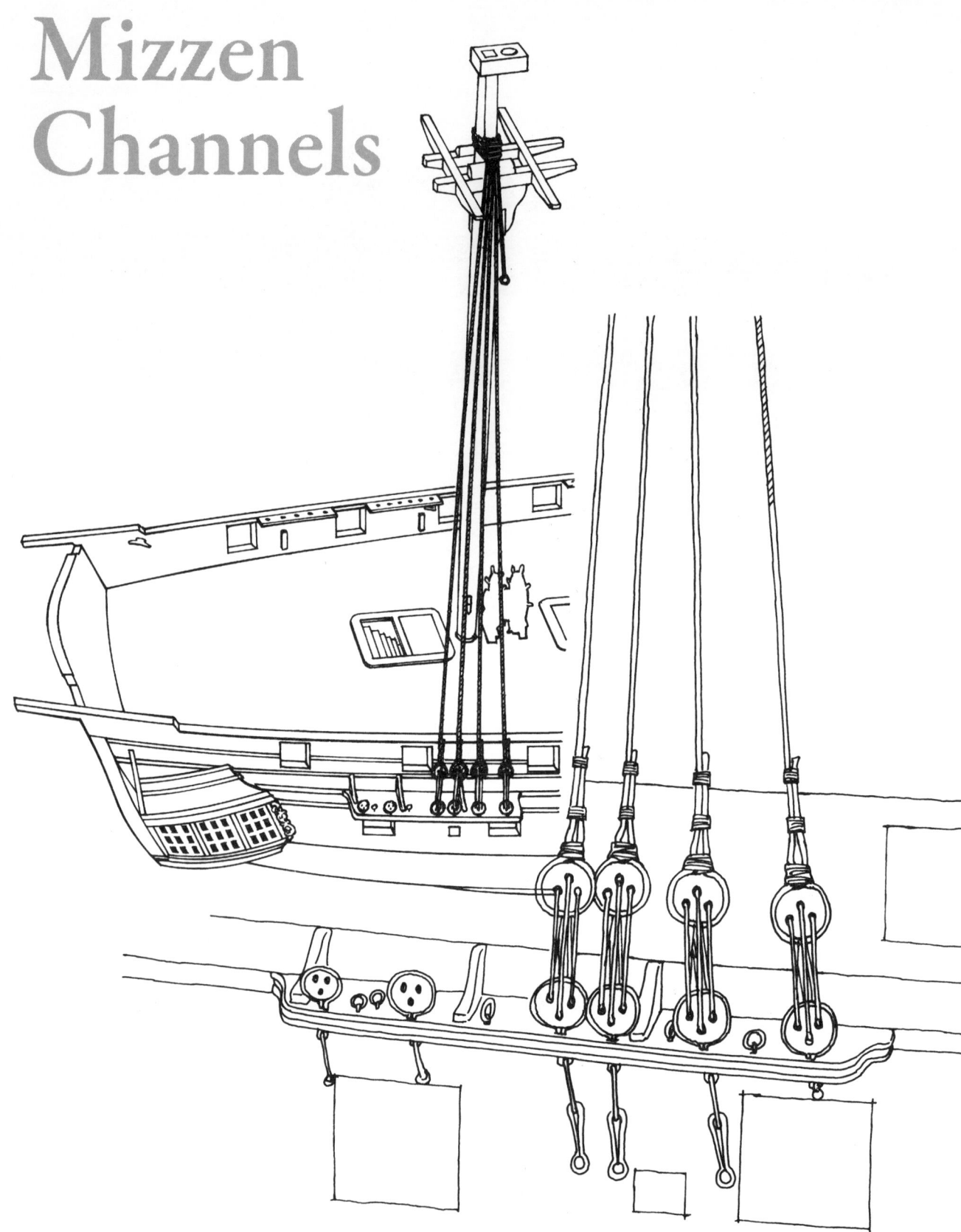

Fore Shrouds

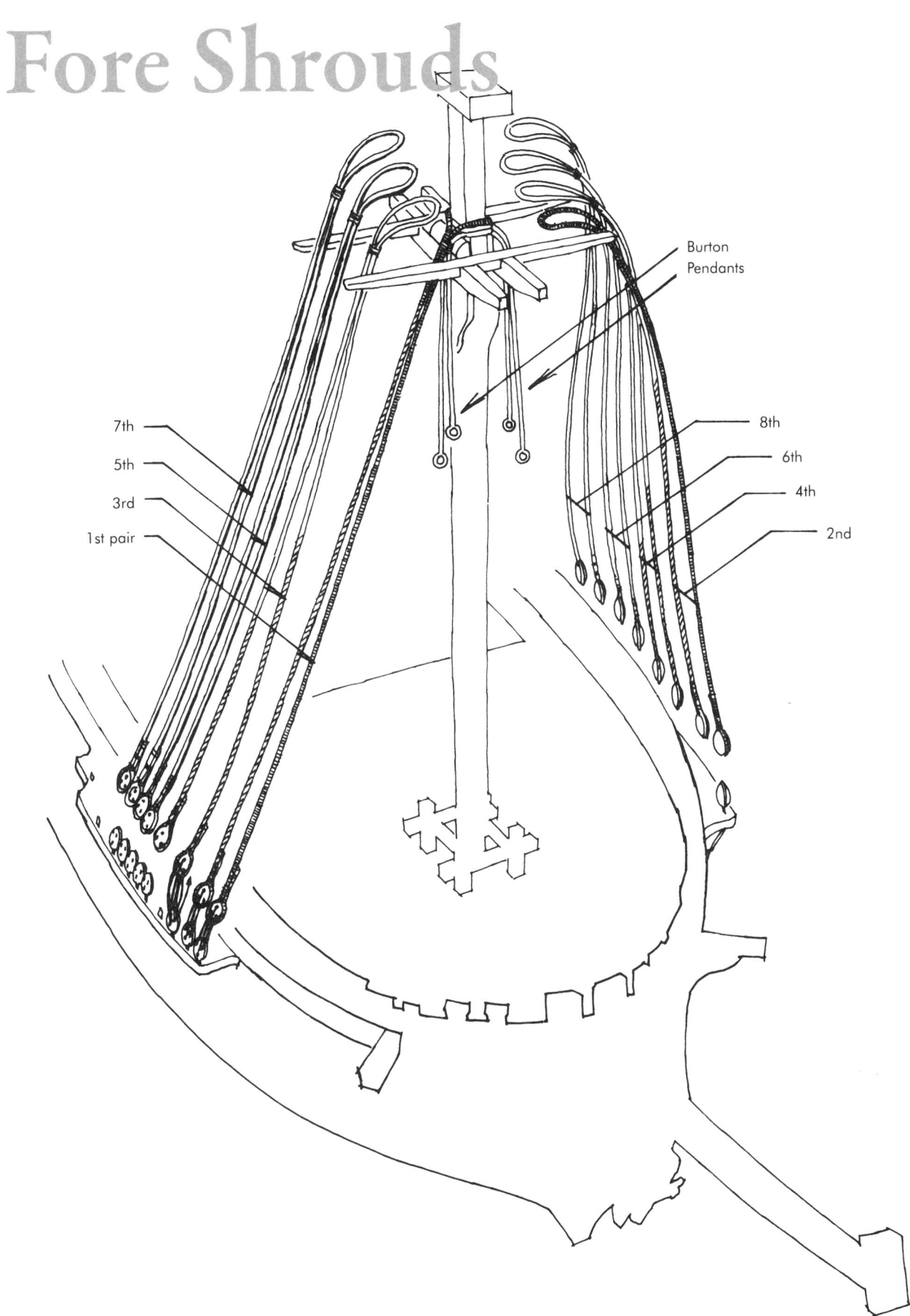

Main & Mizzen Shrouds

Fore Topmast Shrouds

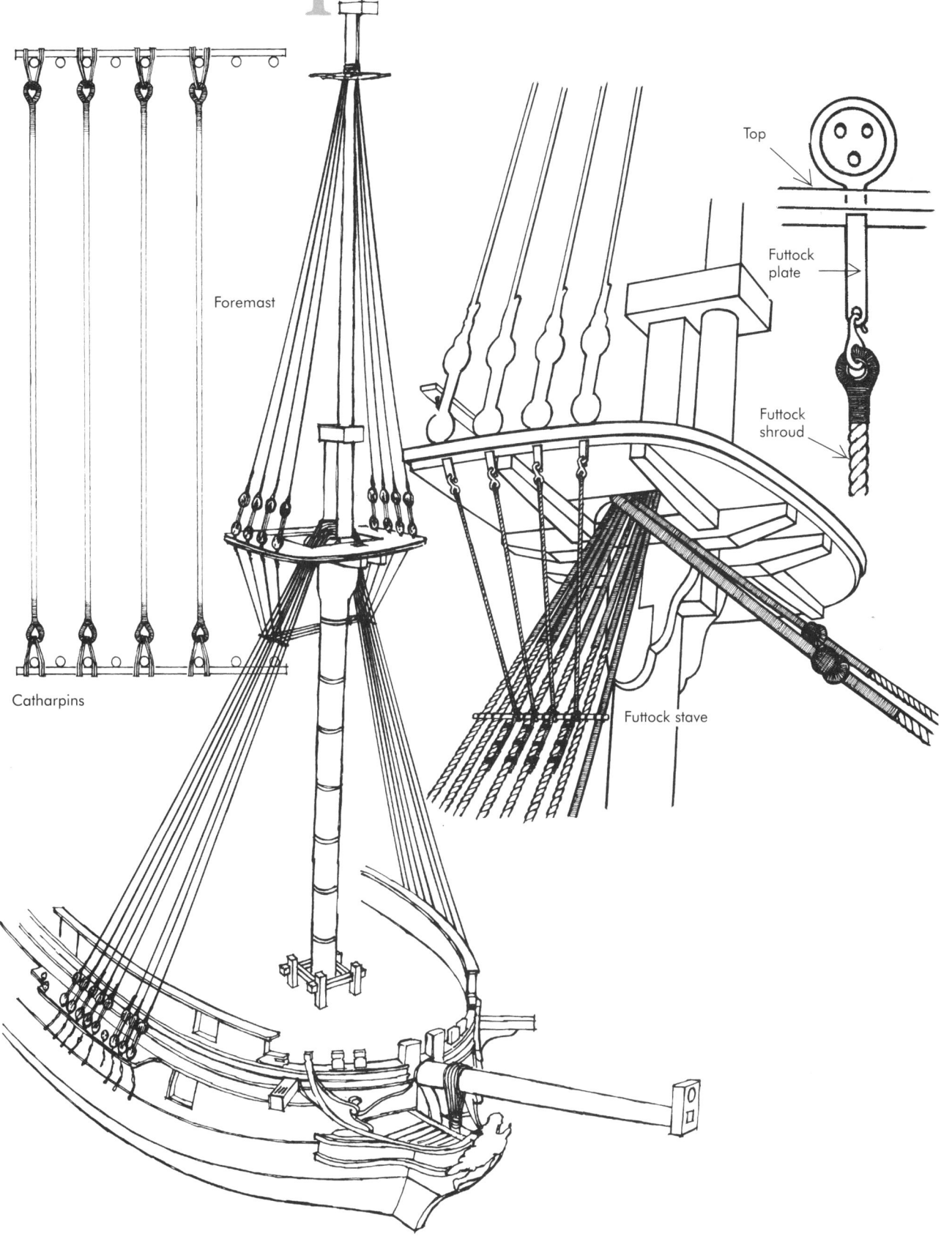

Mizzen Backstays

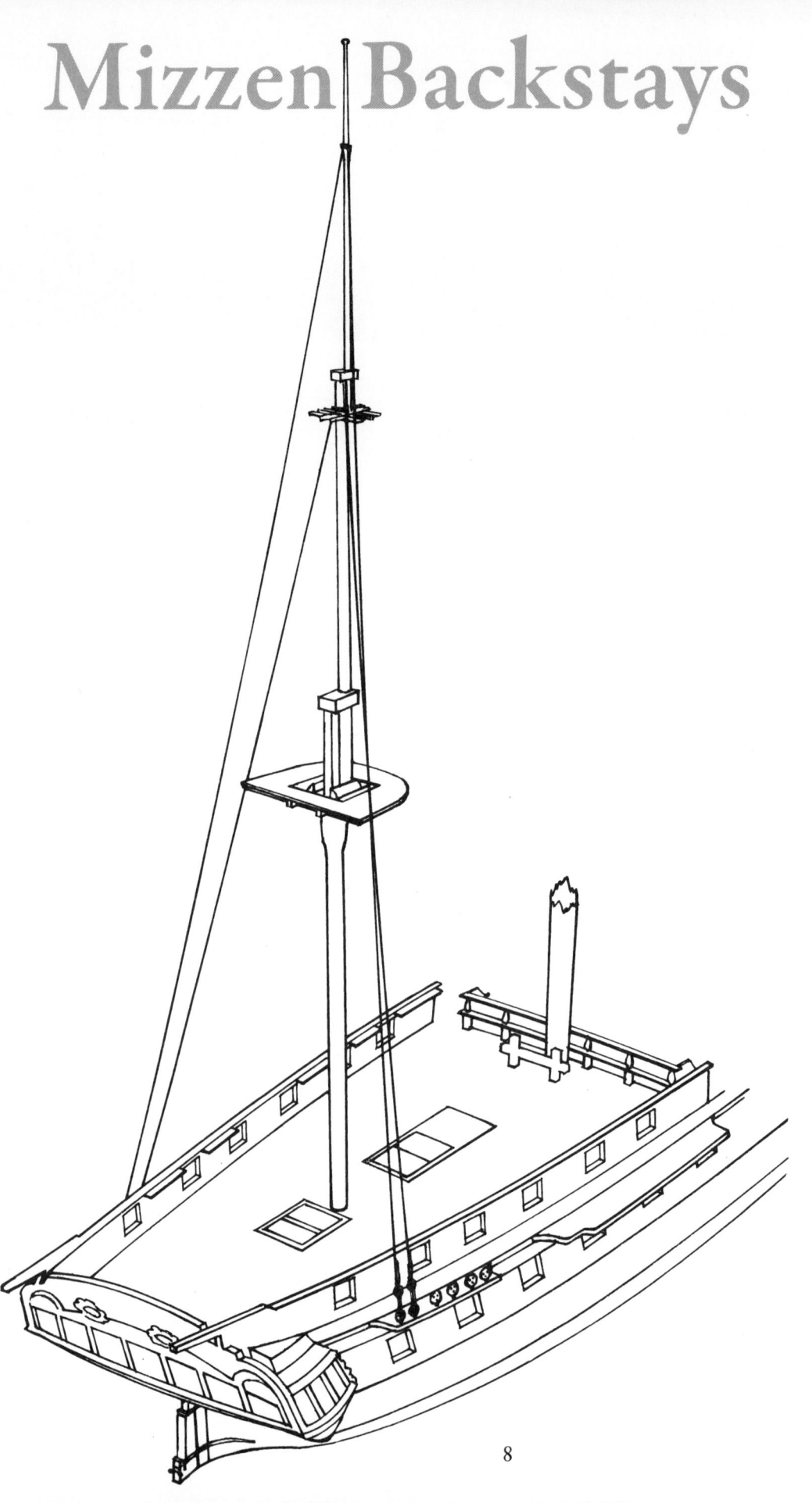

Main Backstays

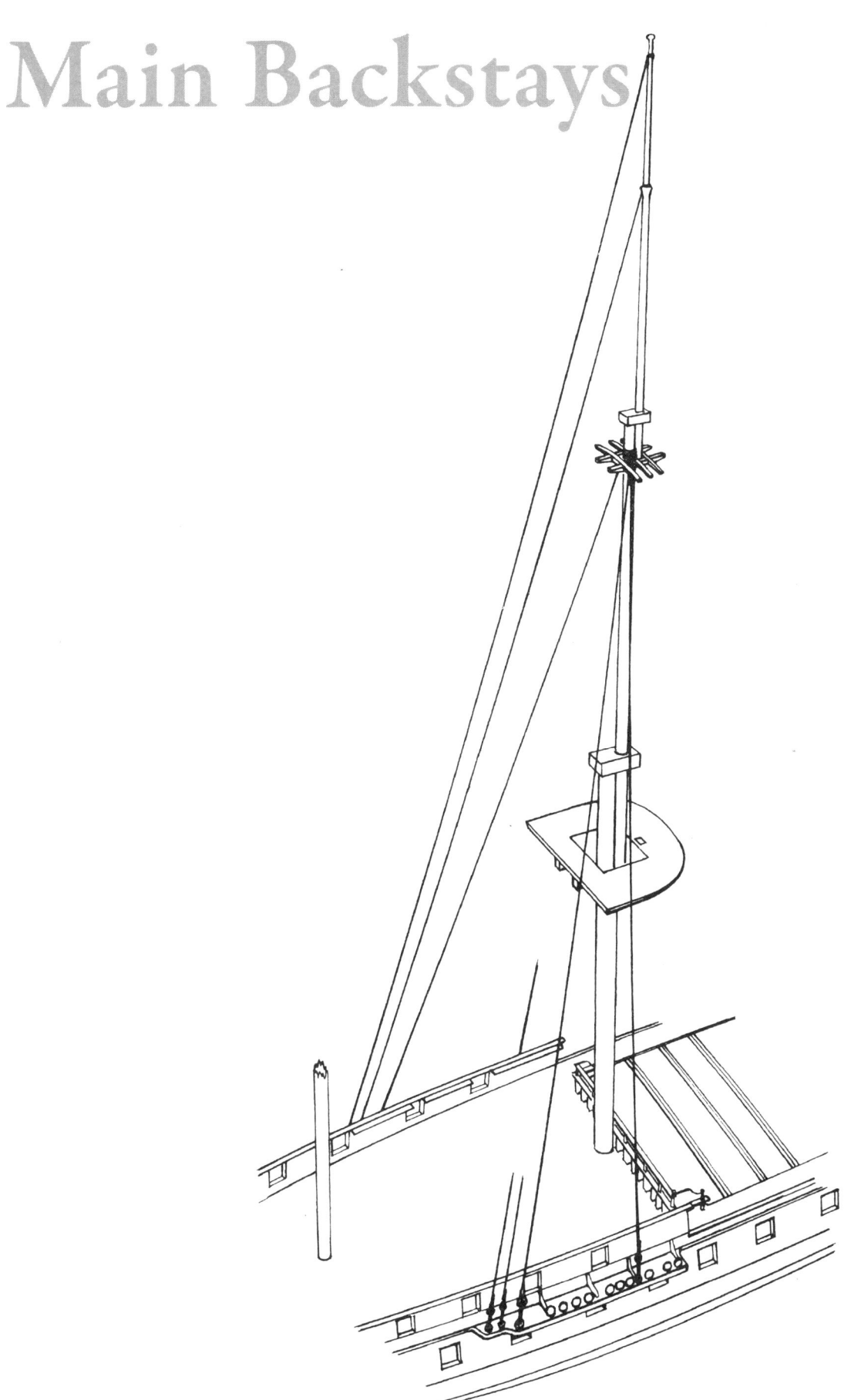

Fore Backstays & Shrouds

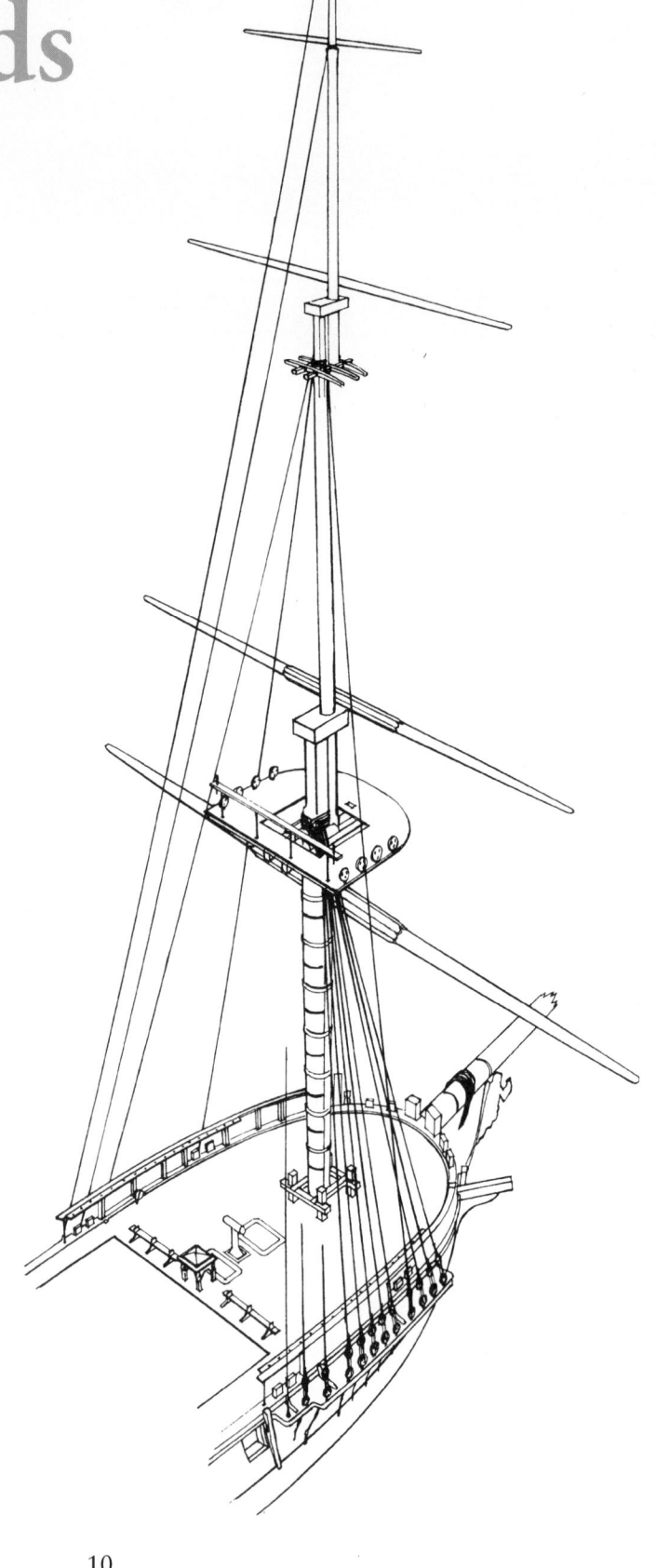

Fore Backstay, Topmast & Topgallant Shrouds

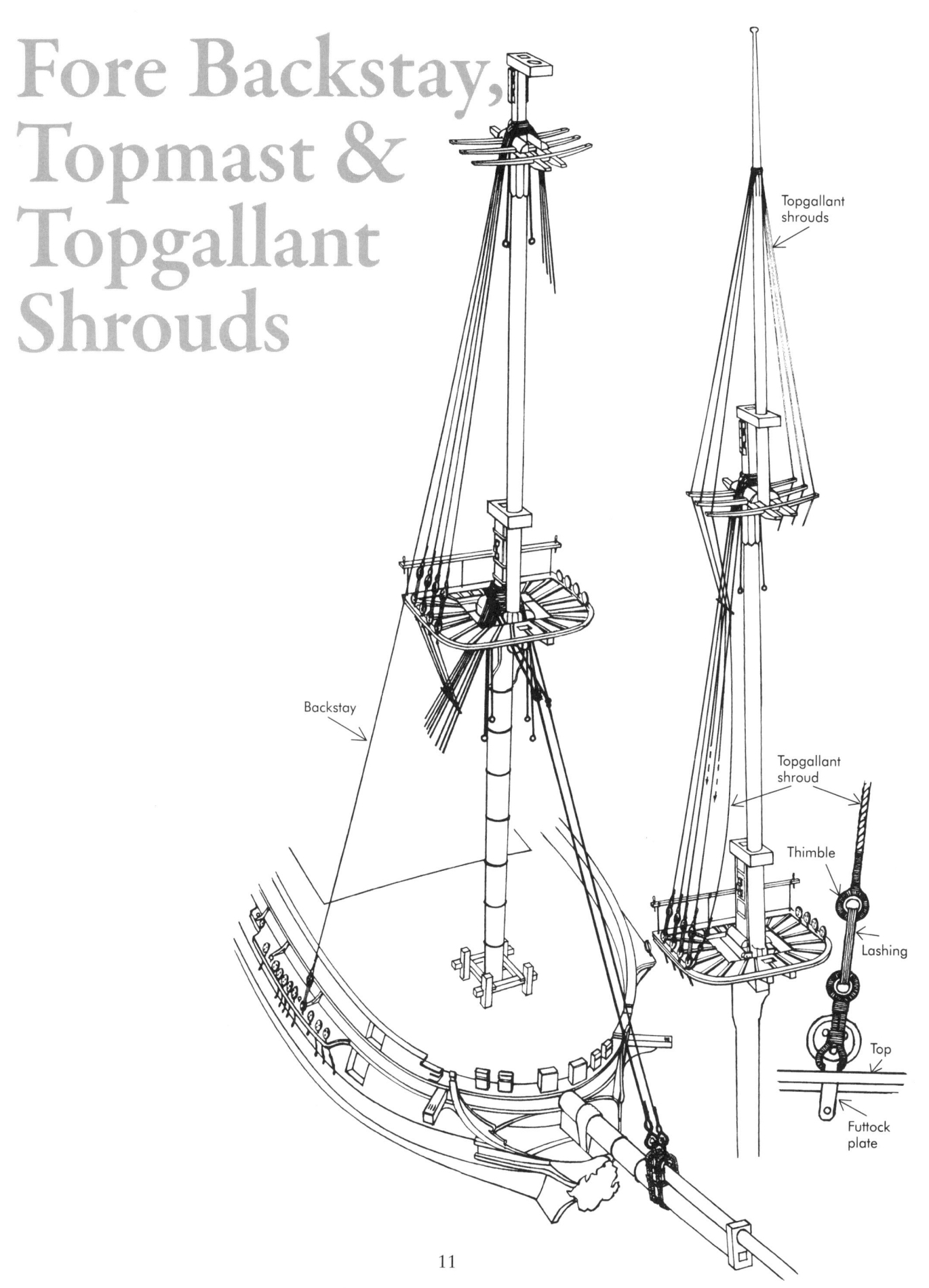

Stays

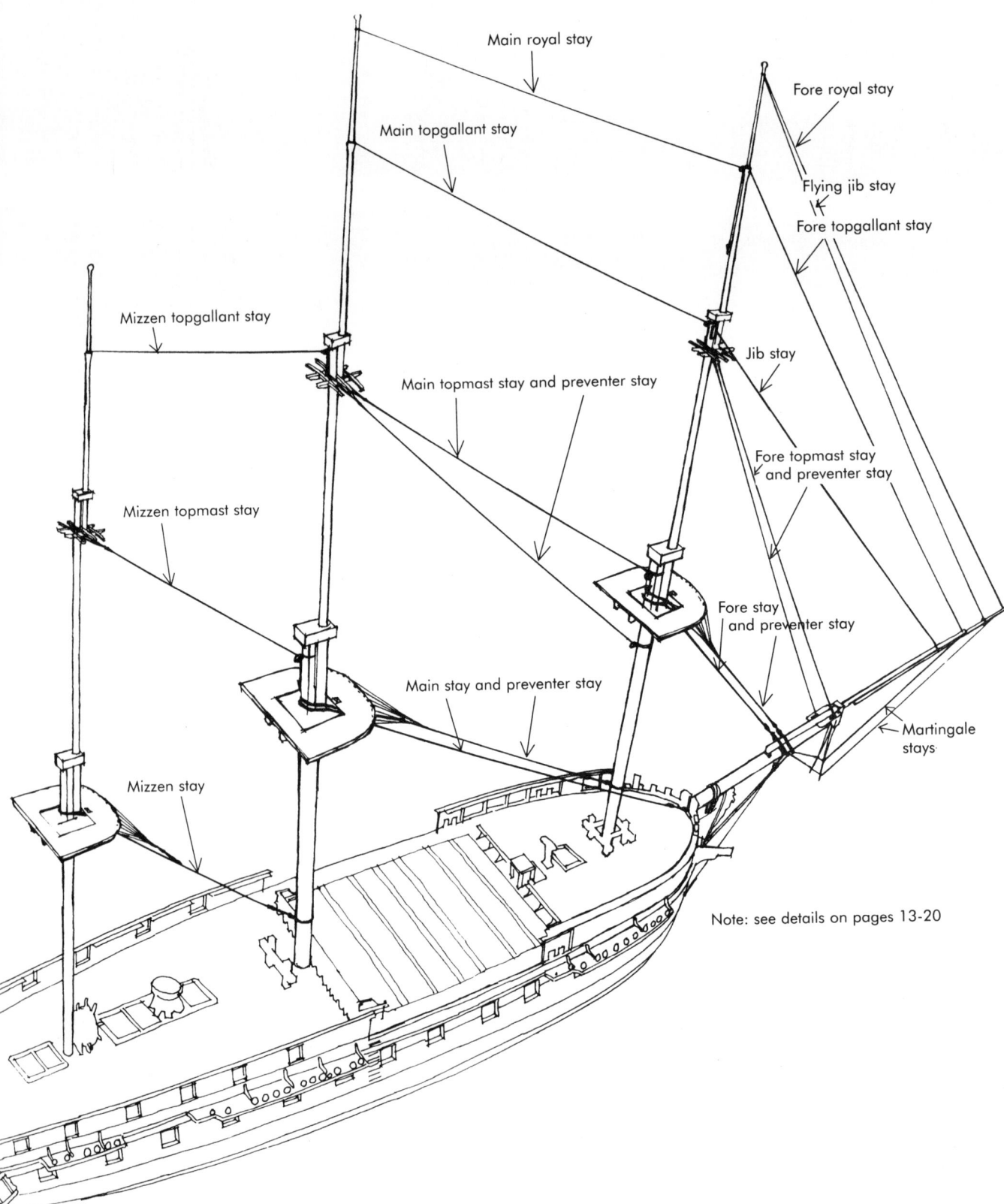

Note: see details on pages 13-20

Mizzen Stay

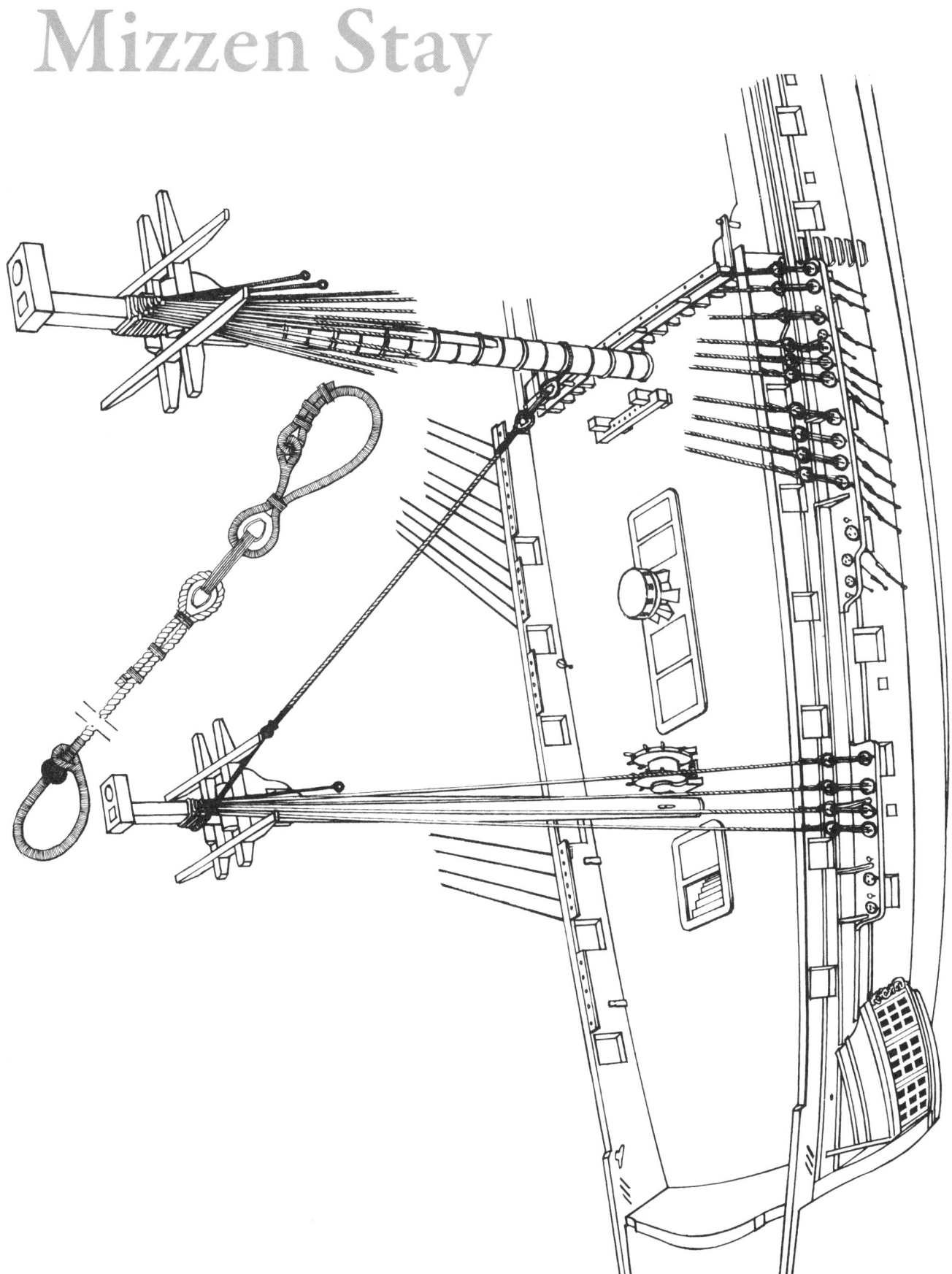

Main Stay & Preventer Stay

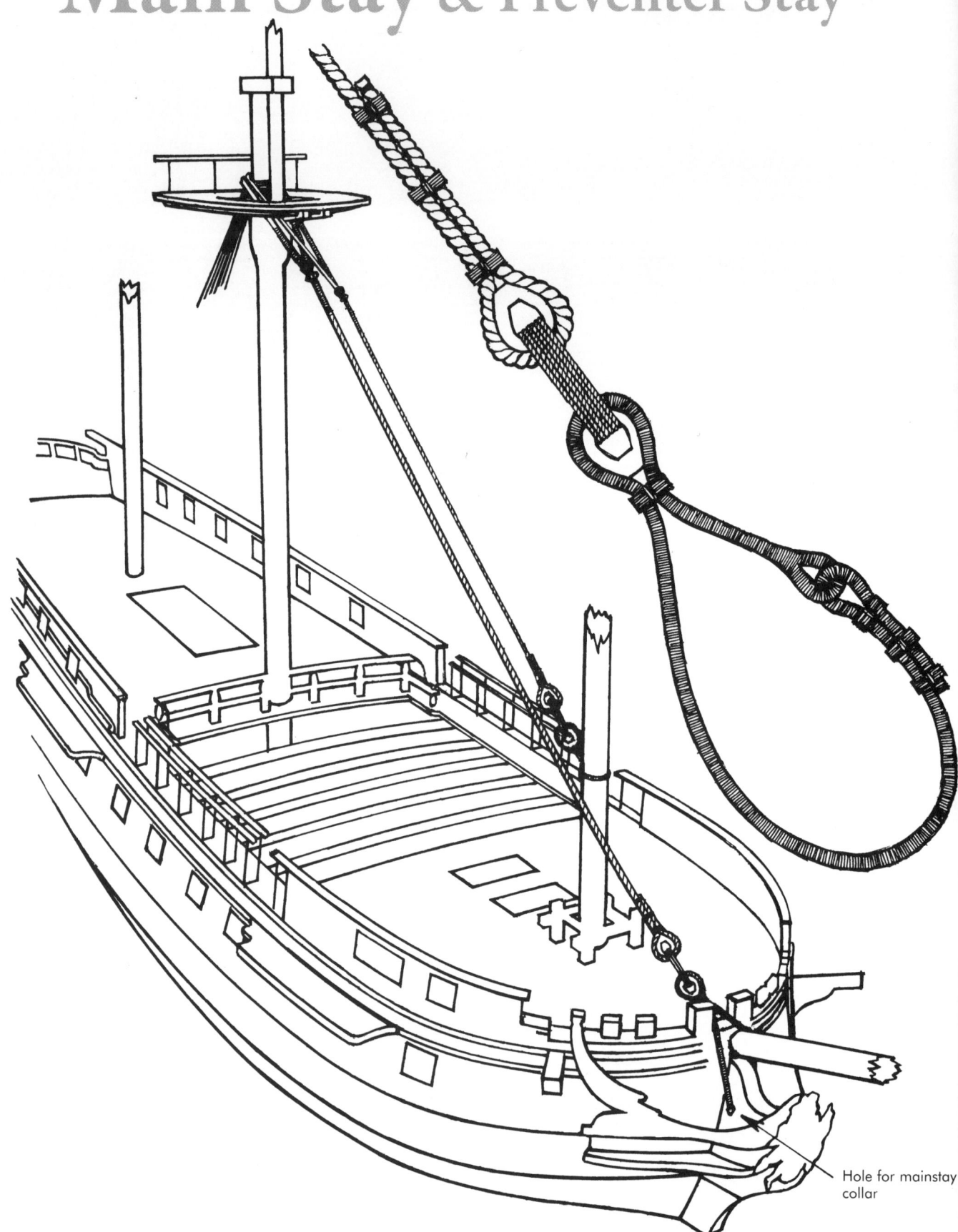

Hole for mainstay collar

Fore Stay & Preventer Stay

- Worming
- Hitched to the previous lead through the top
- Parcelling
- Crowsfeet of the top
- Serving
- Fore stay
- Fore preventer stay
- Splice
- Collar served
- Lashing

Mizzen Topmast Stay & Topgallant Stay

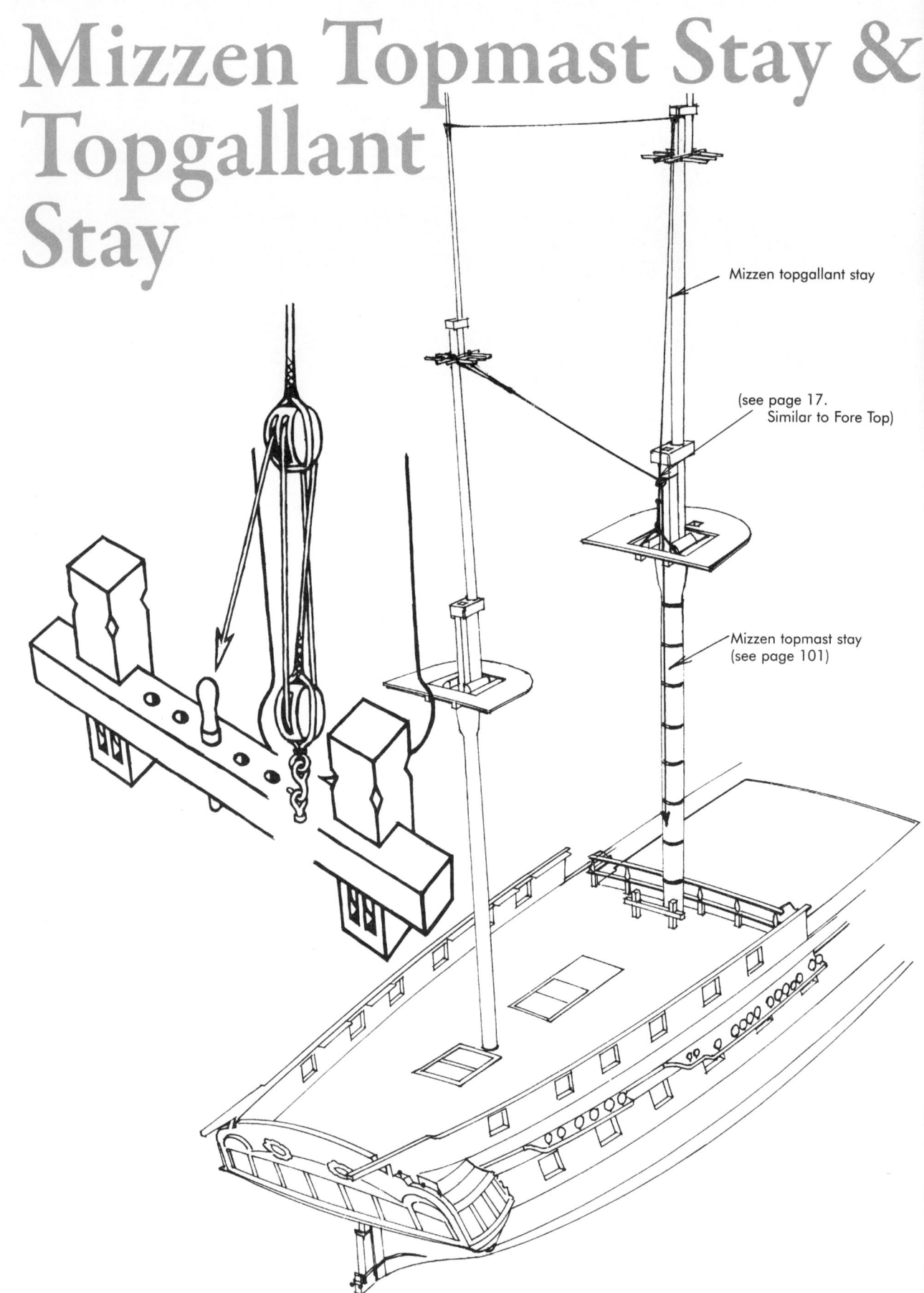

Mizzen topgallant stay

(see page 17. Similar to Fore Top)

Mizzen topmast stay (see page 101)

Main Topmast Stay, Preventer Stay, Topgallant & Royal Stay

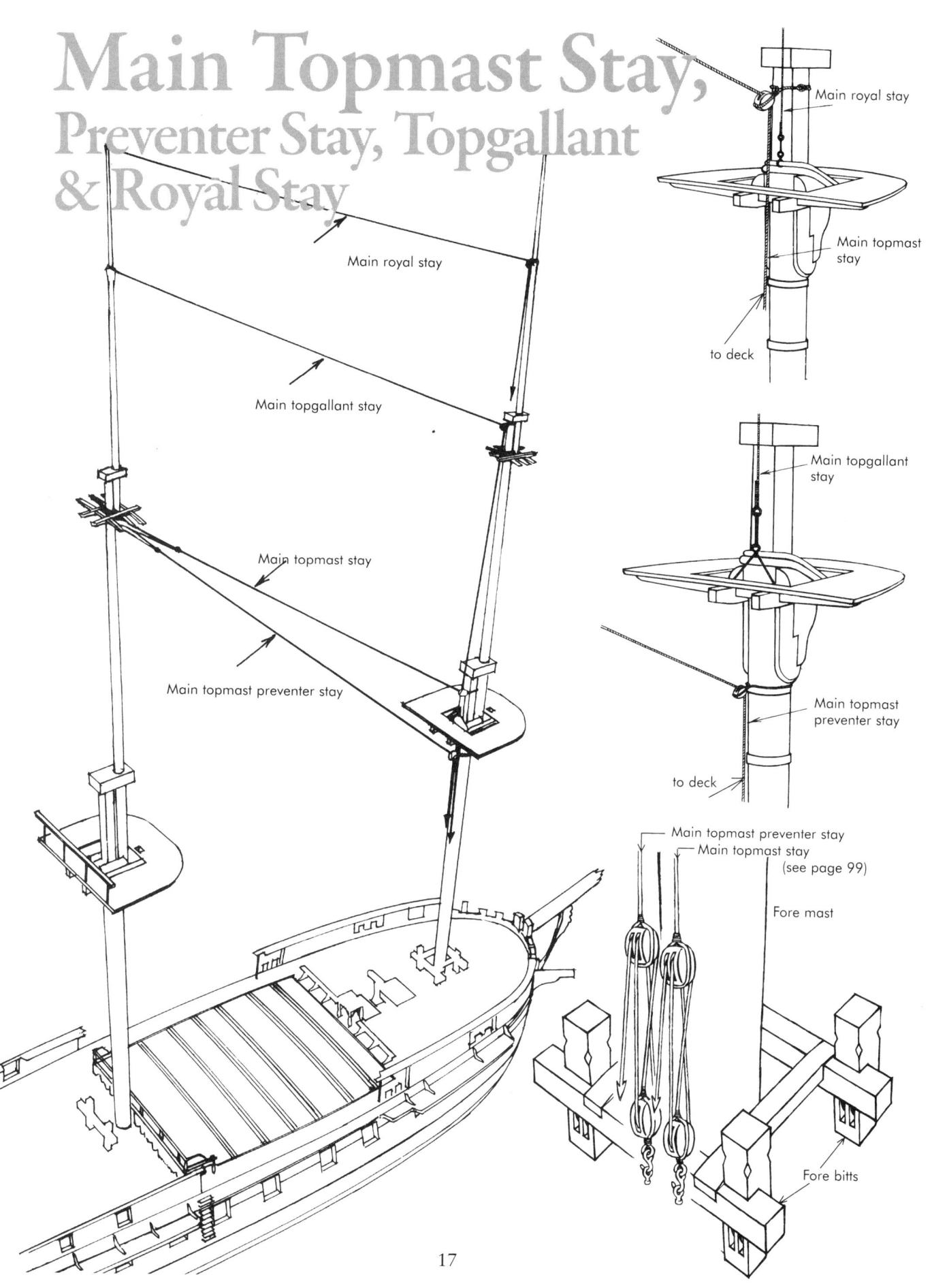

Fore Topmast
& Preventer Stay

Eyebolt in the bows, close to the bowsprit on both sides

Lanyard frapped round itself 10 times

Fore topmast preventer stay

Fore topmast stay

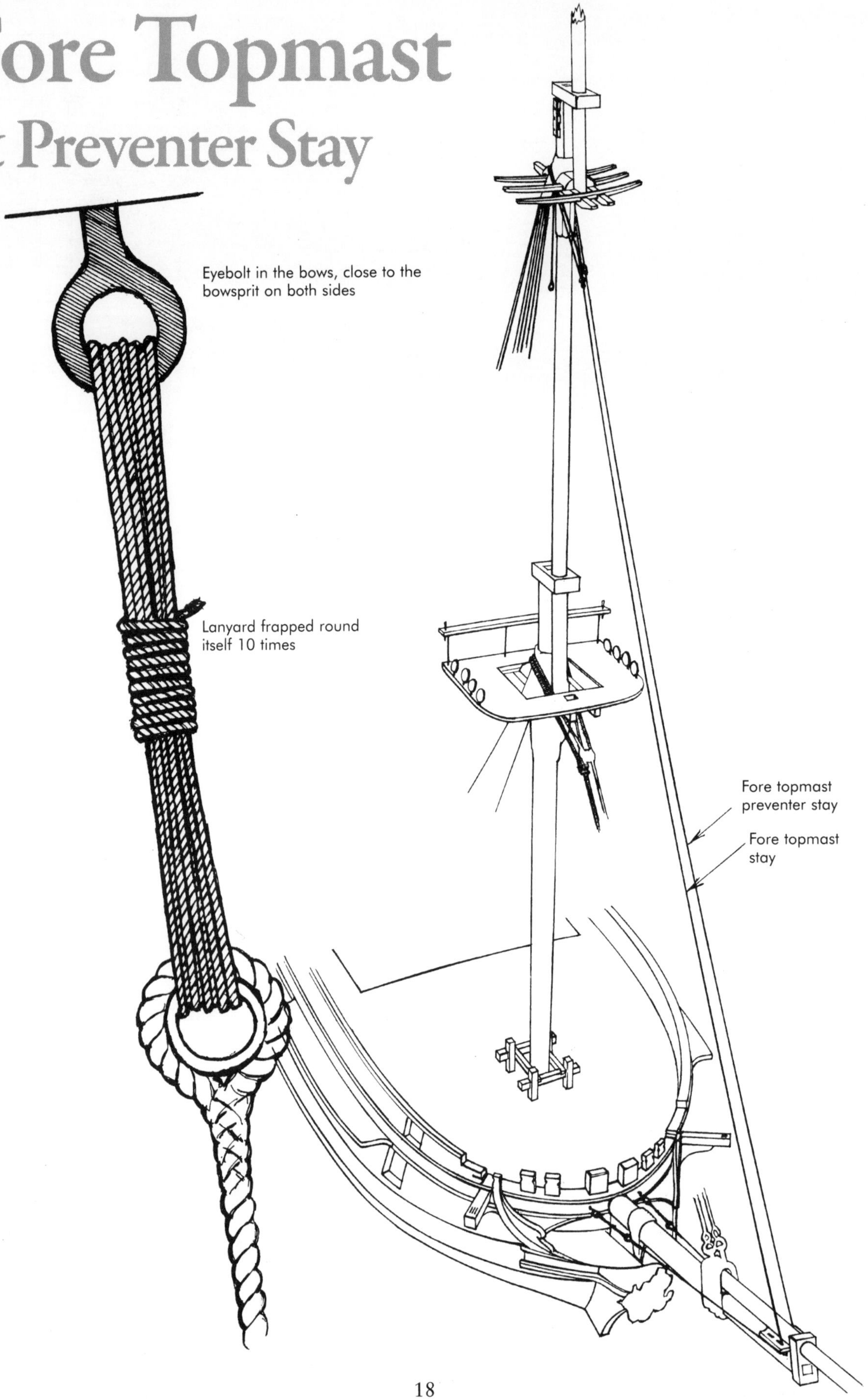

Jibstay, Fore Topgallant Flying Jib & Royal Stay

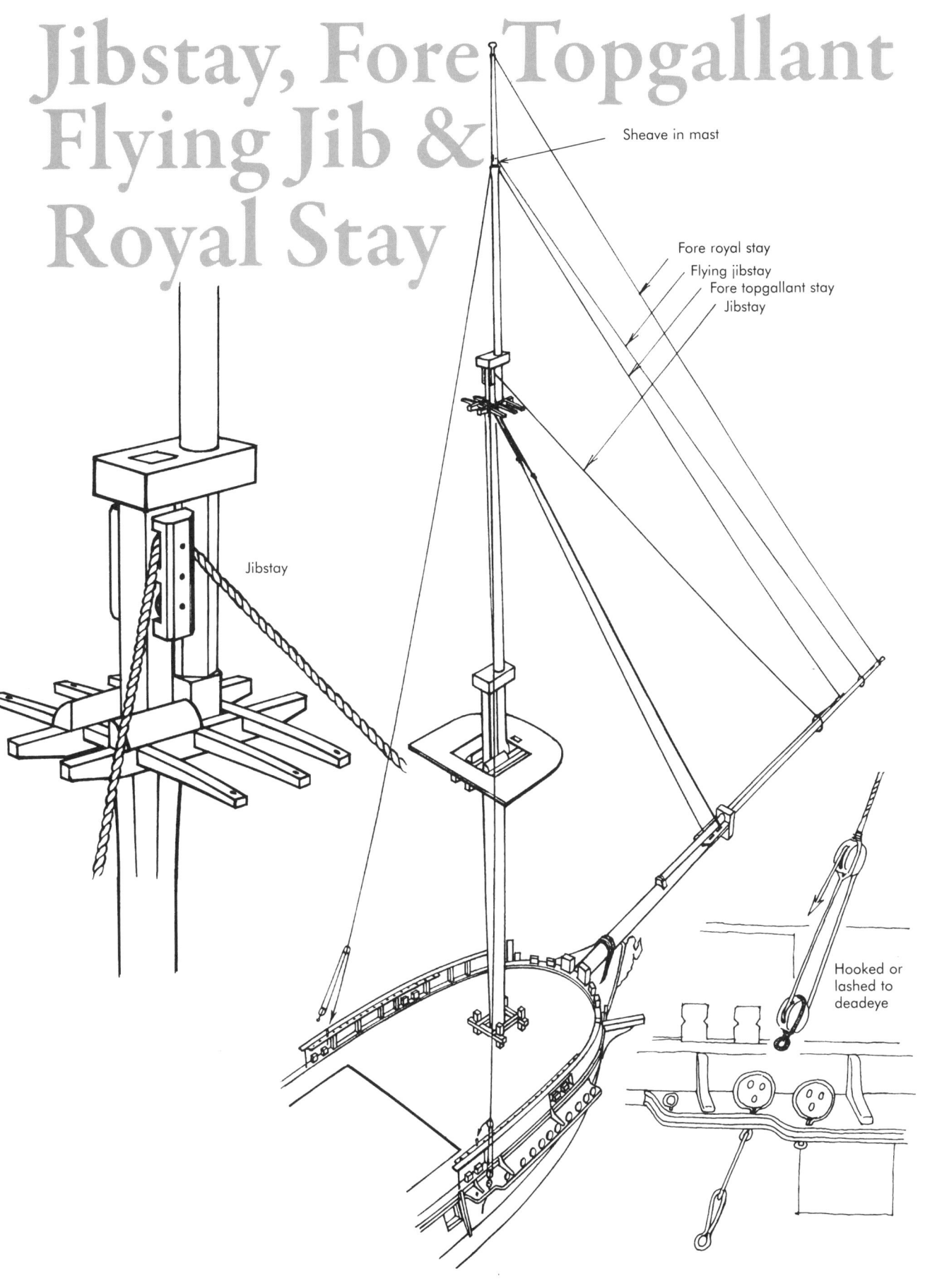

Bobstay, Bowsprit Shrouds

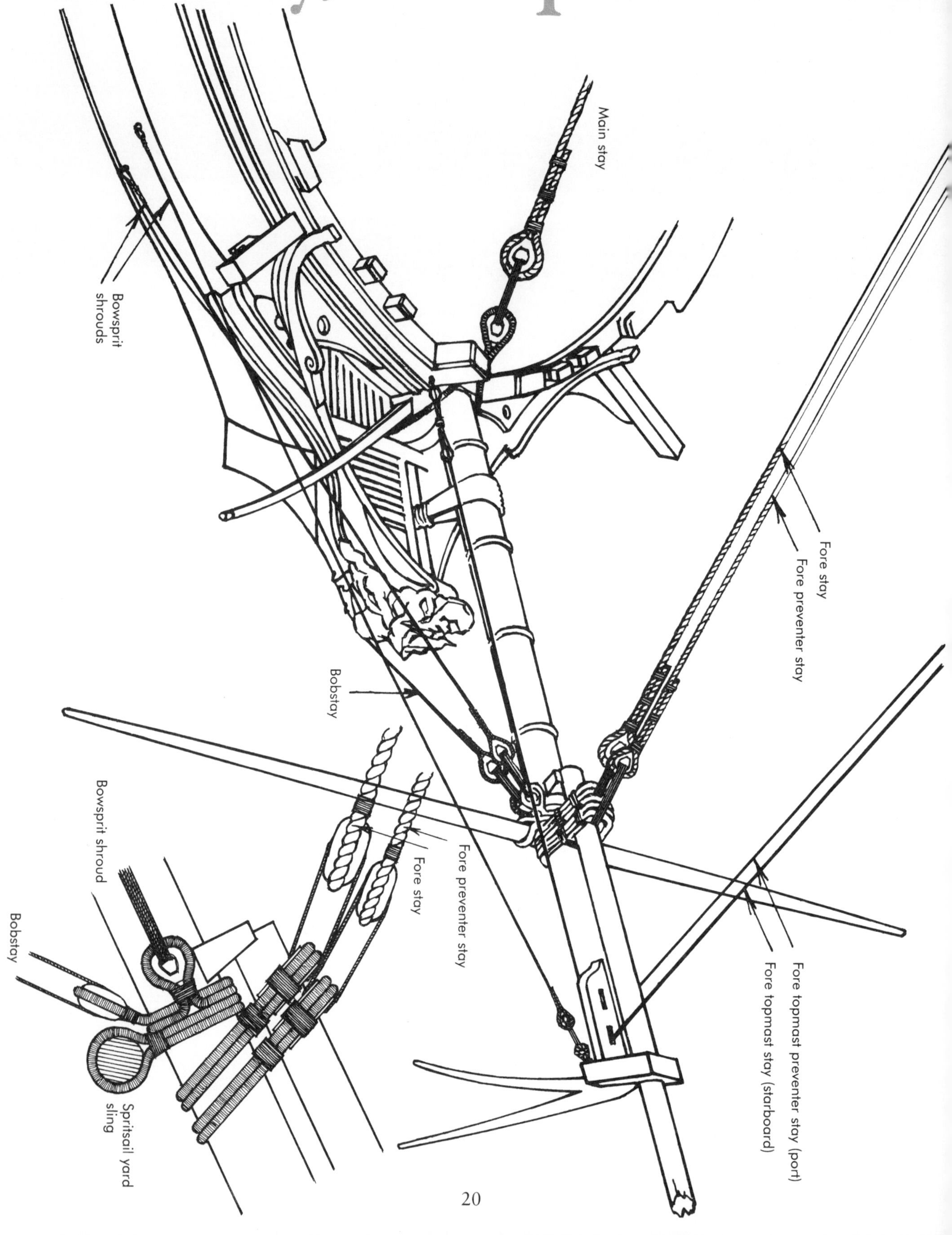

- Main stay
- Bowsprit shrouds
- Bobstay
- Fore stay
- Fore preventer stay
- Bowsprit shroud
- Fore stay
- Fore preventer stay
- Bobstay
- Spritsail yard sling
- Fore topmast preventer stay (port)
- Fore topmast stay (starboard)

Jibstay & Martingale Stays

Cross Jack Truss Pendant

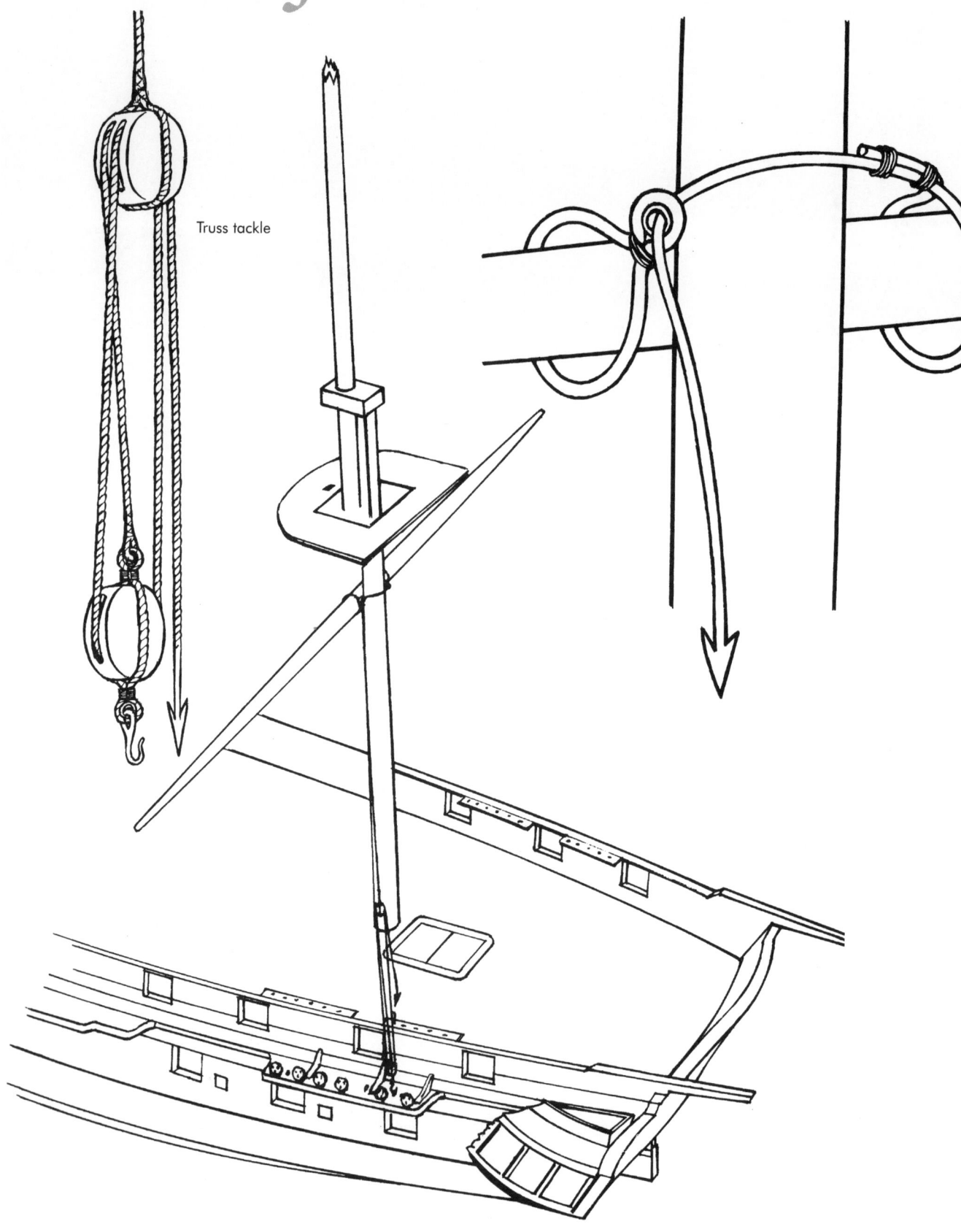

Truss tackle

Cross Jack Sling

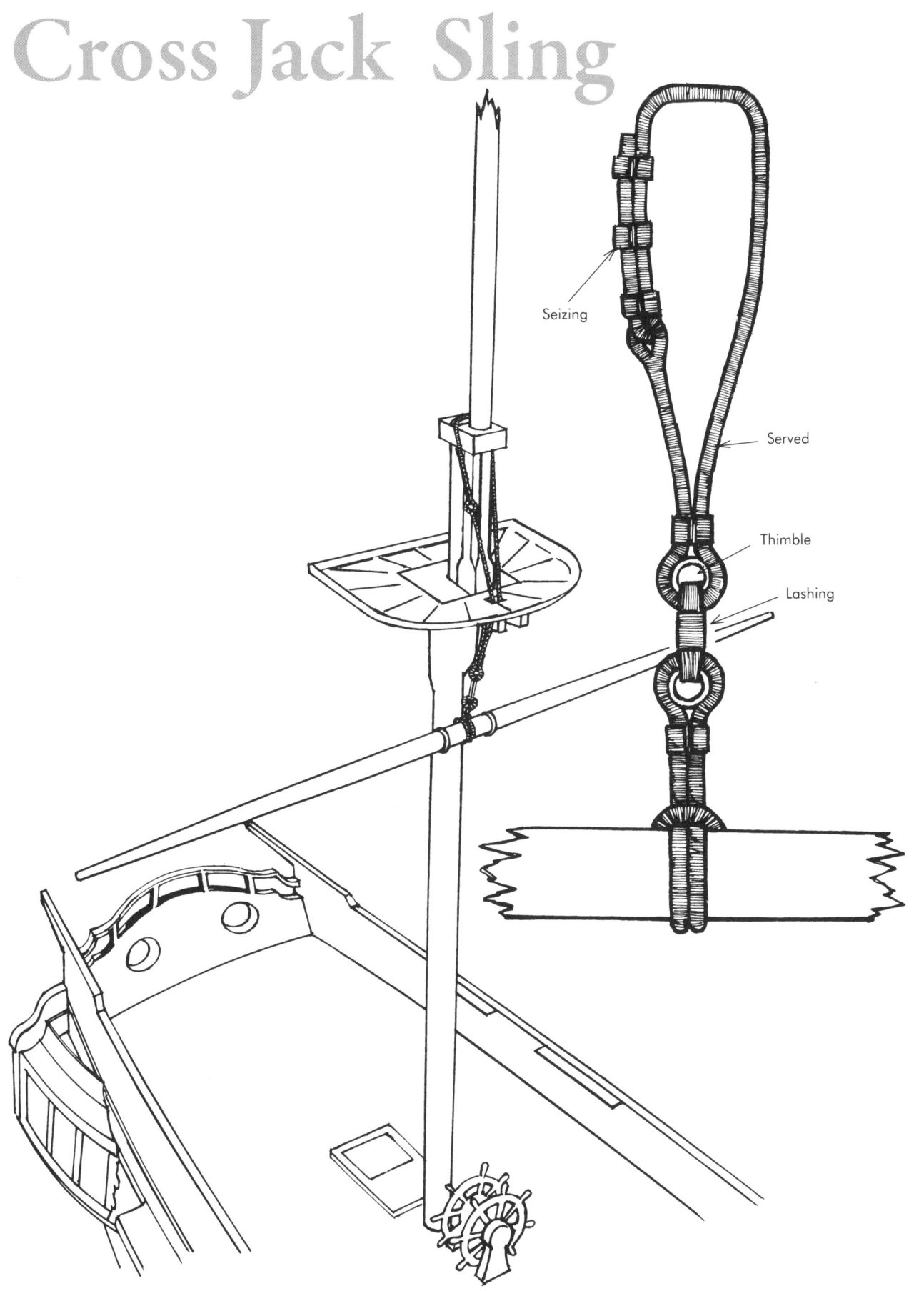

Cross Jack Lift

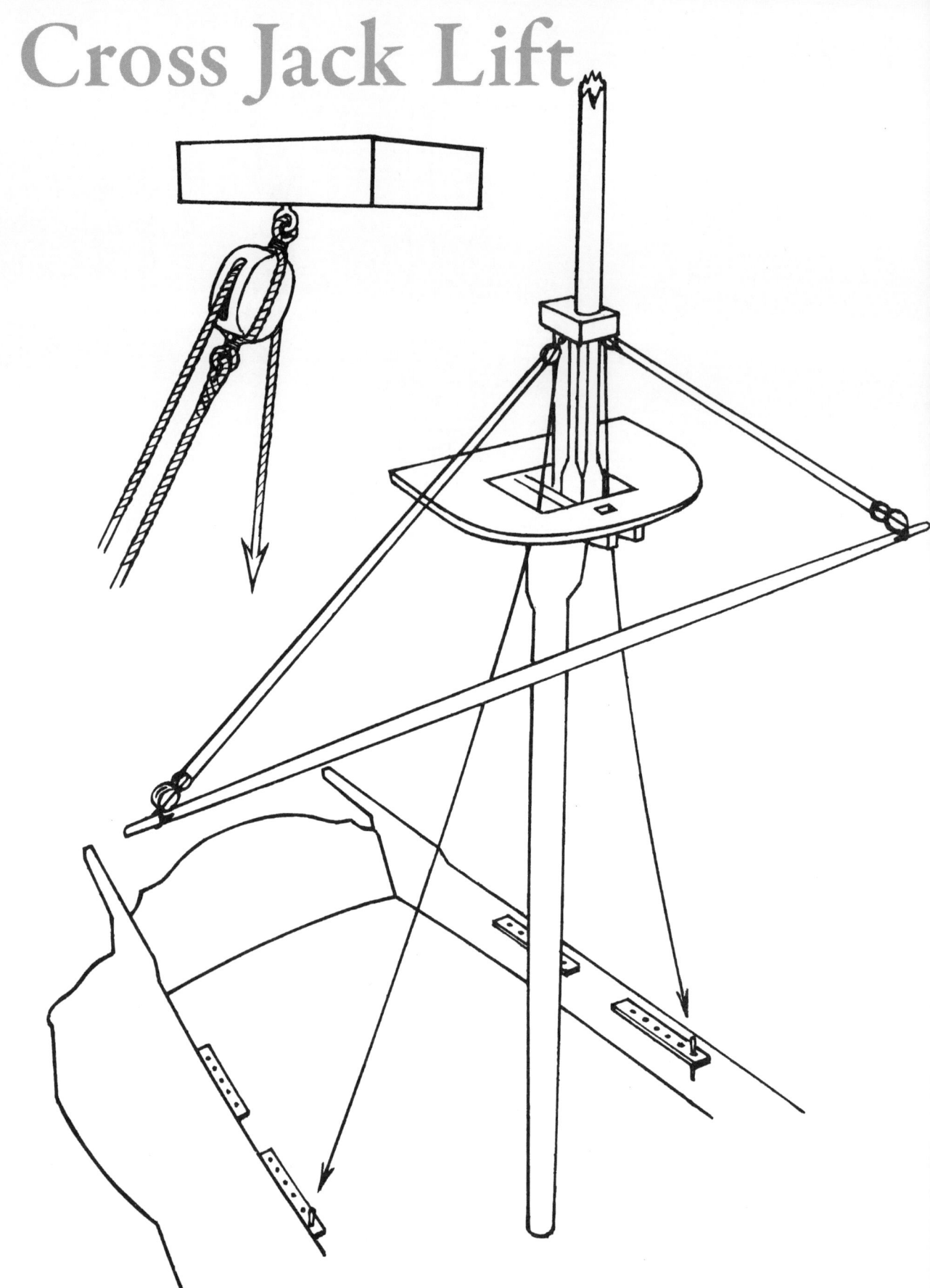

Spanker Boom Sheet & Guy Pendants

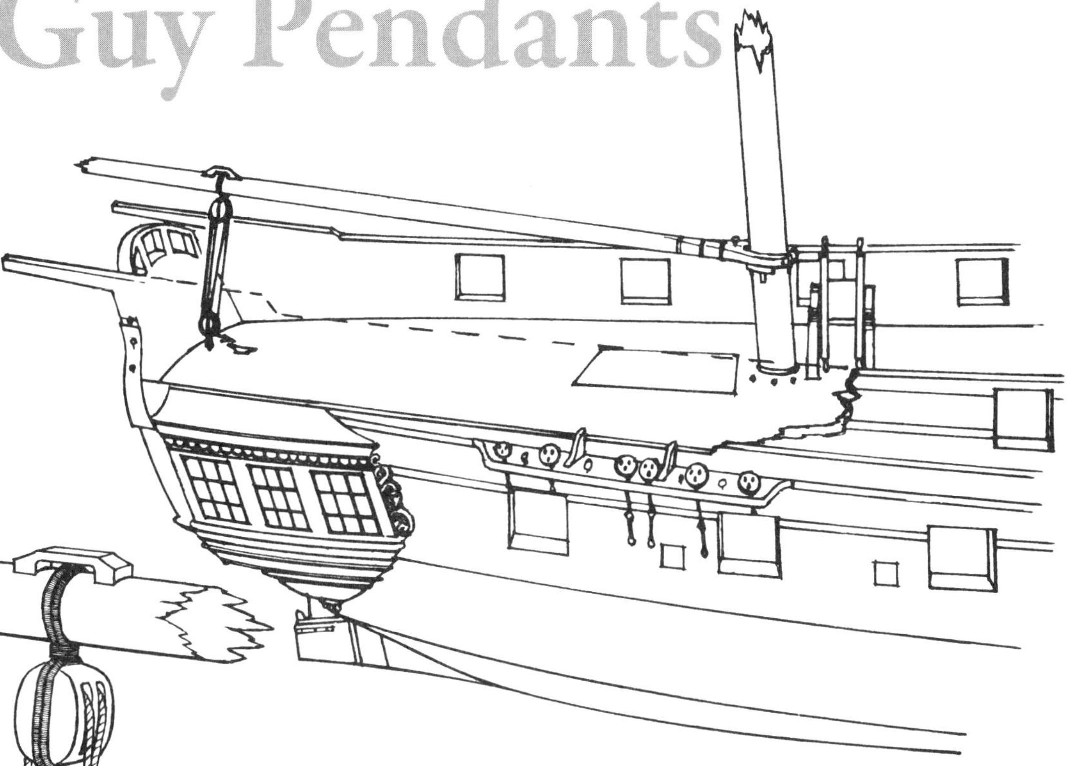

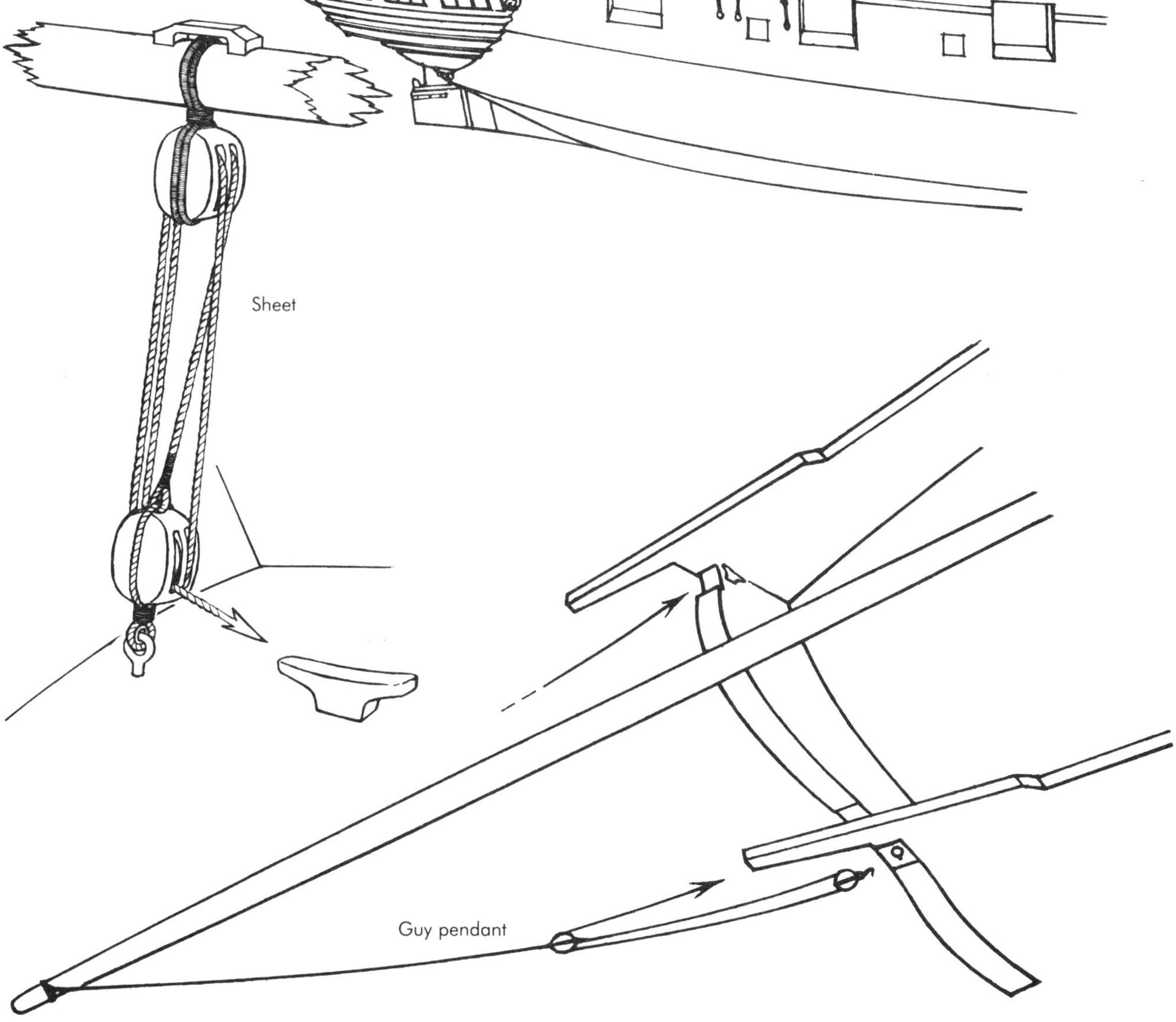

Sheet

Guy pendant

Boom Topping Lift

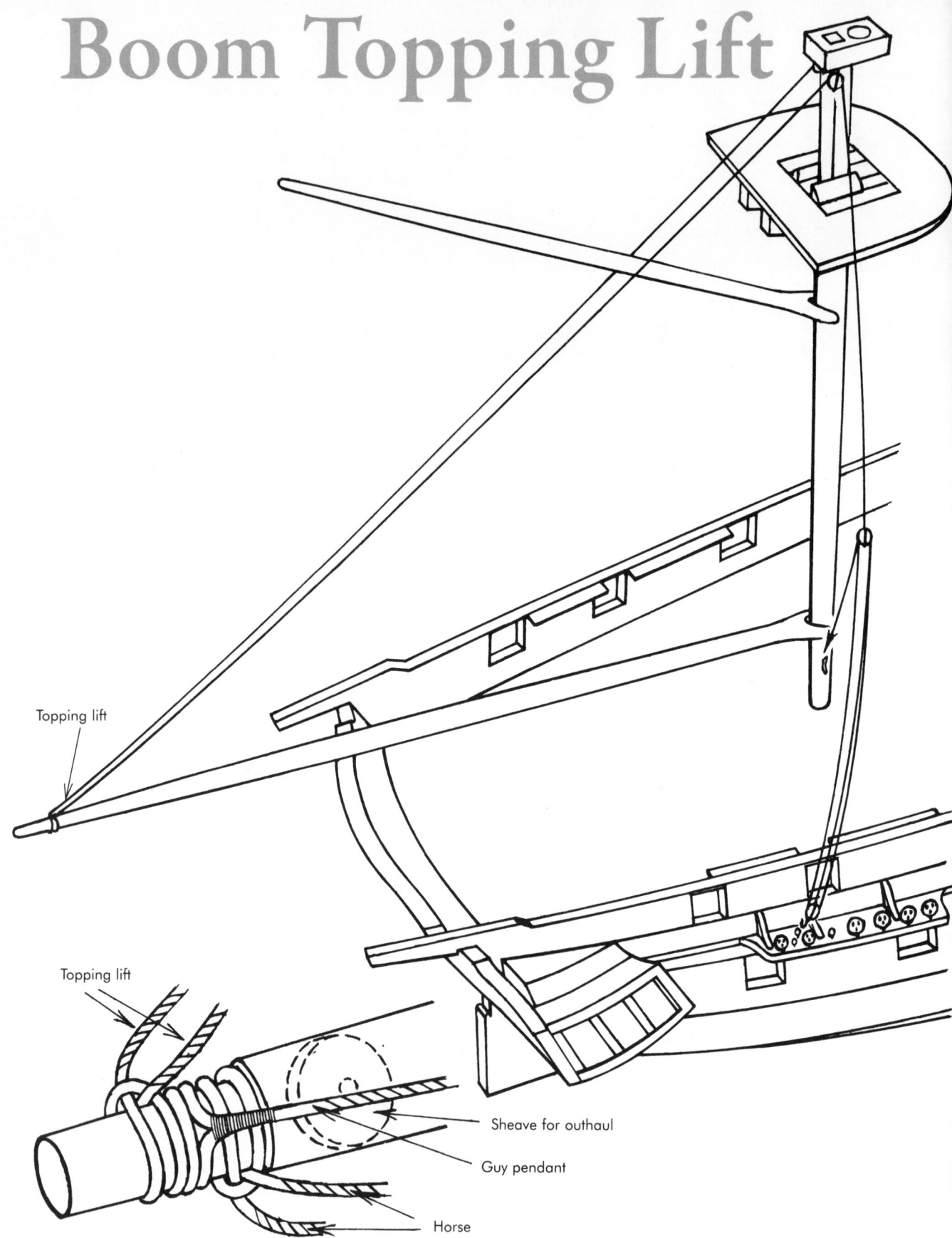

Topping lift

Topping lift

Sheave for outhaul
Guy pendant
Horse

Vangs

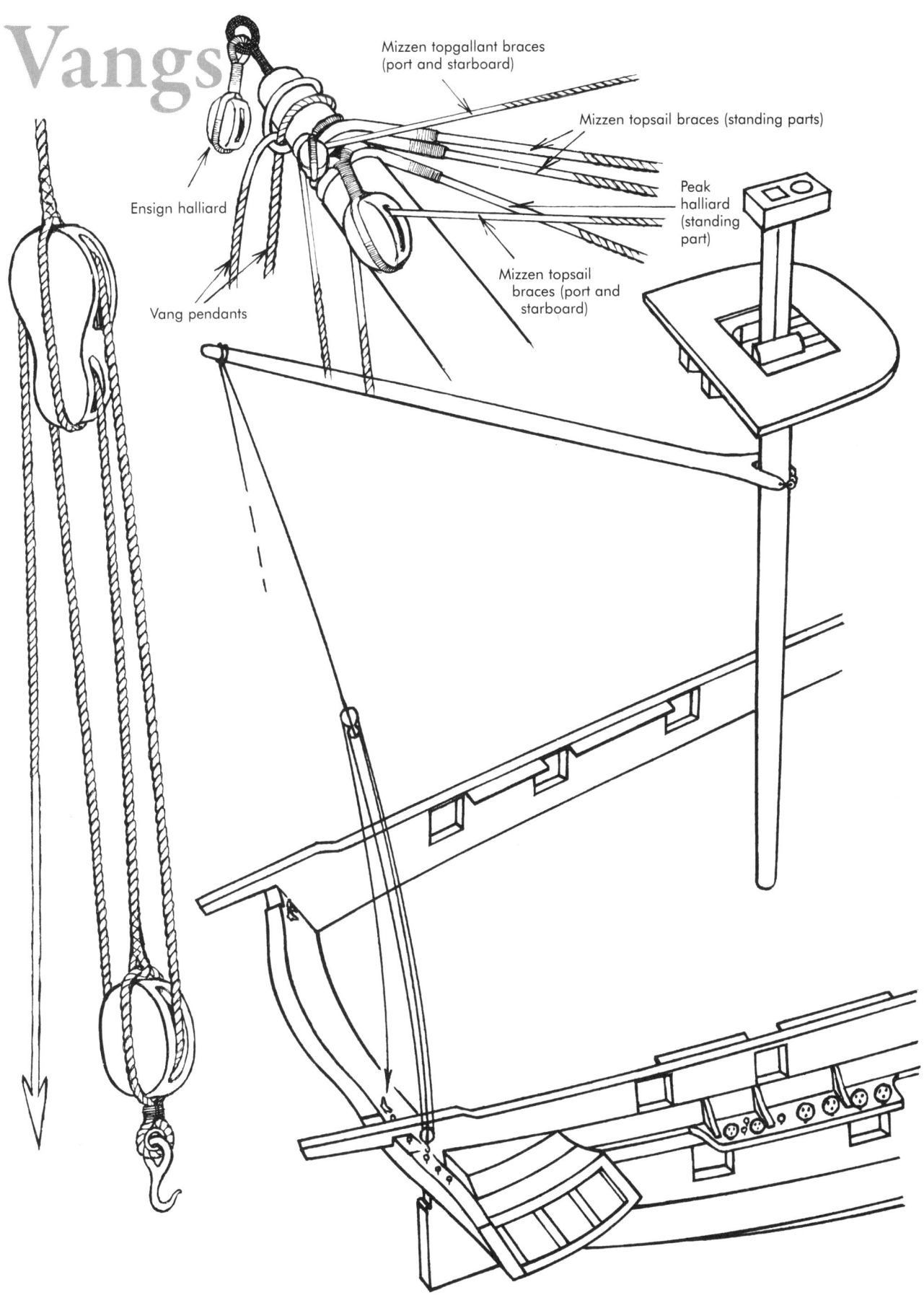

Peak Halliard

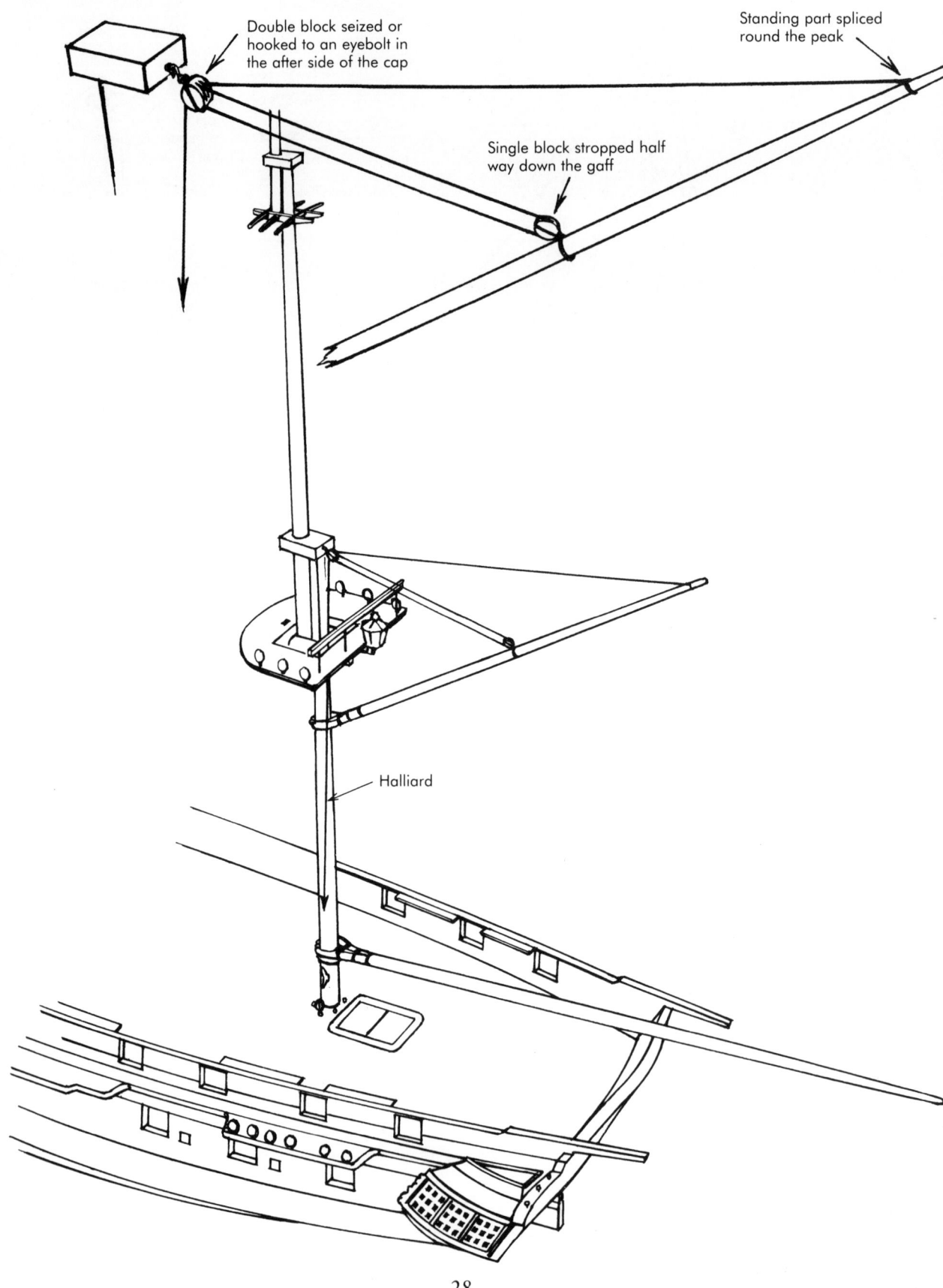

Throat Halliard

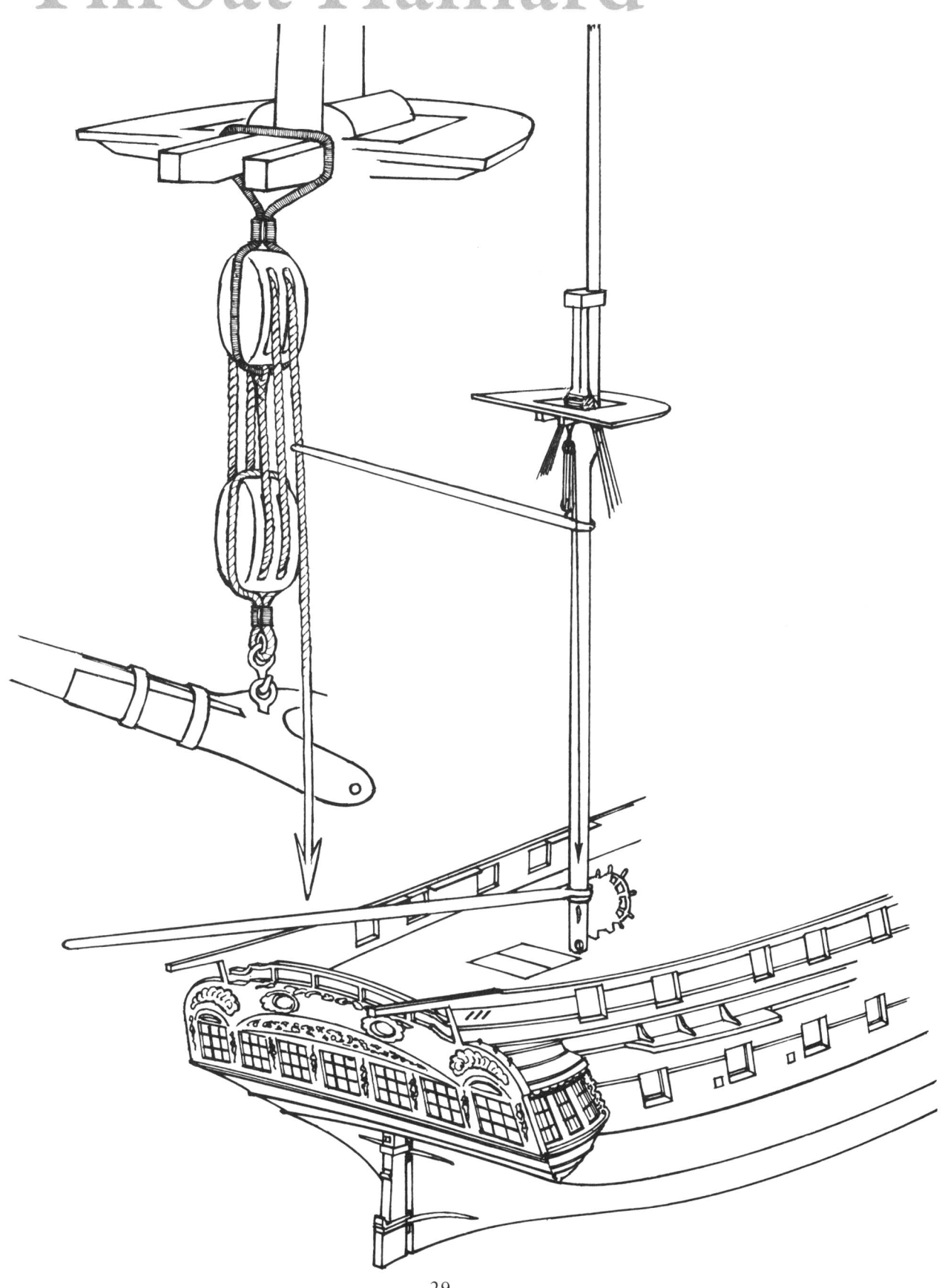

Mizzen Tyes: Topsail, Topgallant & Royal Yard

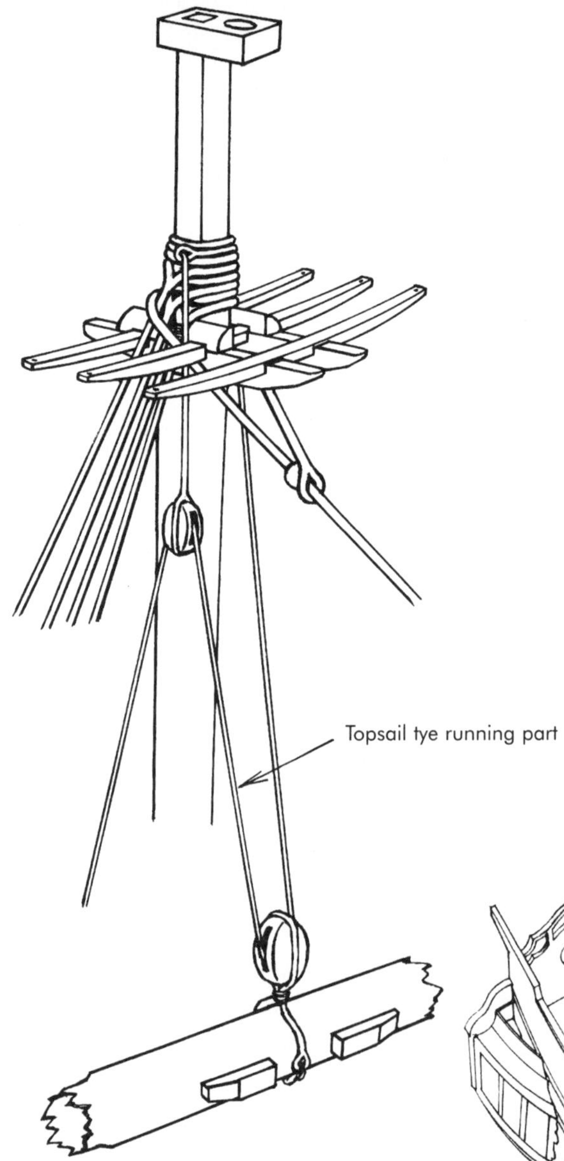

Through a sheave in the mast

Royal halliard to crosstrees

Topgallant halliard

Topsail tye running part

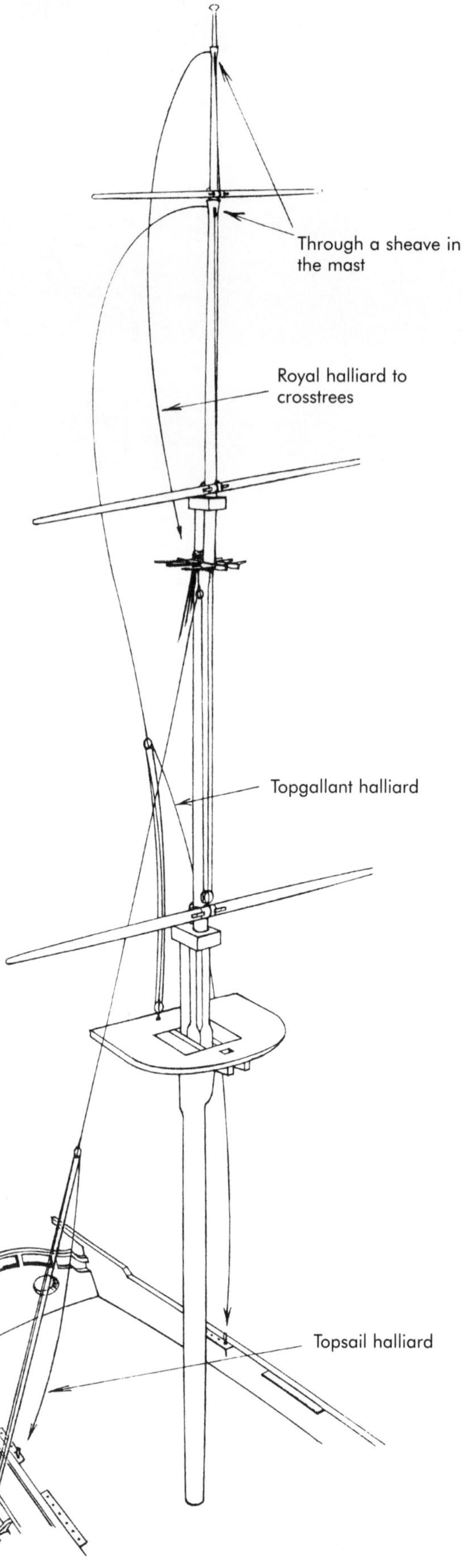

Topsail halliard

Mizzen Lifts: Topsail & Topgallant

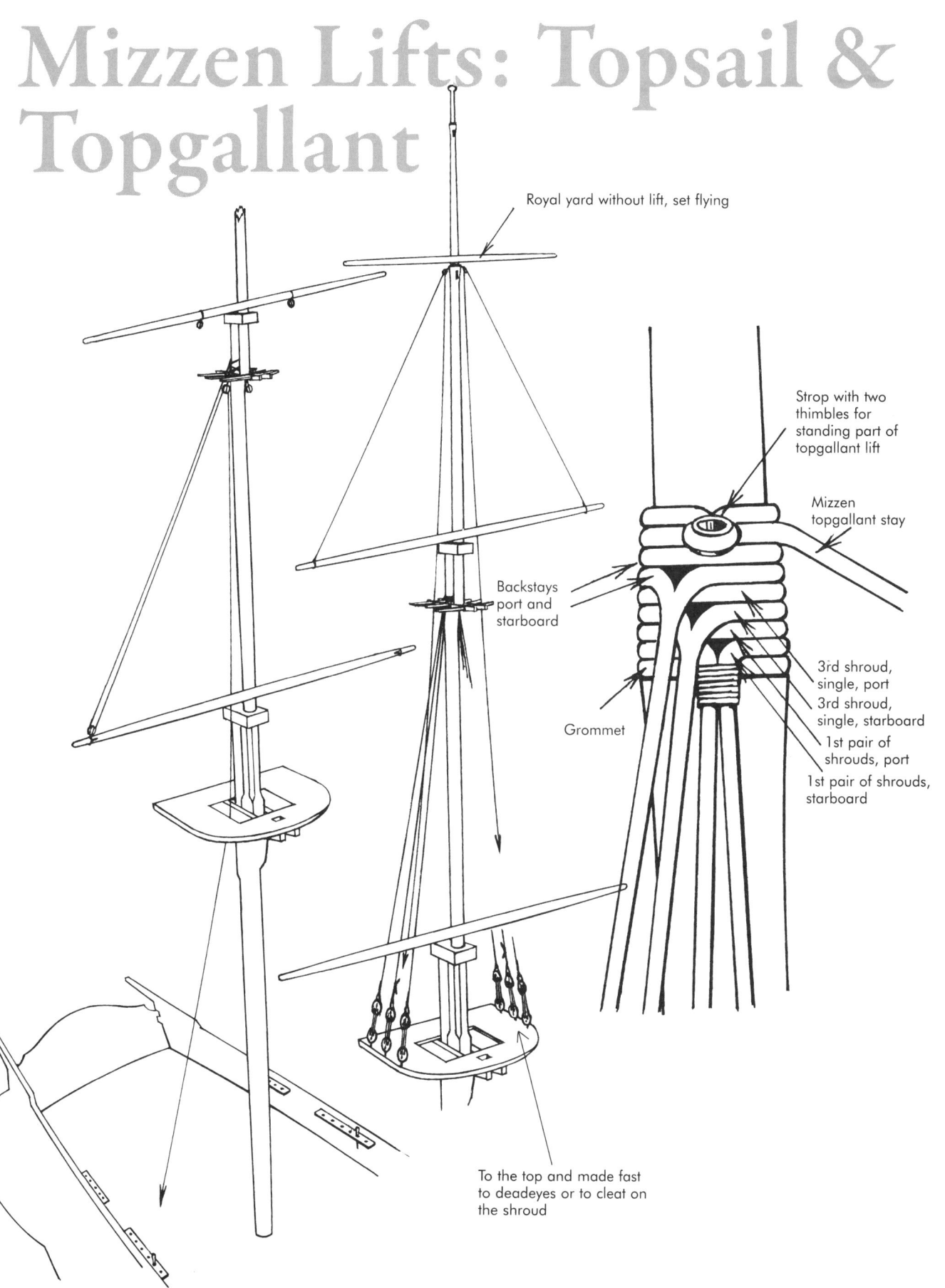

Cross Jack Braces

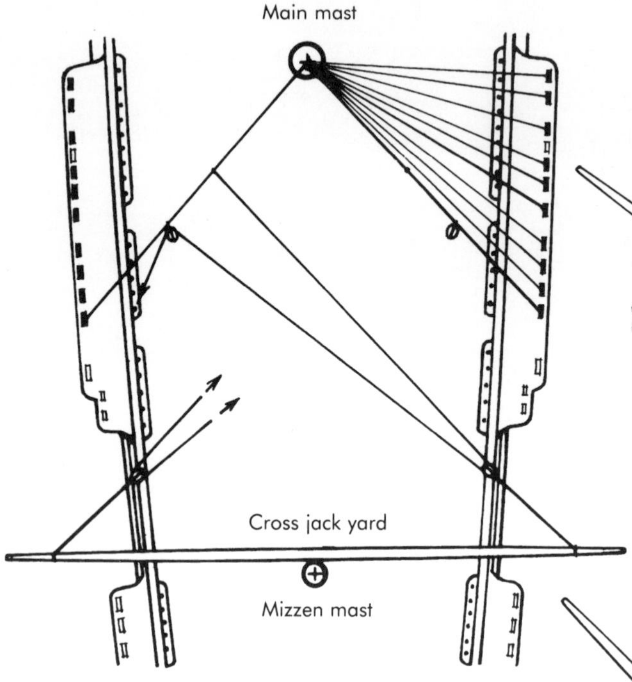

Main mast

Cross jack yard

Mizzen mast

The braces were taken forward, crossing each other, port brace reeving through the block on the aftermost starboard shroud, starboard brace reeving through the port block

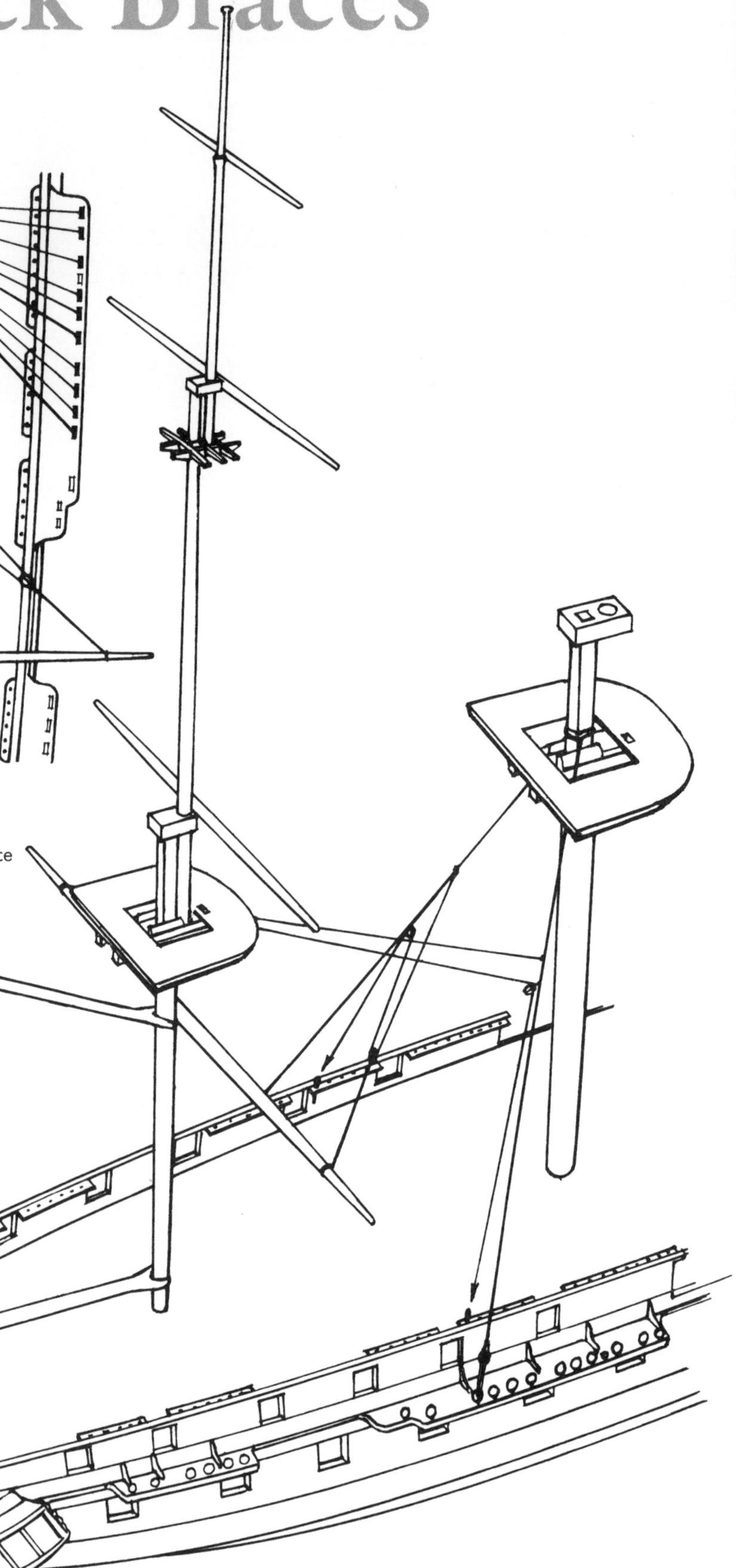

Mizzen Topsail & Topgallant Braces

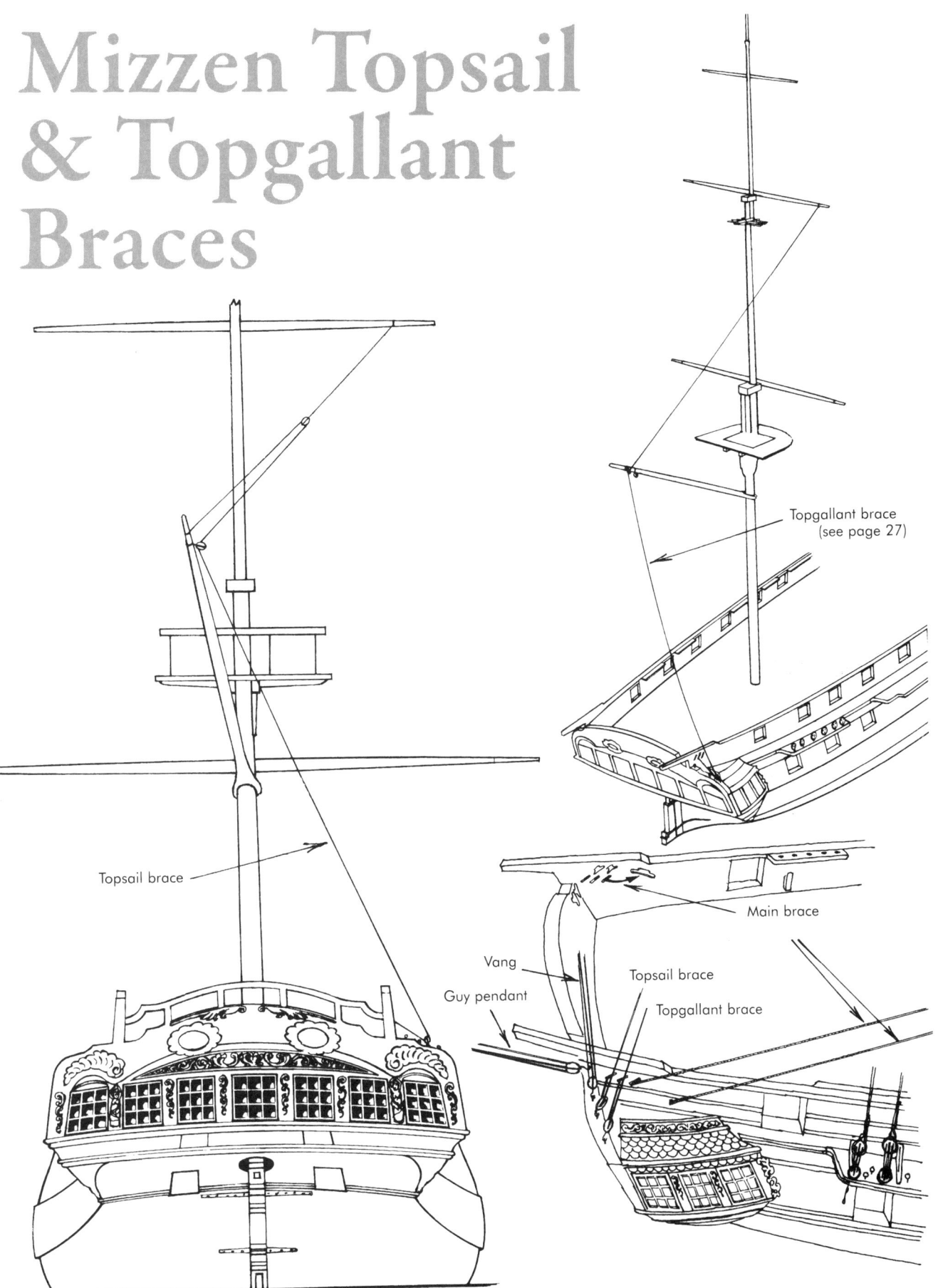

Fore & Main Slings

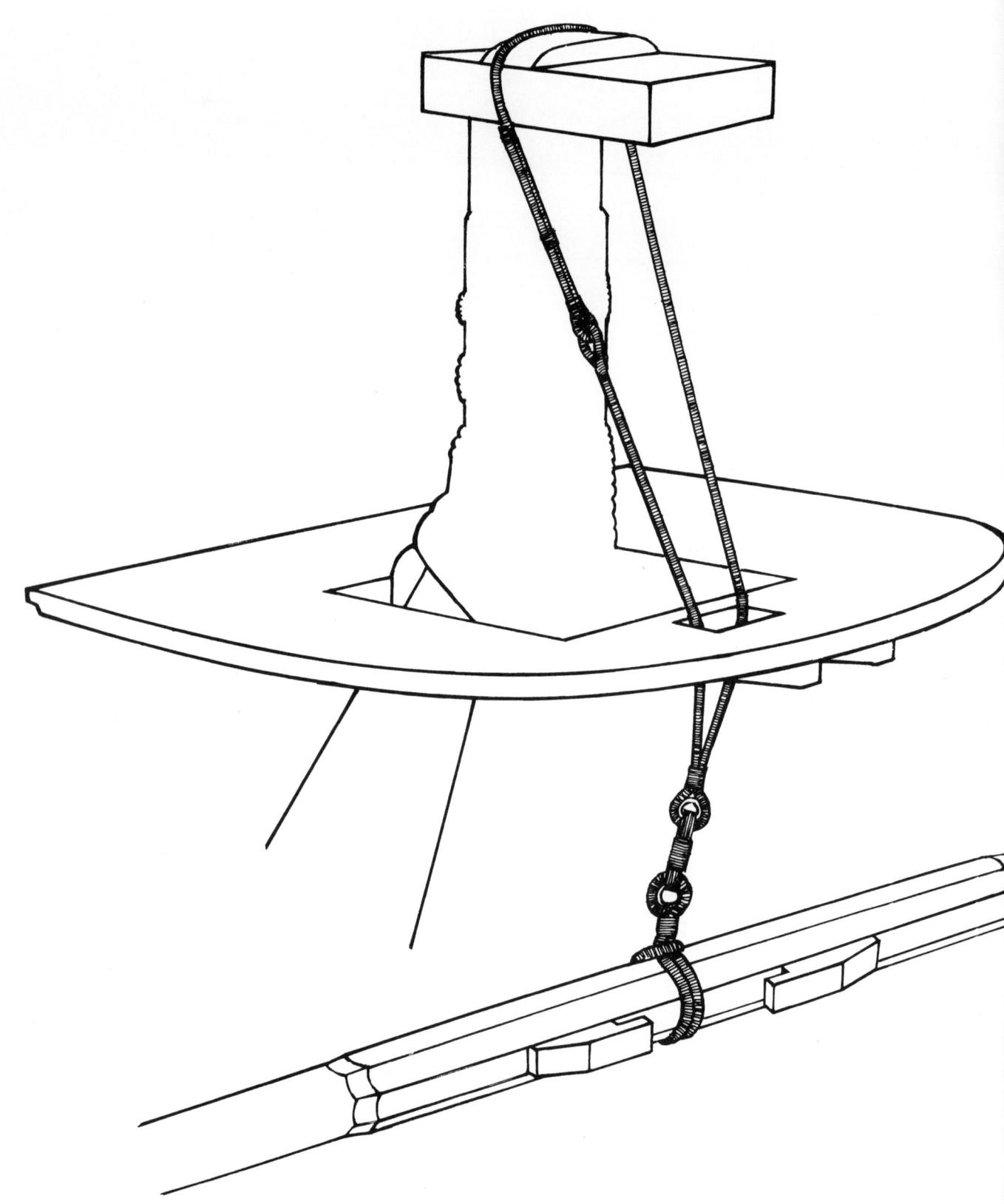

Fore & Main Jeers

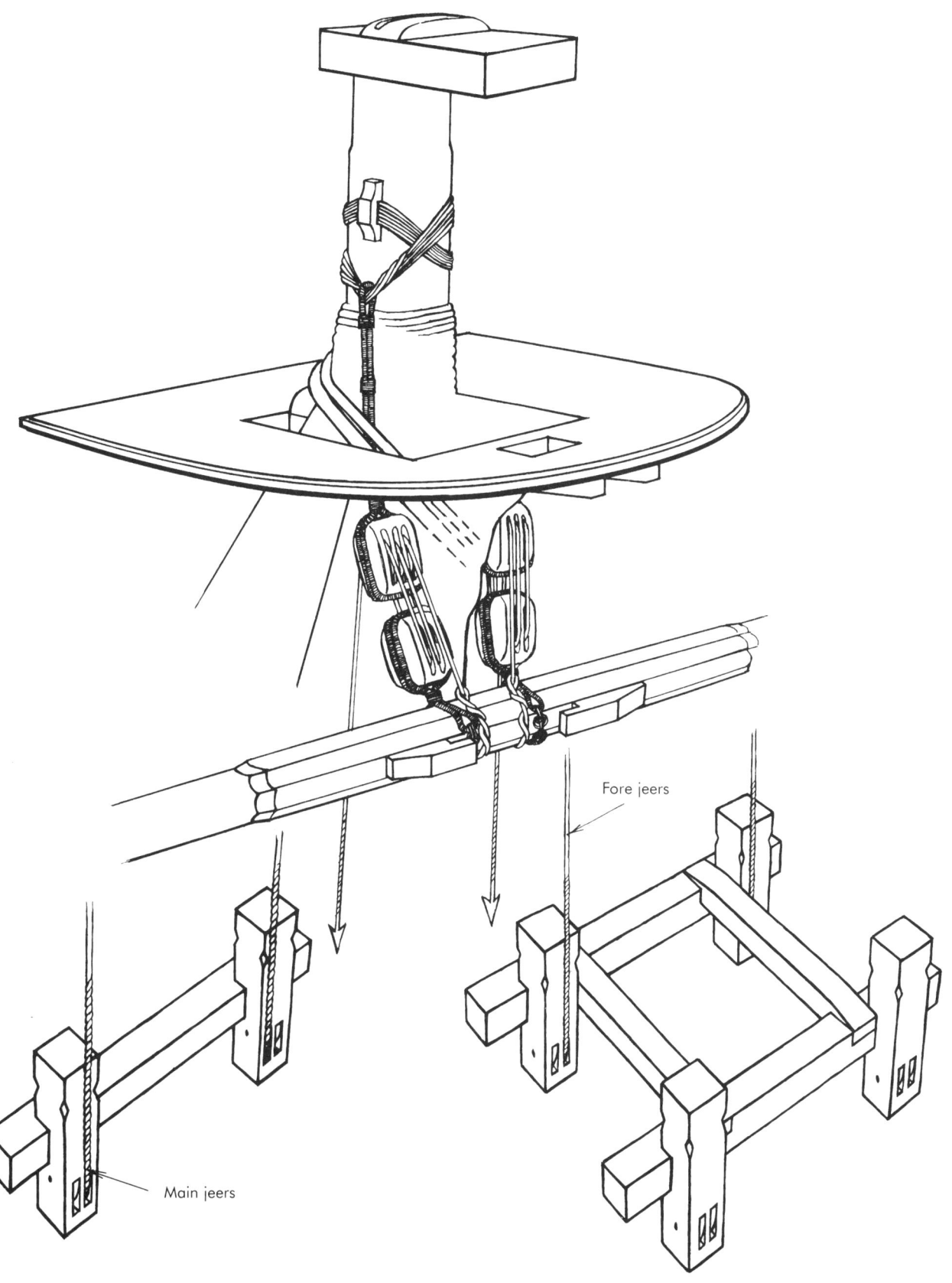

Truss Pendants
& Nave Line

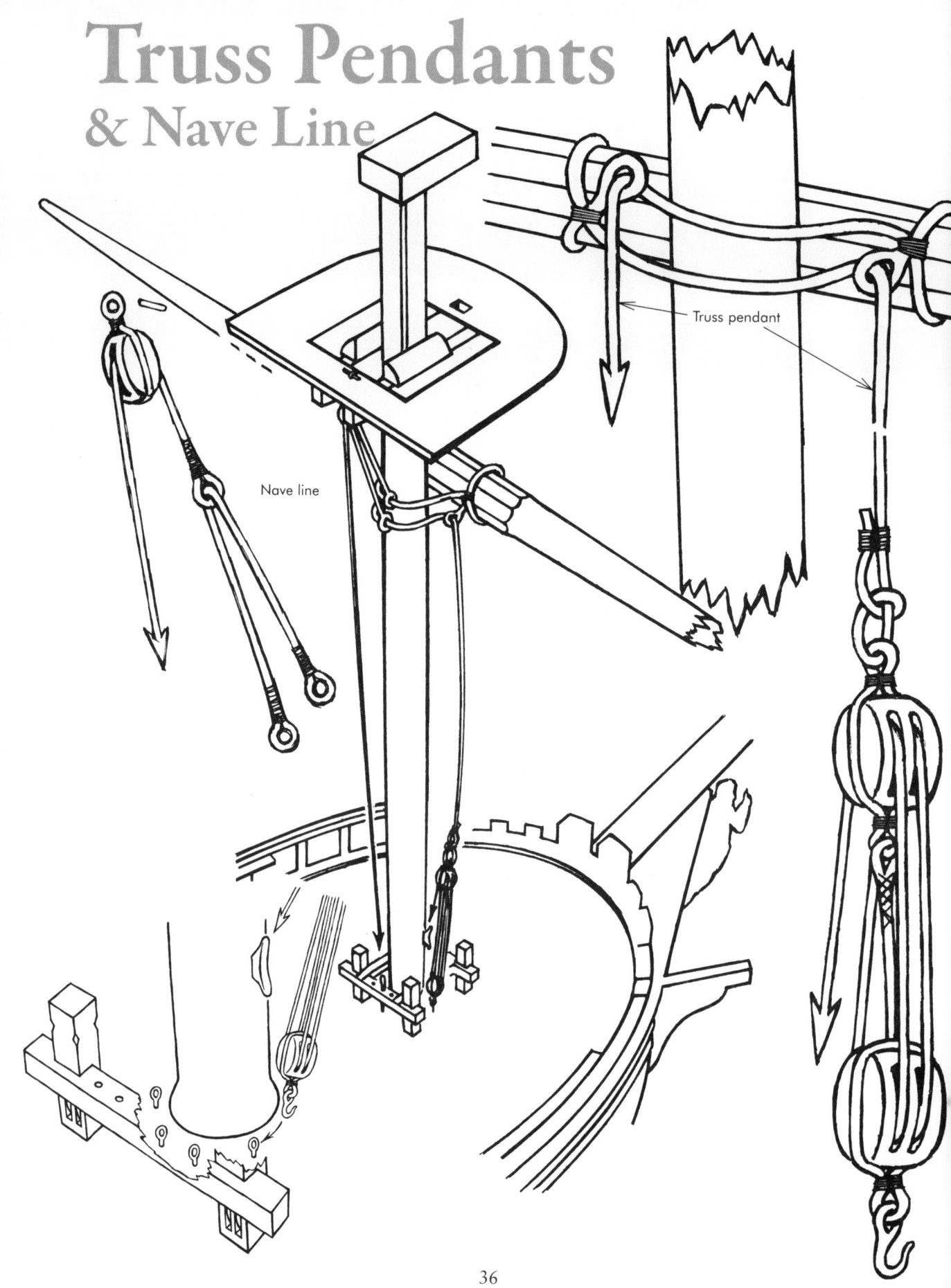

Truss pendant

Nave line

Main Lift

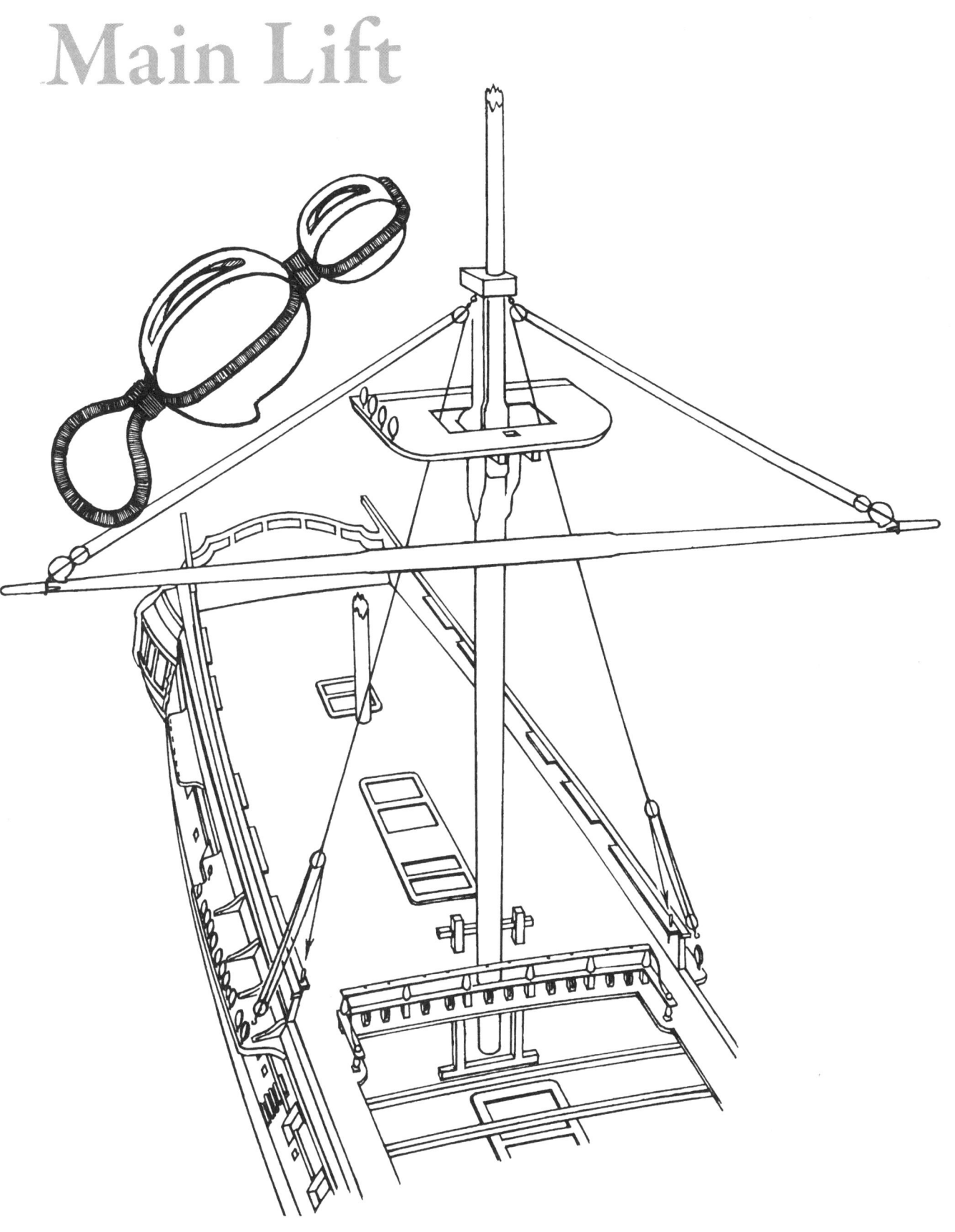

Fore Lift

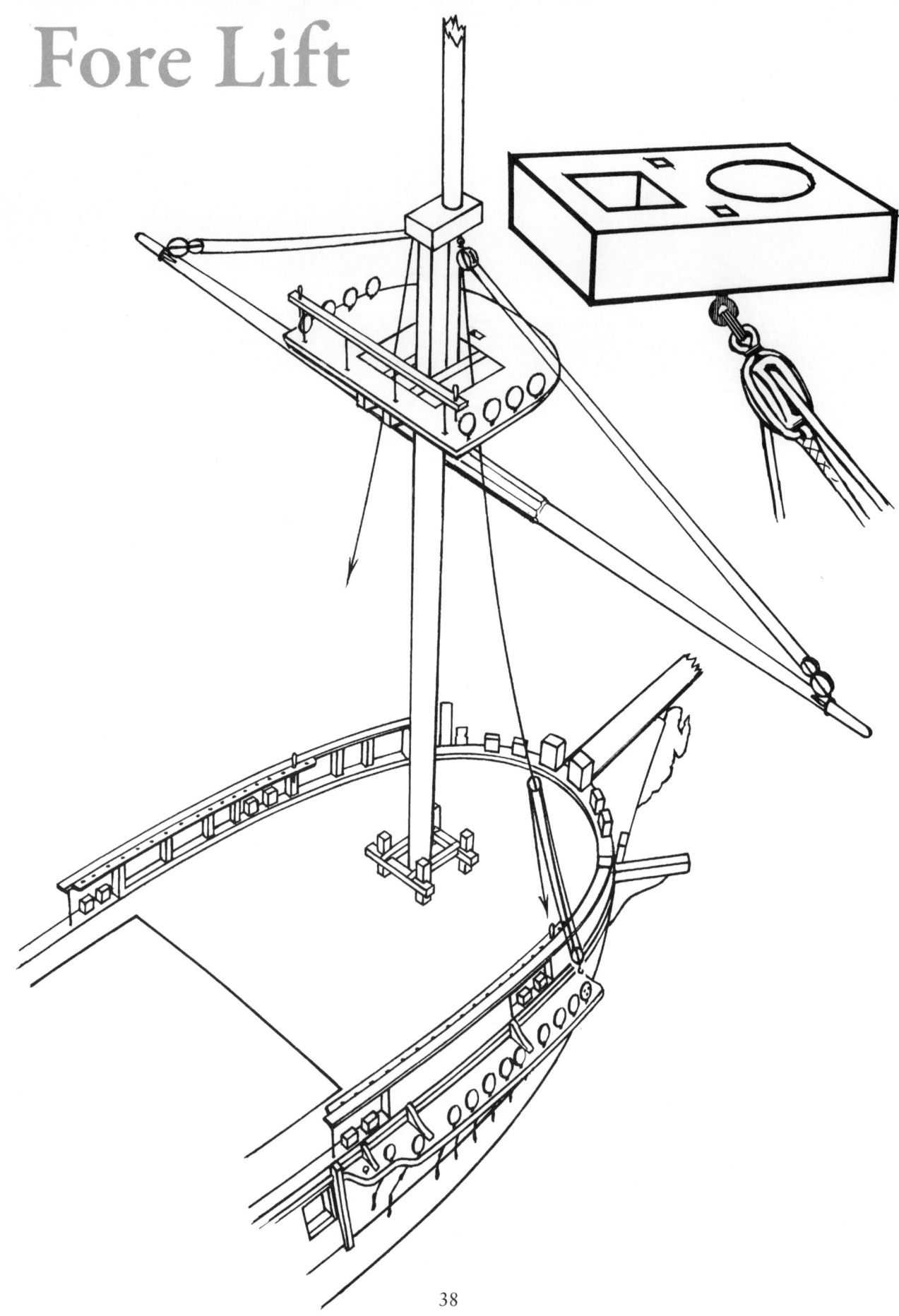

Main Topsail Yard Tye
& Halliard

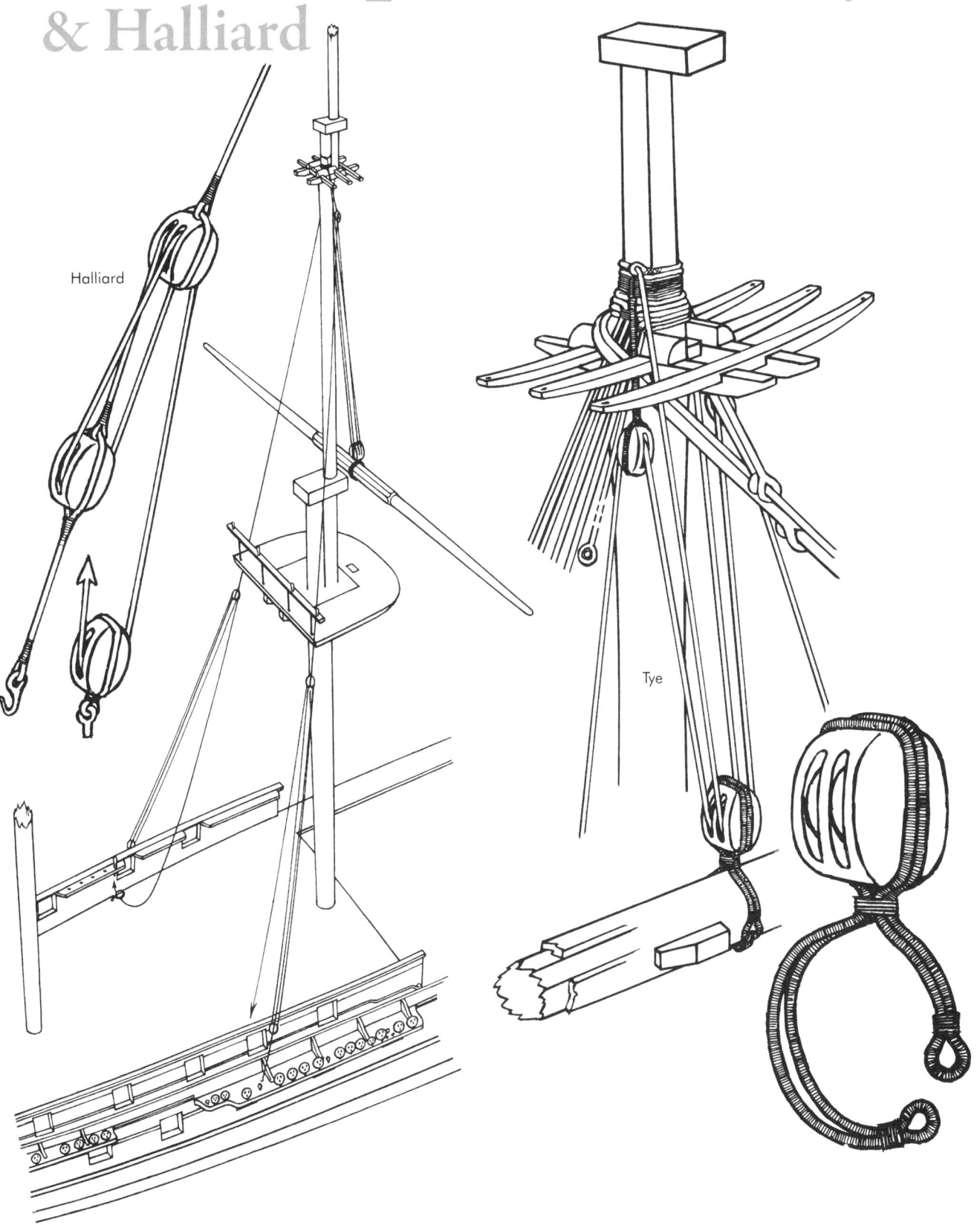

Halliard

Tye

Fore Topsail Yard Tye
& Halliard

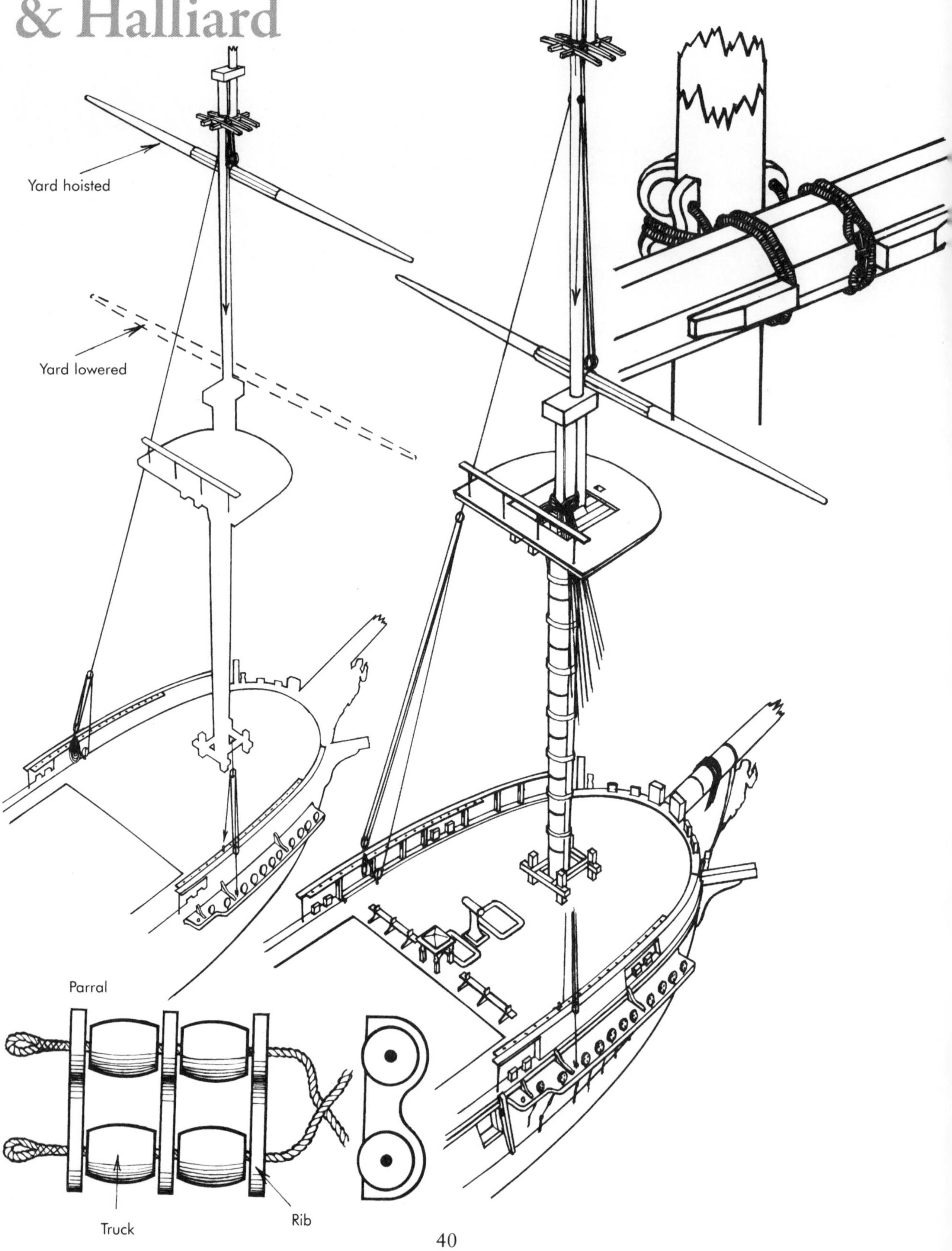

Yard hoisted

Yard lowered

Parral

Truck

Rib

40

Fore Topgallant/Royal Tye & Halliard

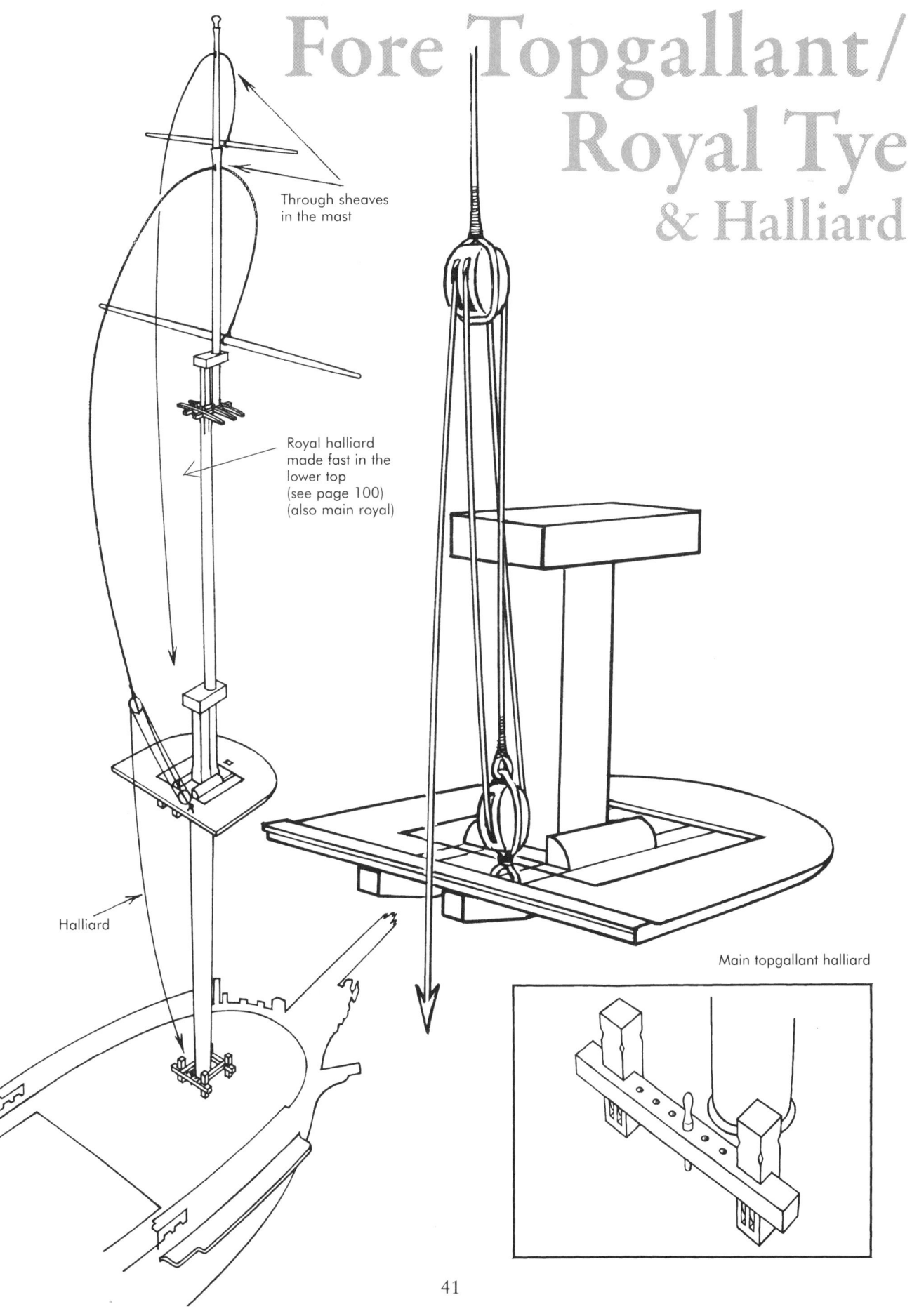

Main topgallant halliard

Fore Topsail Topgallant & Royal Lifts

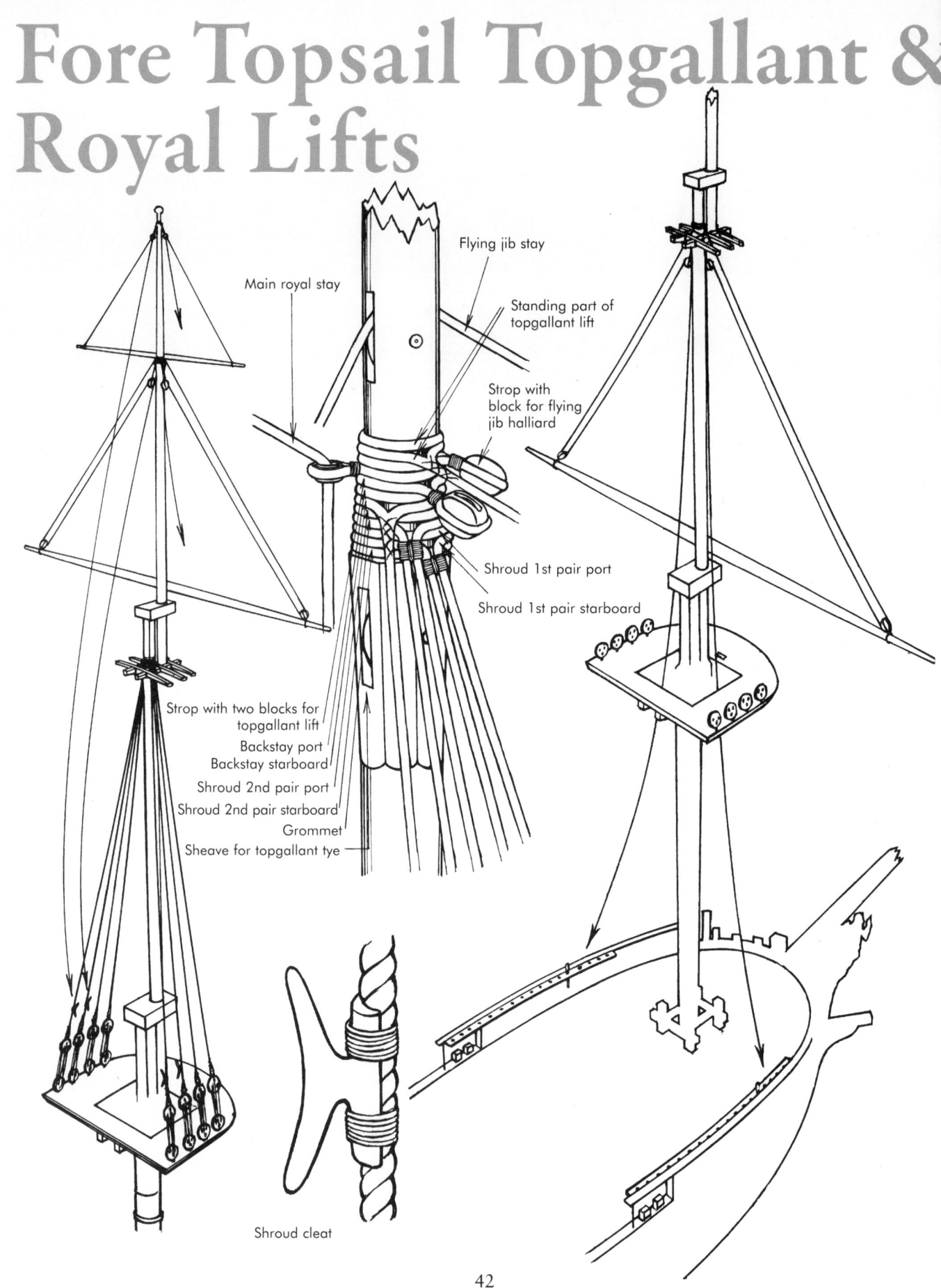

Main & Main Topsail Braces

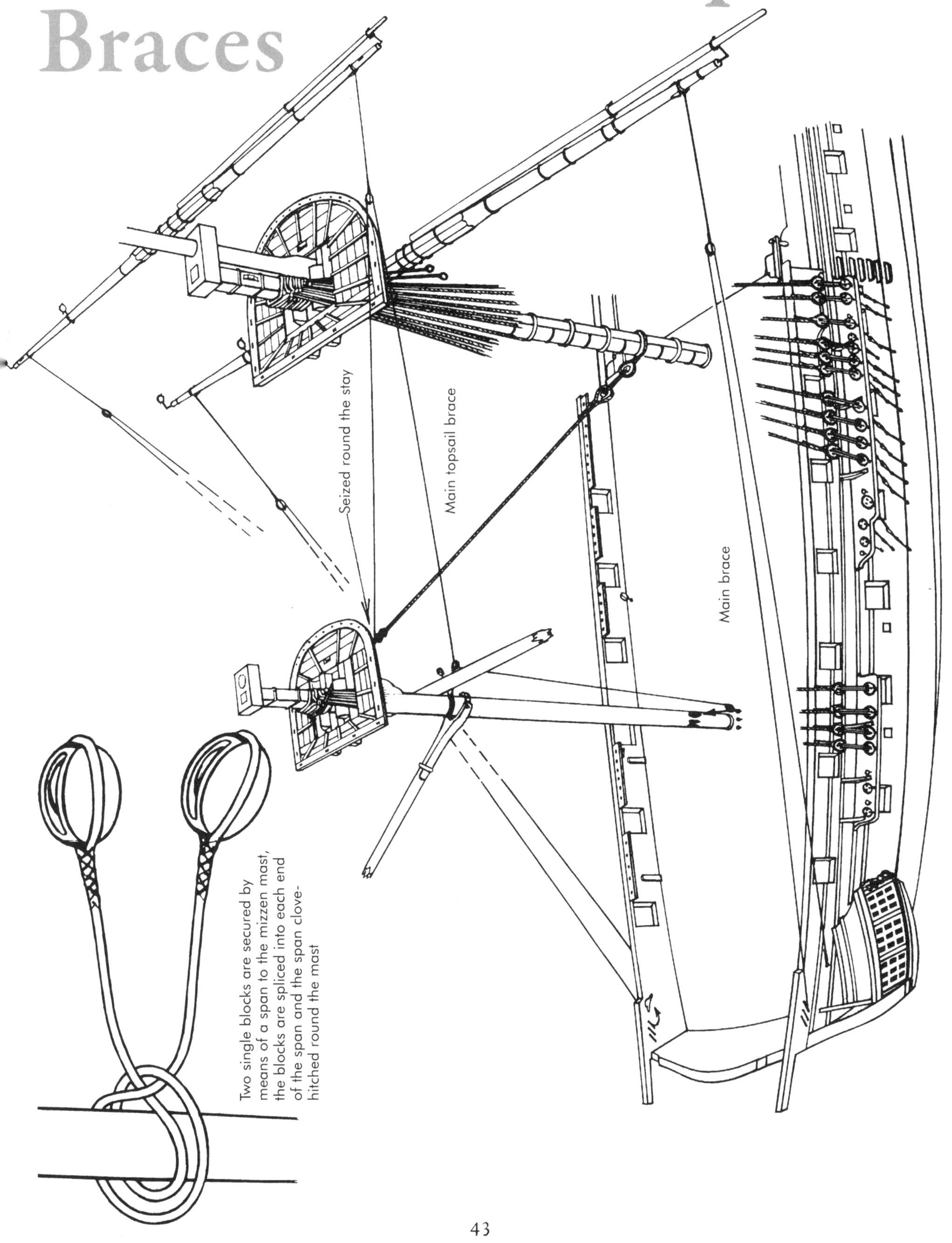

Seized round the stay

Main topsail brace

Main brace

Two single blocks are secured by means of a span to the mizzen mast, the blocks are spliced into each end of the span and the span clove-hitched round the mast

Fore & Fore Topsail Braces

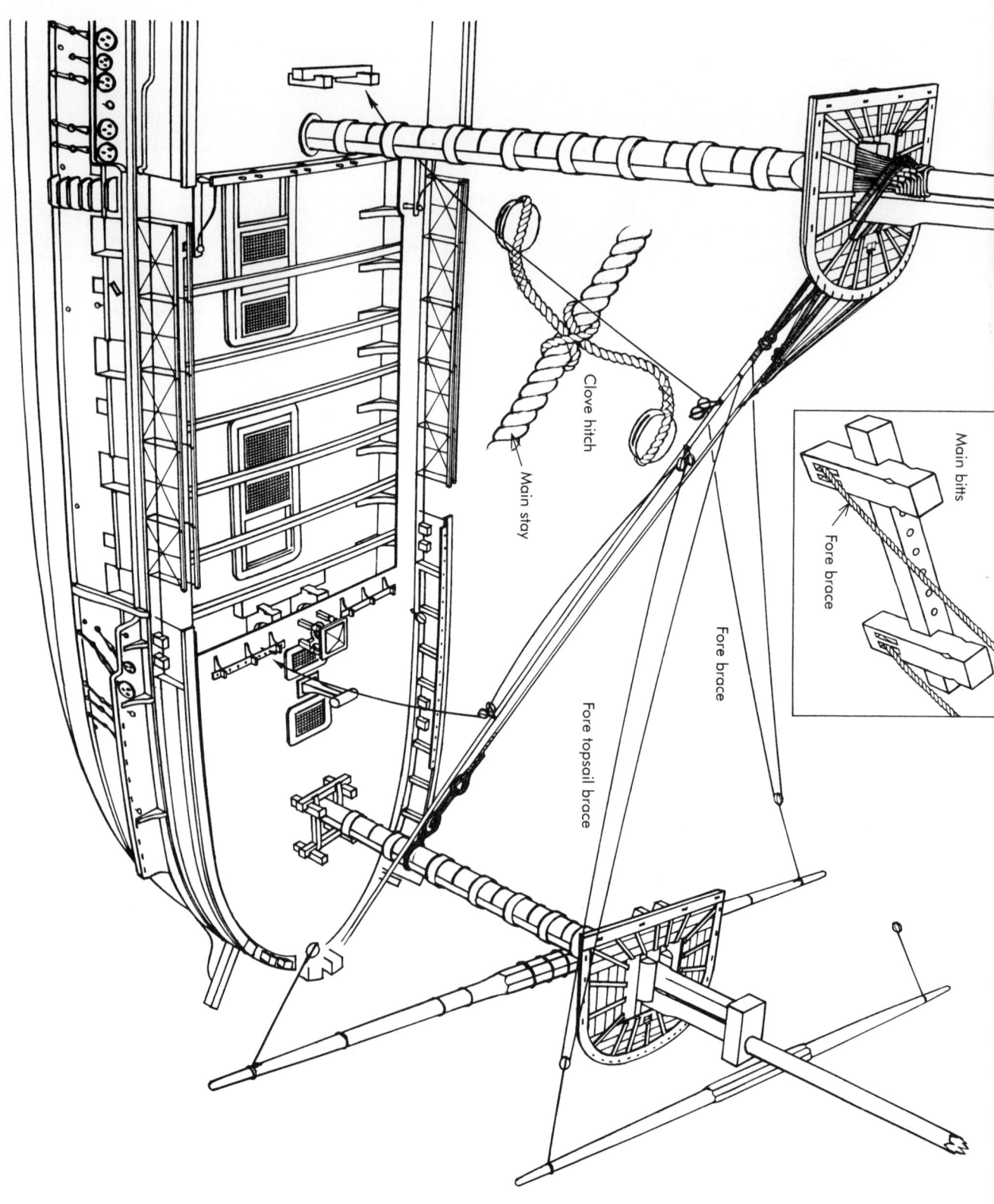

Fore & Main Topgallant Braces

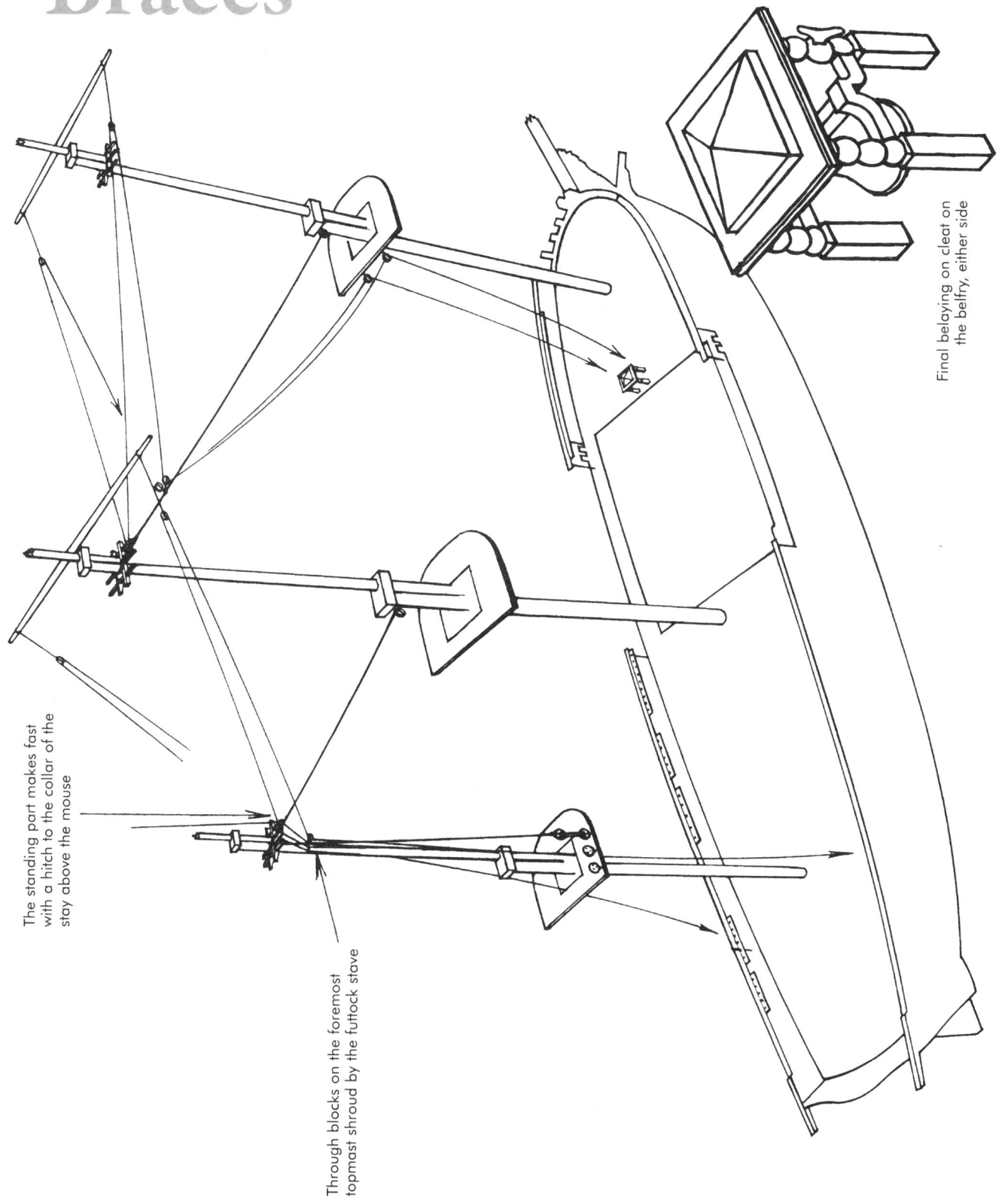

Fore & Main Royal Braces

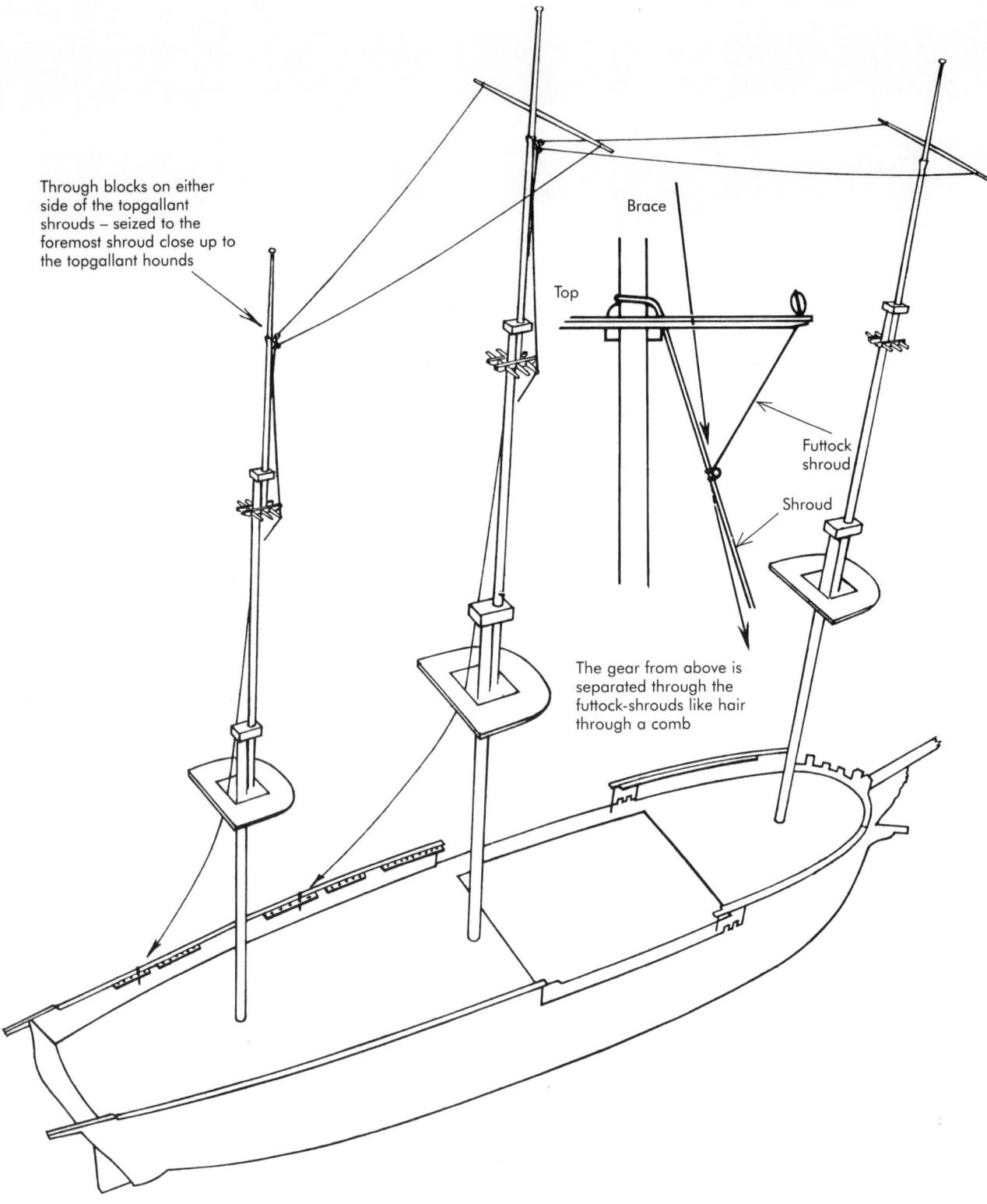

Through blocks on either side of the topgallant shrouds – seized to the foremost shroud close up to the topgallant hounds

Brace

Top

Futtock shroud

Shroud

The gear from above is separated through the futtock-shrouds like hair through a comb

Spritsail & Spritsail Topsail Braces

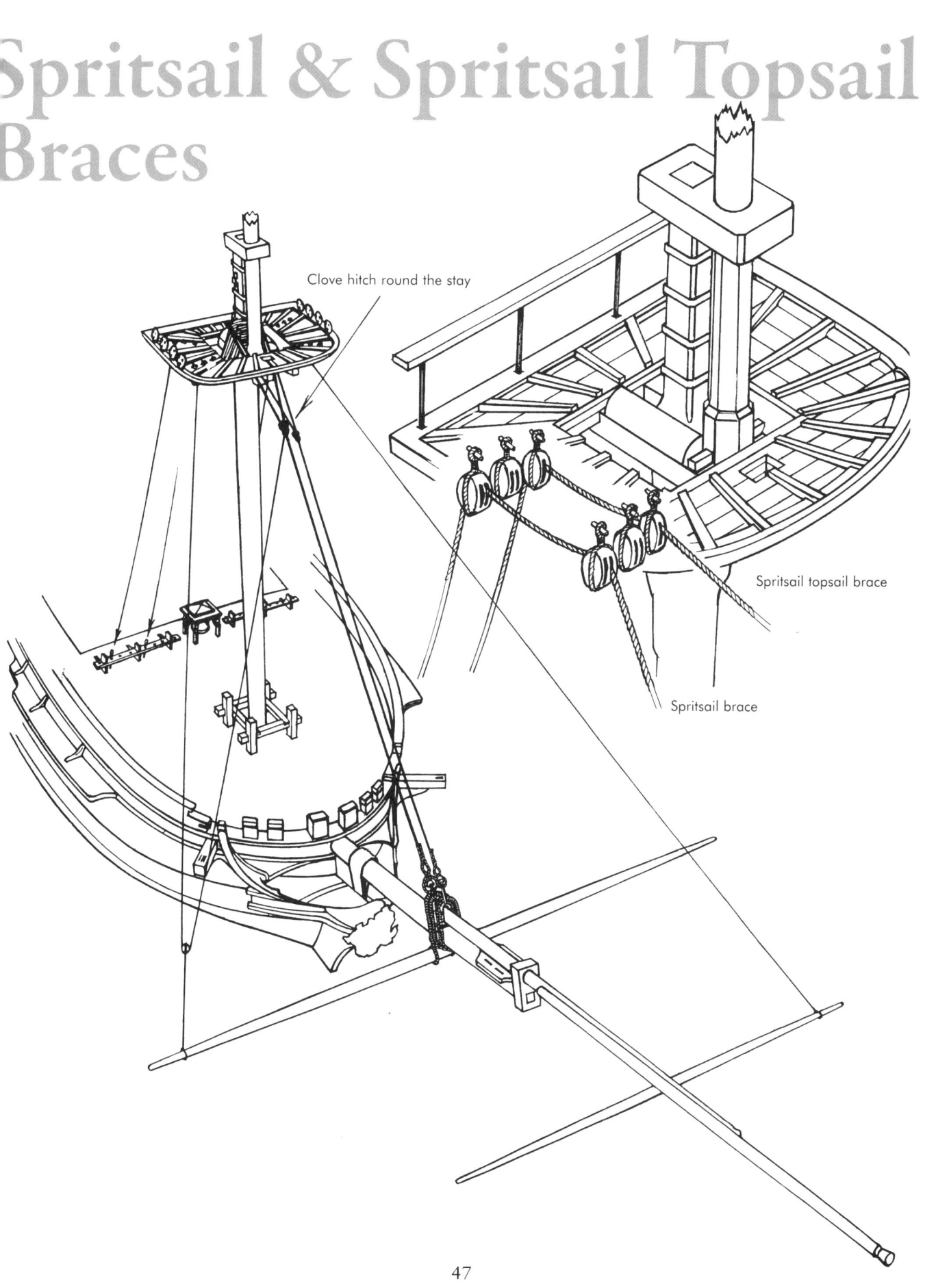

Fore Sheet, Tack & Clueline

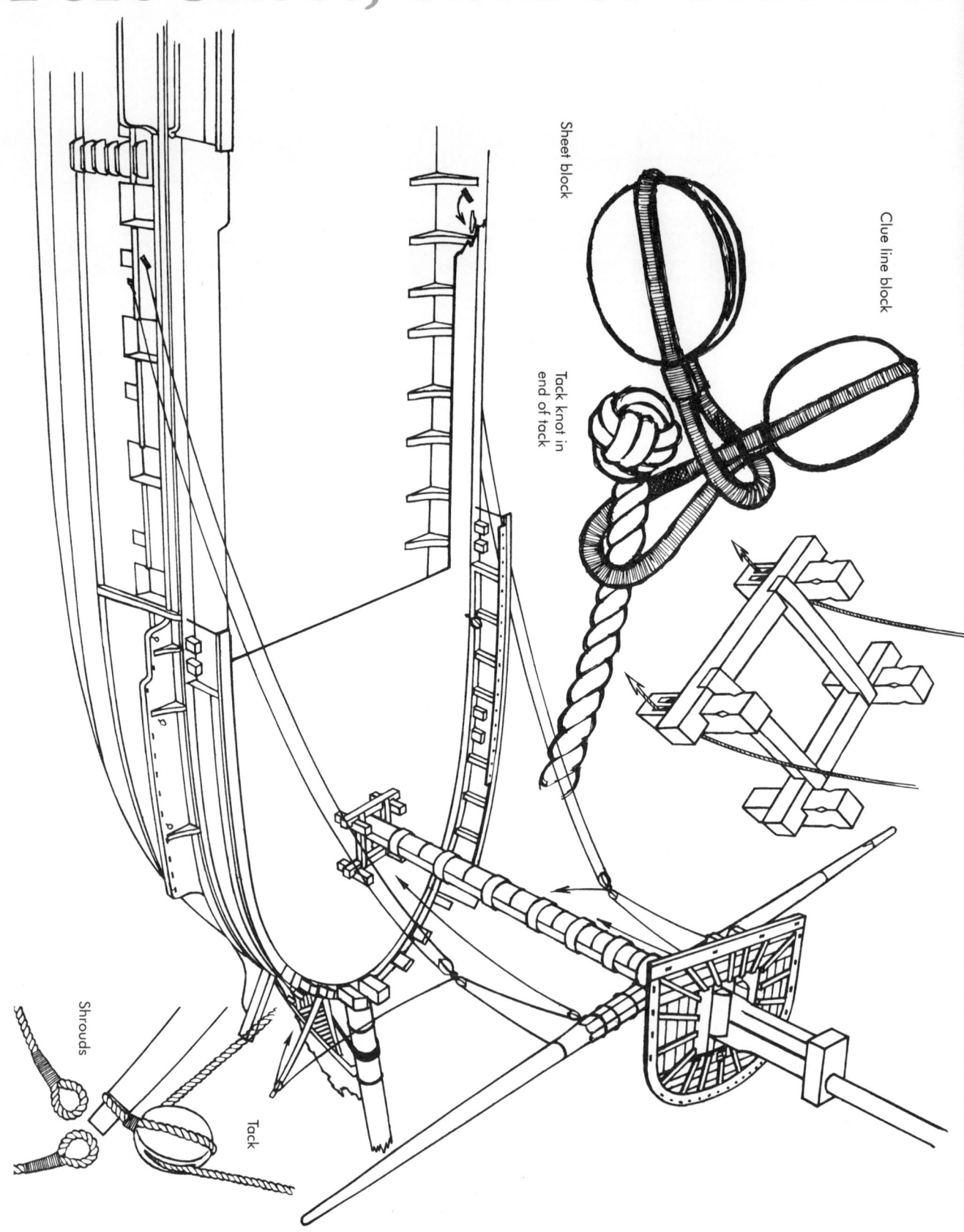

Fore Topsail Sheet & Clueline

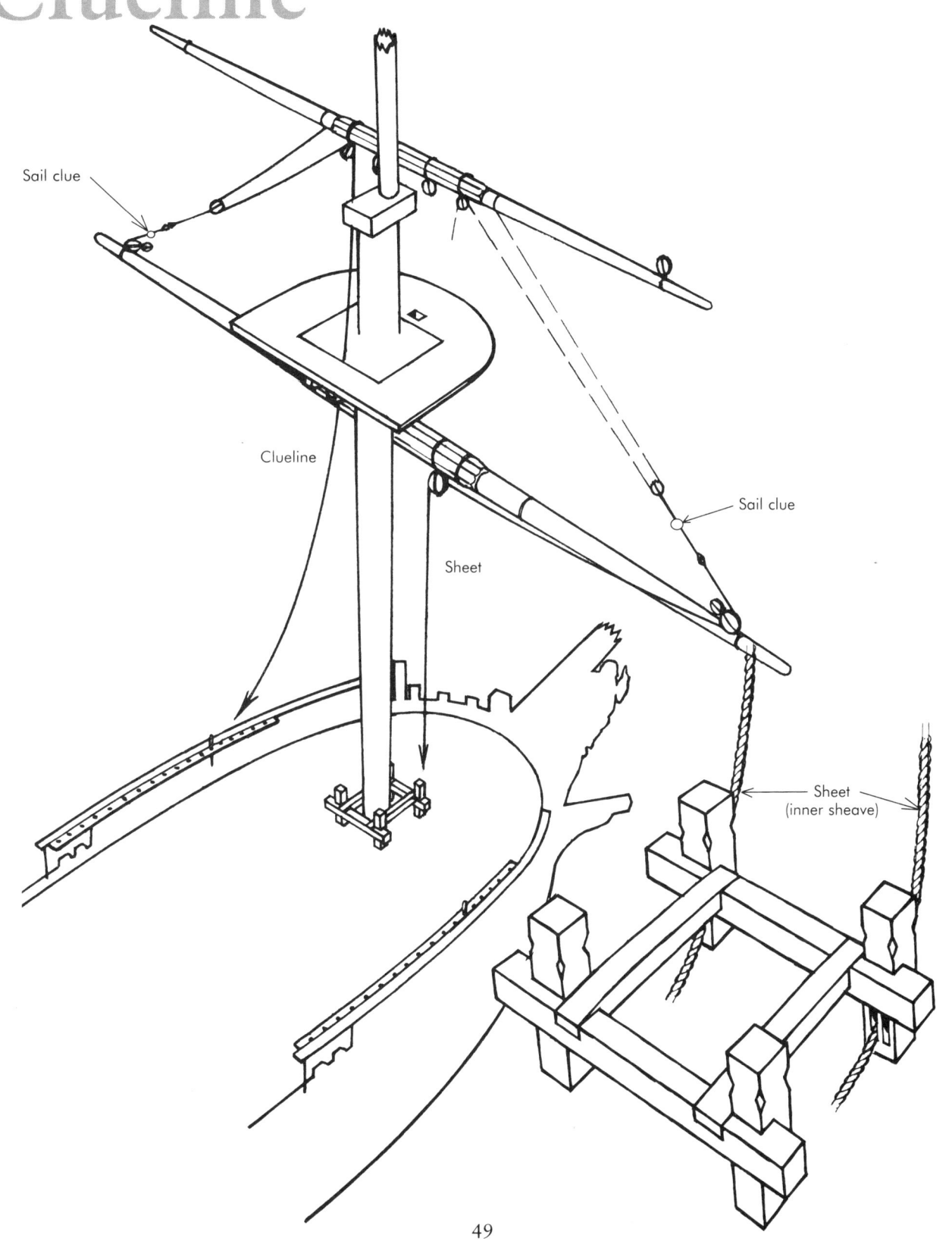

Fore Topgallant & Royal Sheet, Fore Topgallant Clueline

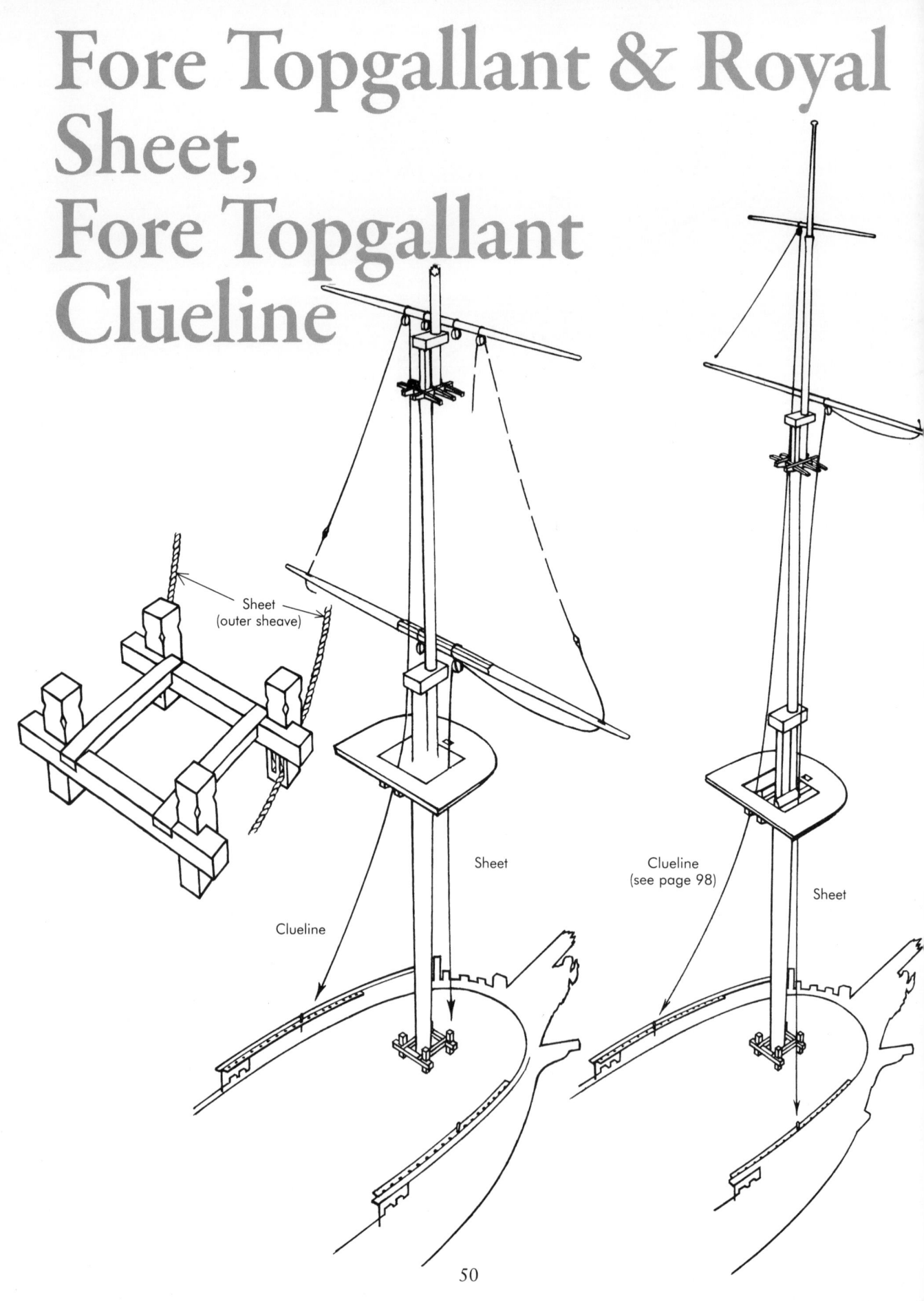

Main Sheet, Clueline & Tack

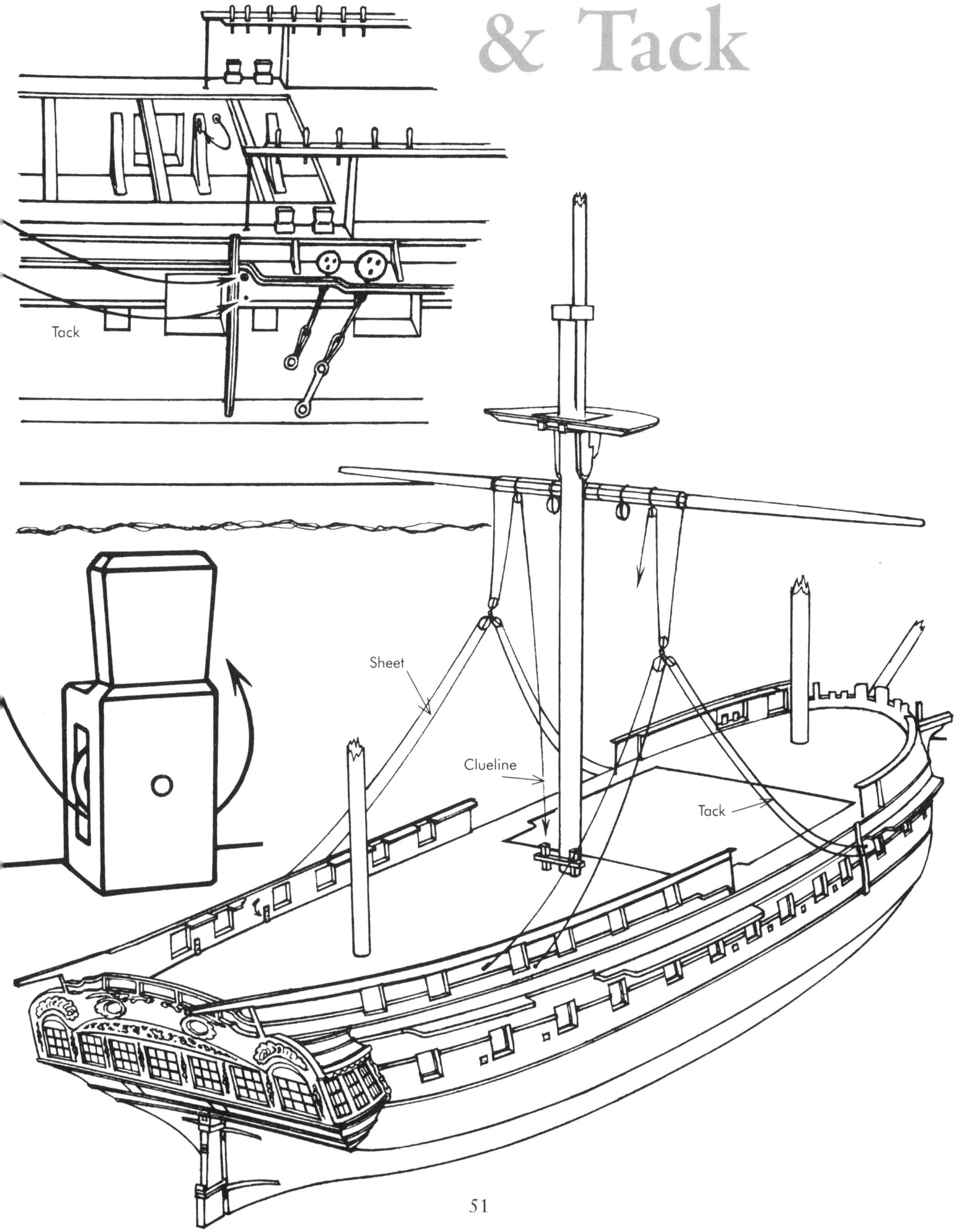

Tack

Sheet

Clueline

Tack

51

Main Topsail Sheet

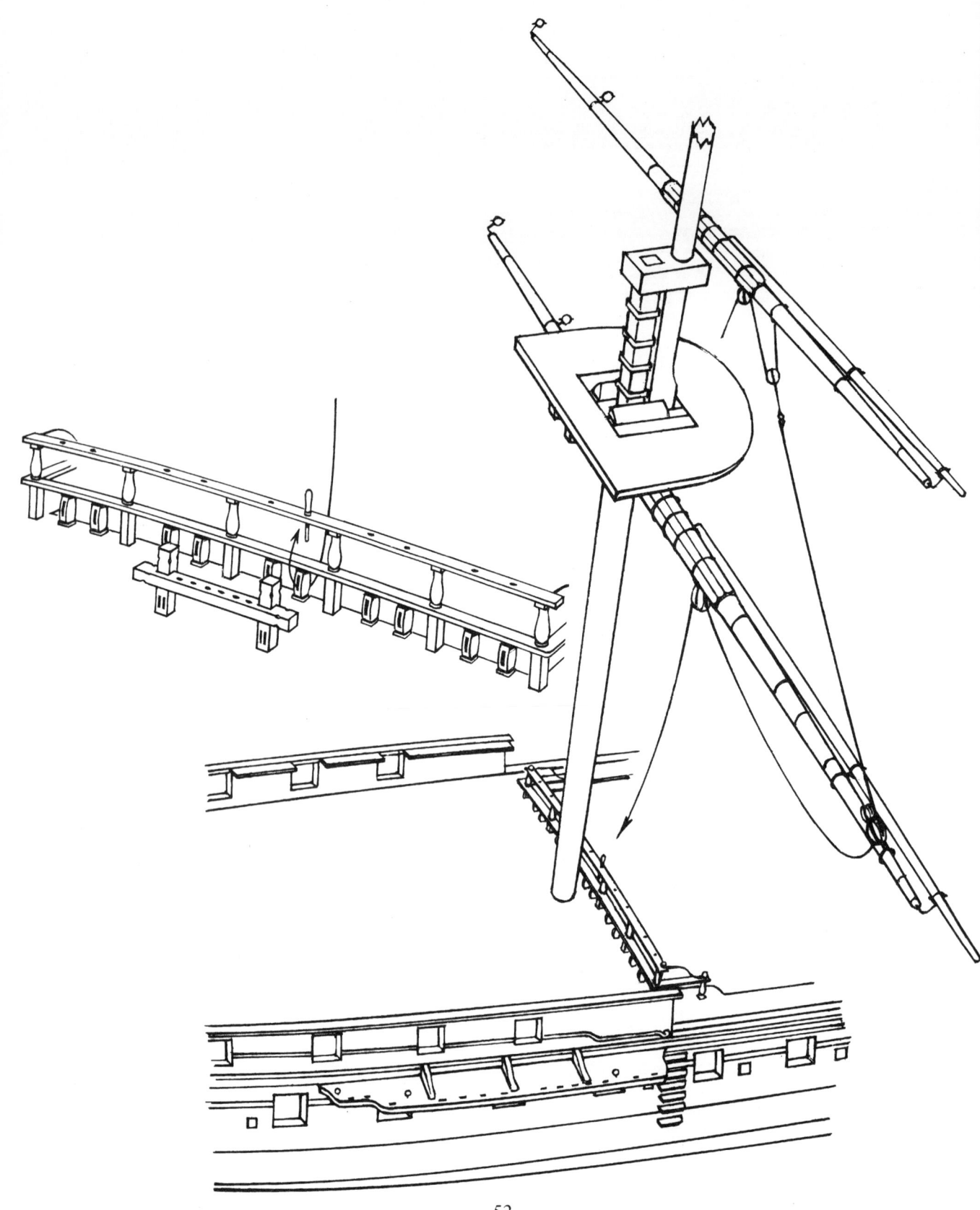

Main Topsail Lift

Topgallant & Royal Lifts

These were rigged in the same way as those on the fore topgallant and royal yard.
See page 42.

Main Topsail Clueline

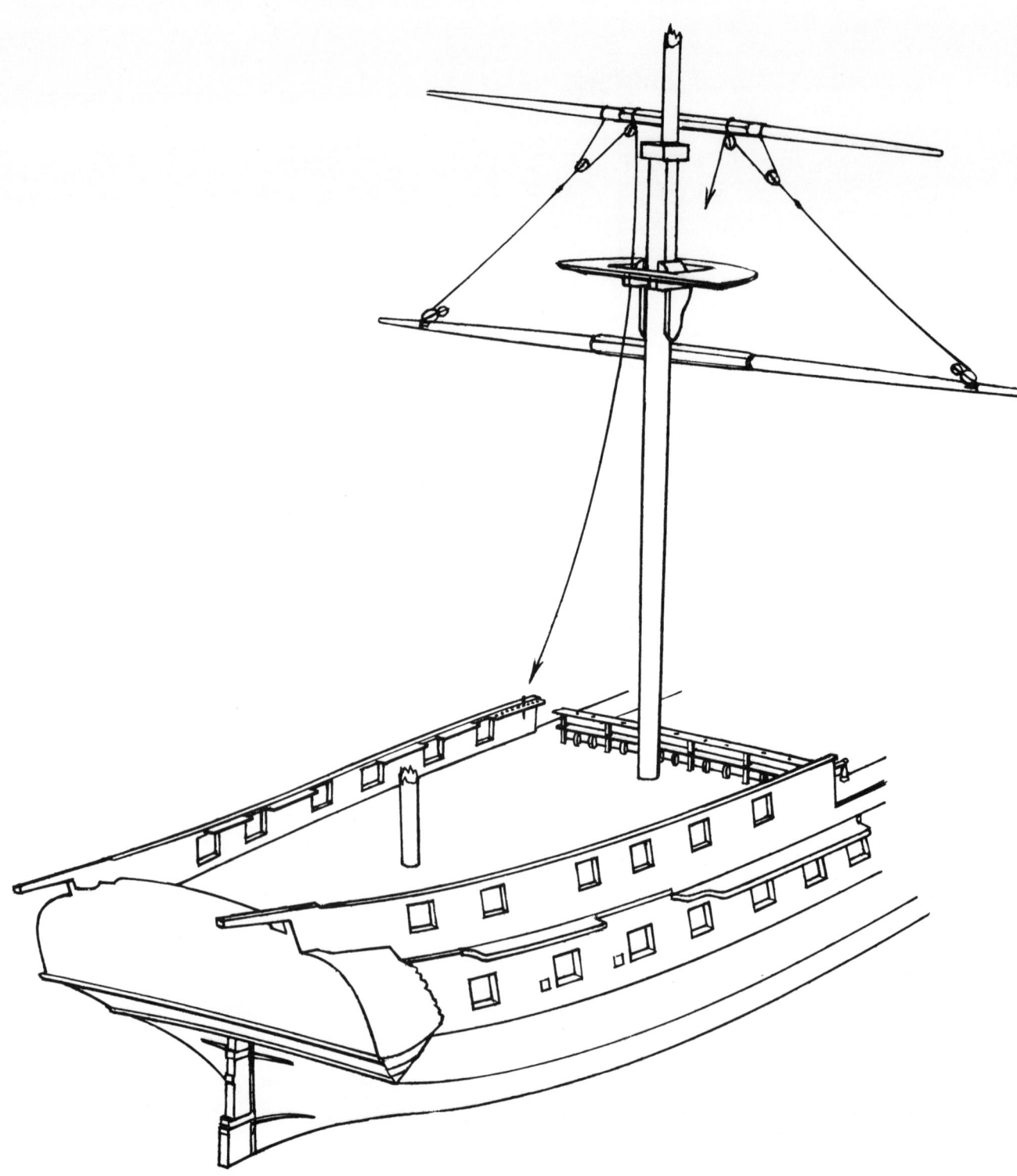

Main Topgallant Sheet & Clueline, Main Royal Sheet

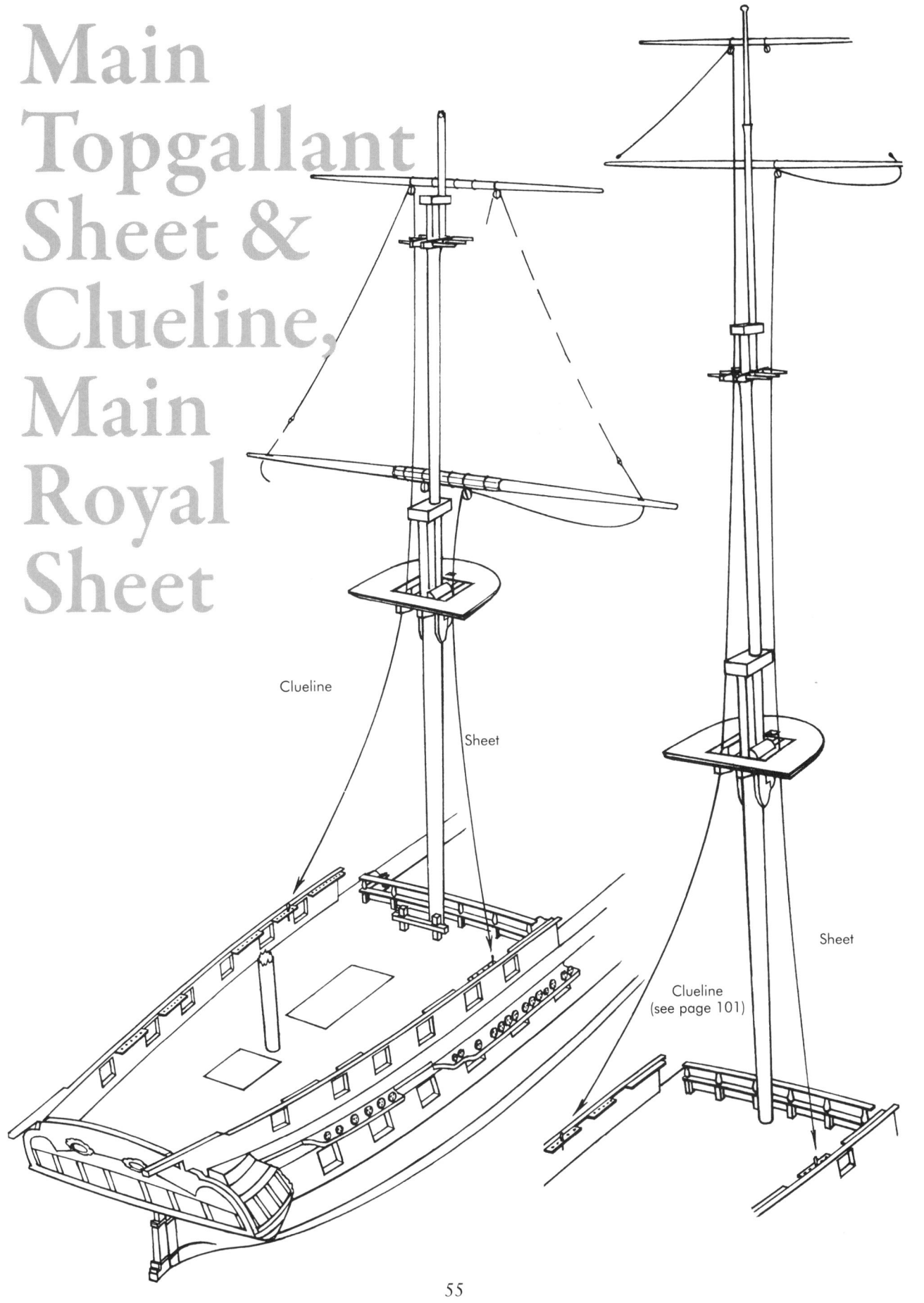

Mizzen Topsail Sheet & Clueline

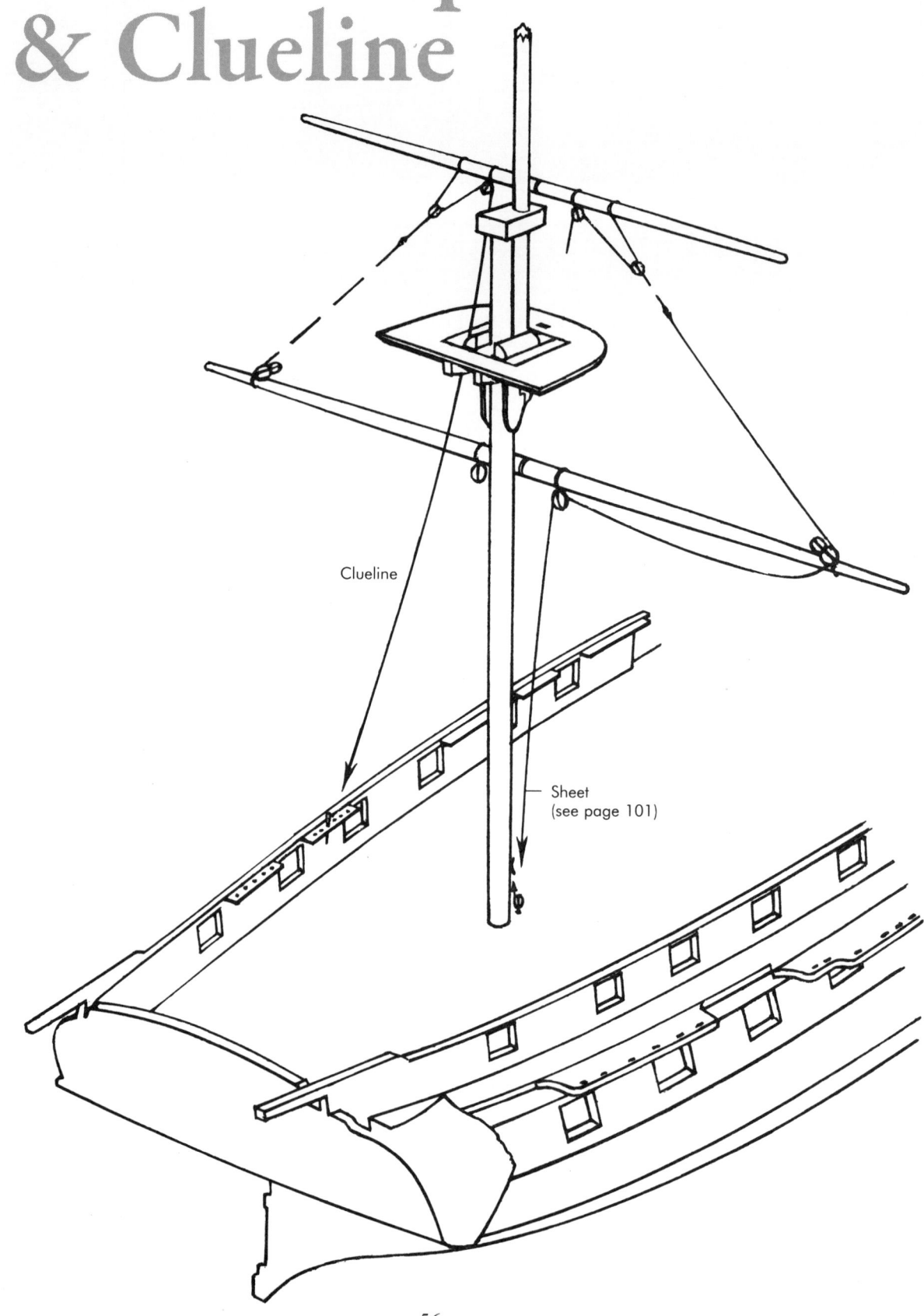

Mizzen Topgallant Sheet & Clueline, Mizzen Royal Sheet

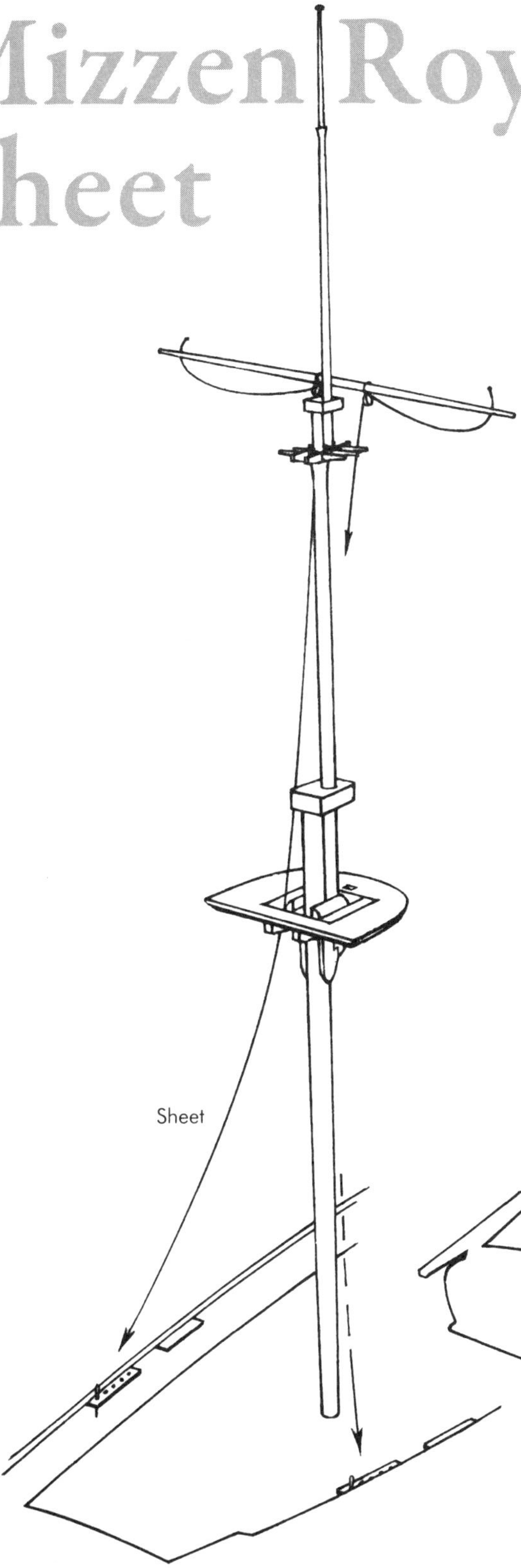

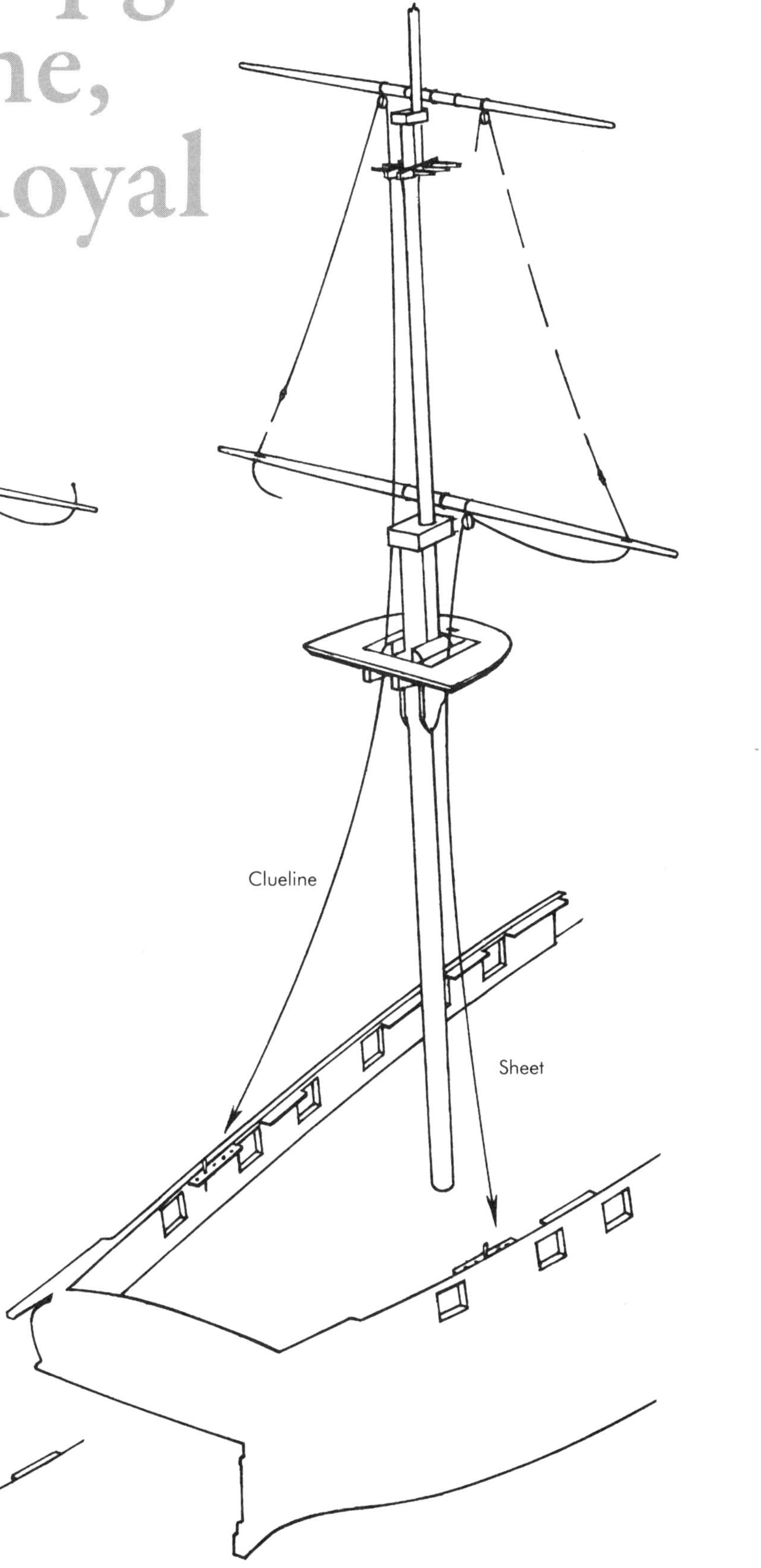

Clueline

Sheet

Sheet

57

Jibboom & Flying Jibboom Guys

Through thimbles strapped to the top of the spritsail yard

Splice to a single block

Eyebolt on the fore side of the Cathead

Single block stropped or hooked to the eyebolt

Spritsail Sling, Spritsail Yard & Spritsail Topsail Yard Halliards

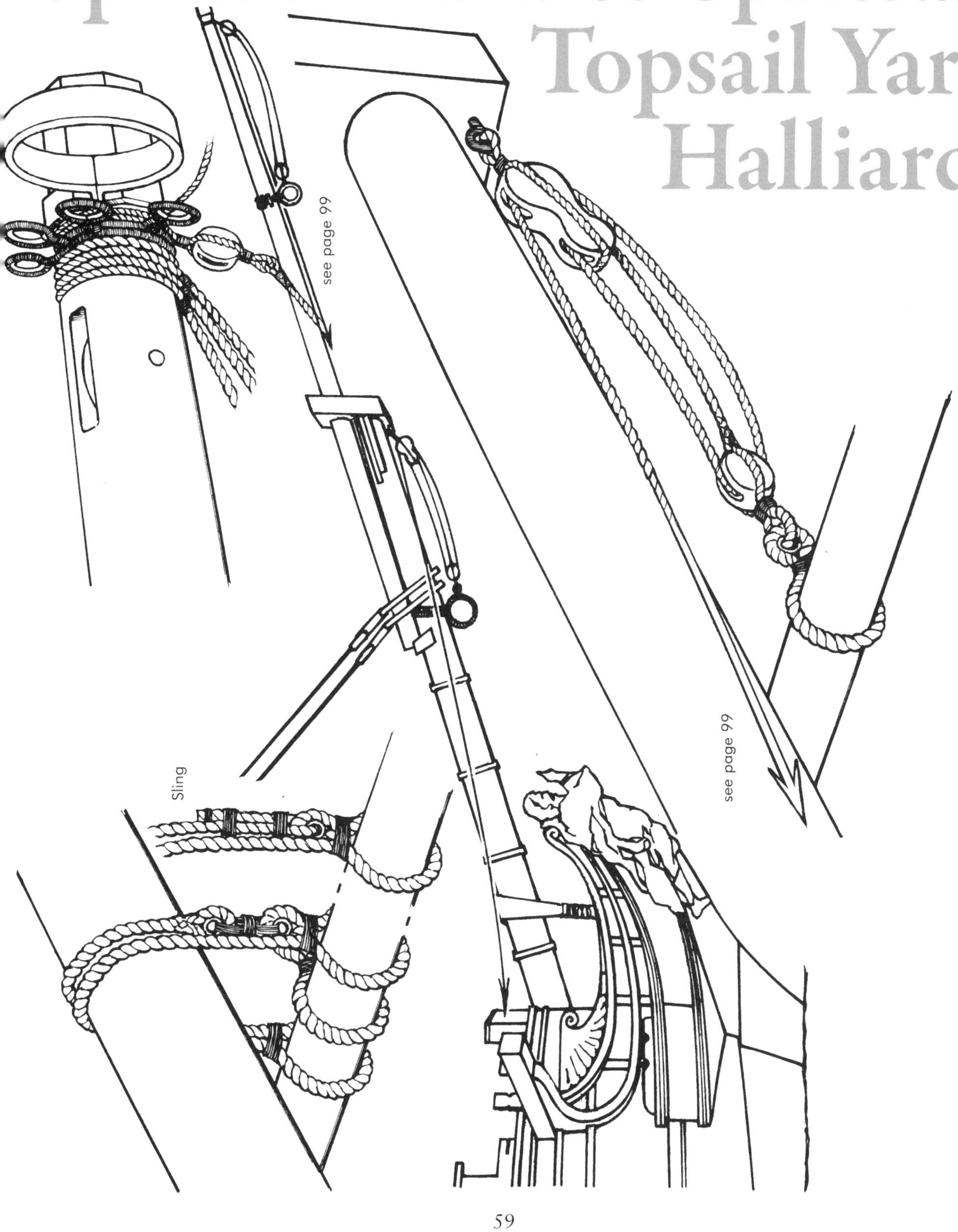

see page 99

Sling

see page 99

59

Royal Stay

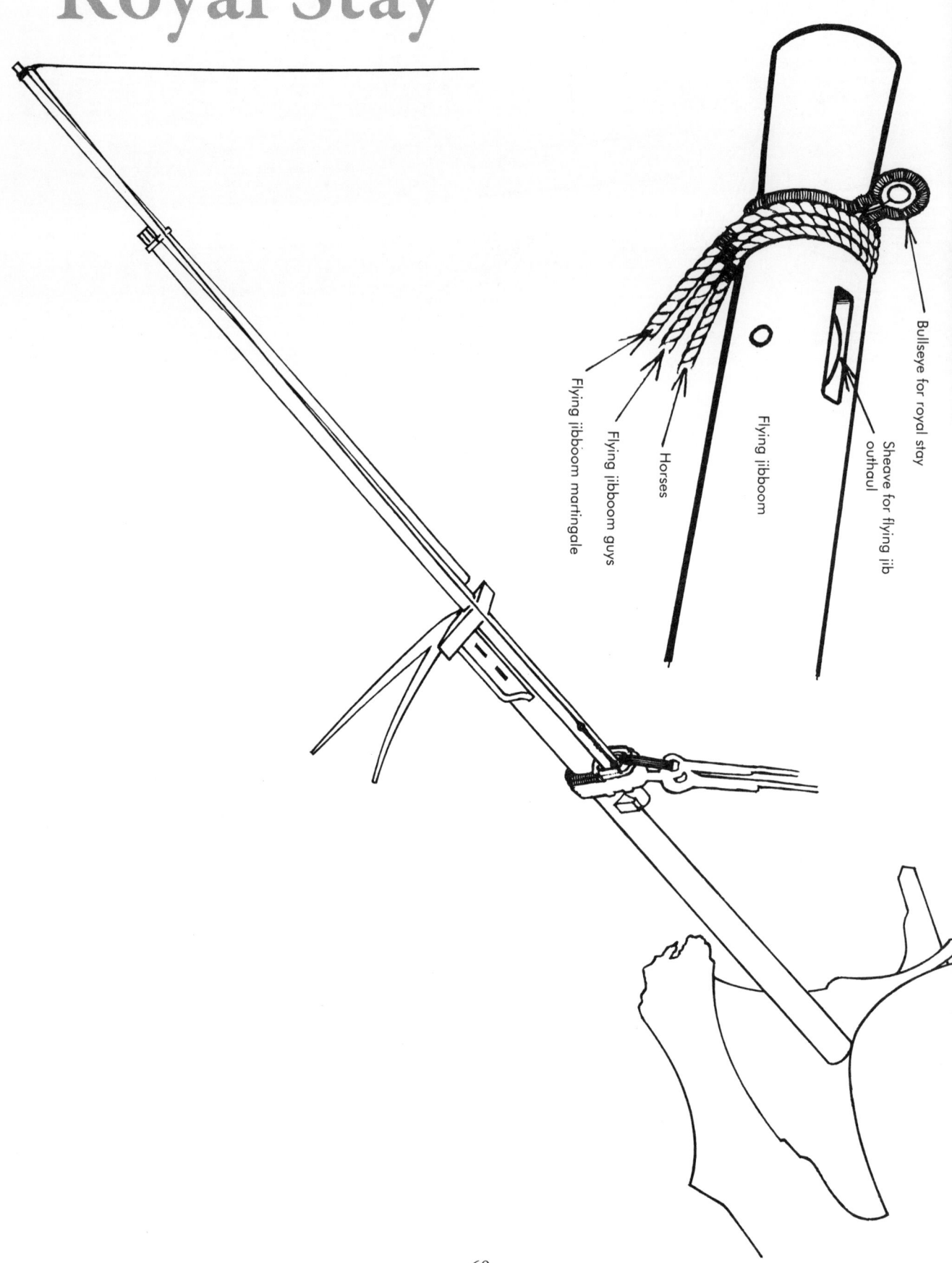

Fore Topgallant Stay & Bumpkin Shrouds

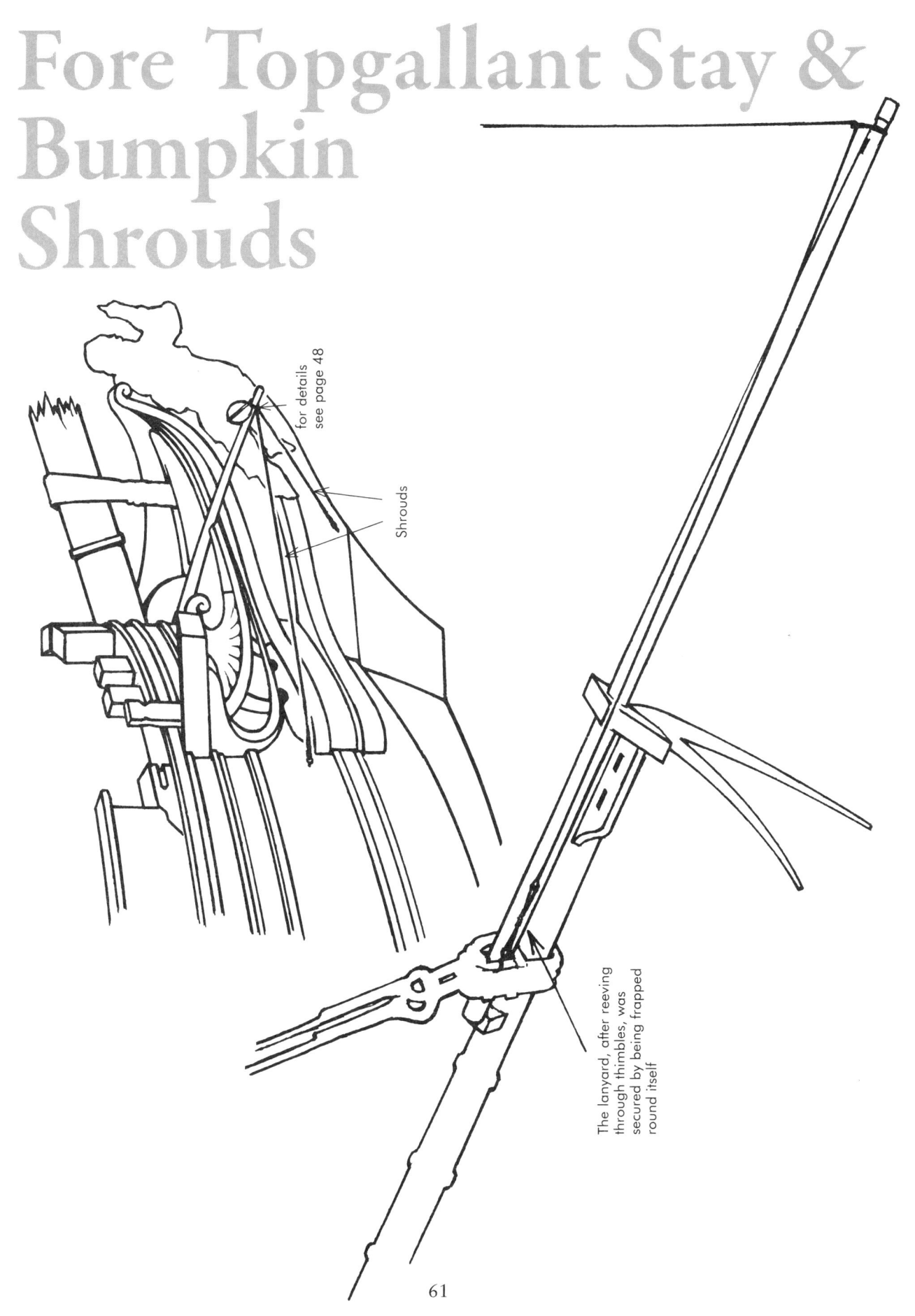

Jib Outhaul

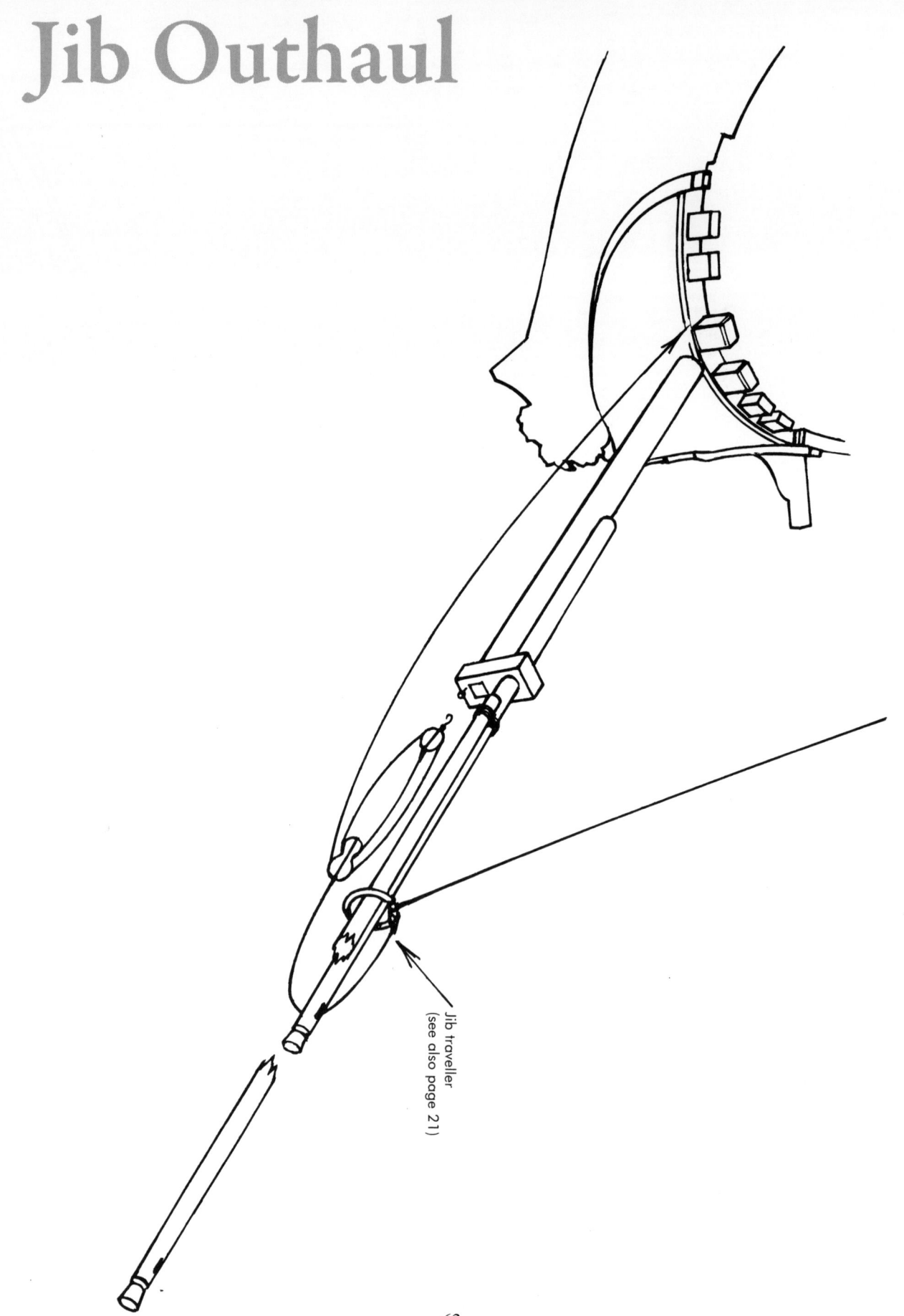

Jib traveller (see also page 21)

Flying Jib Outhaul

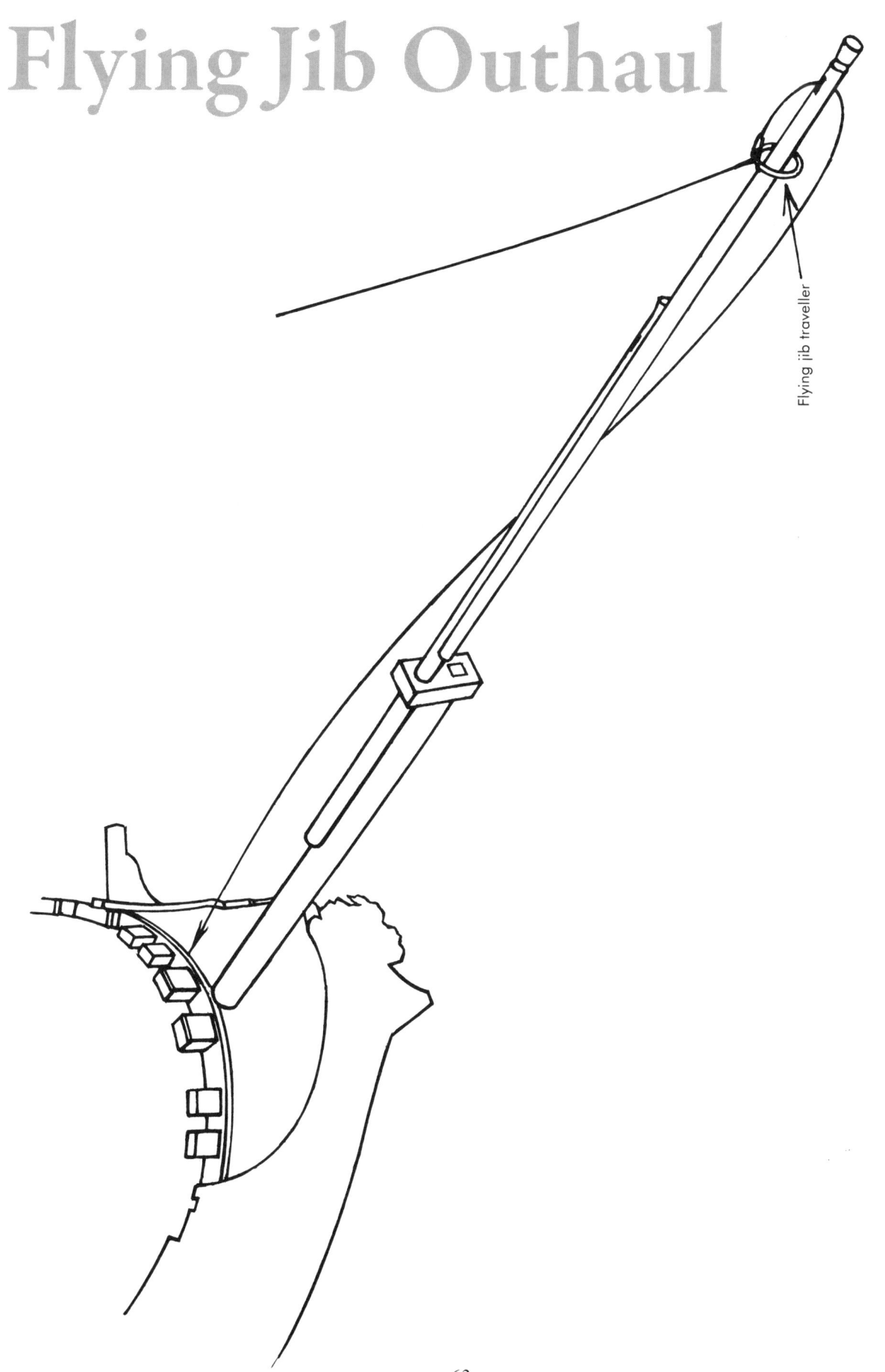

Flying jib traveller

Spritsail Lift, Spritsail Topsail Clueline & Sheet

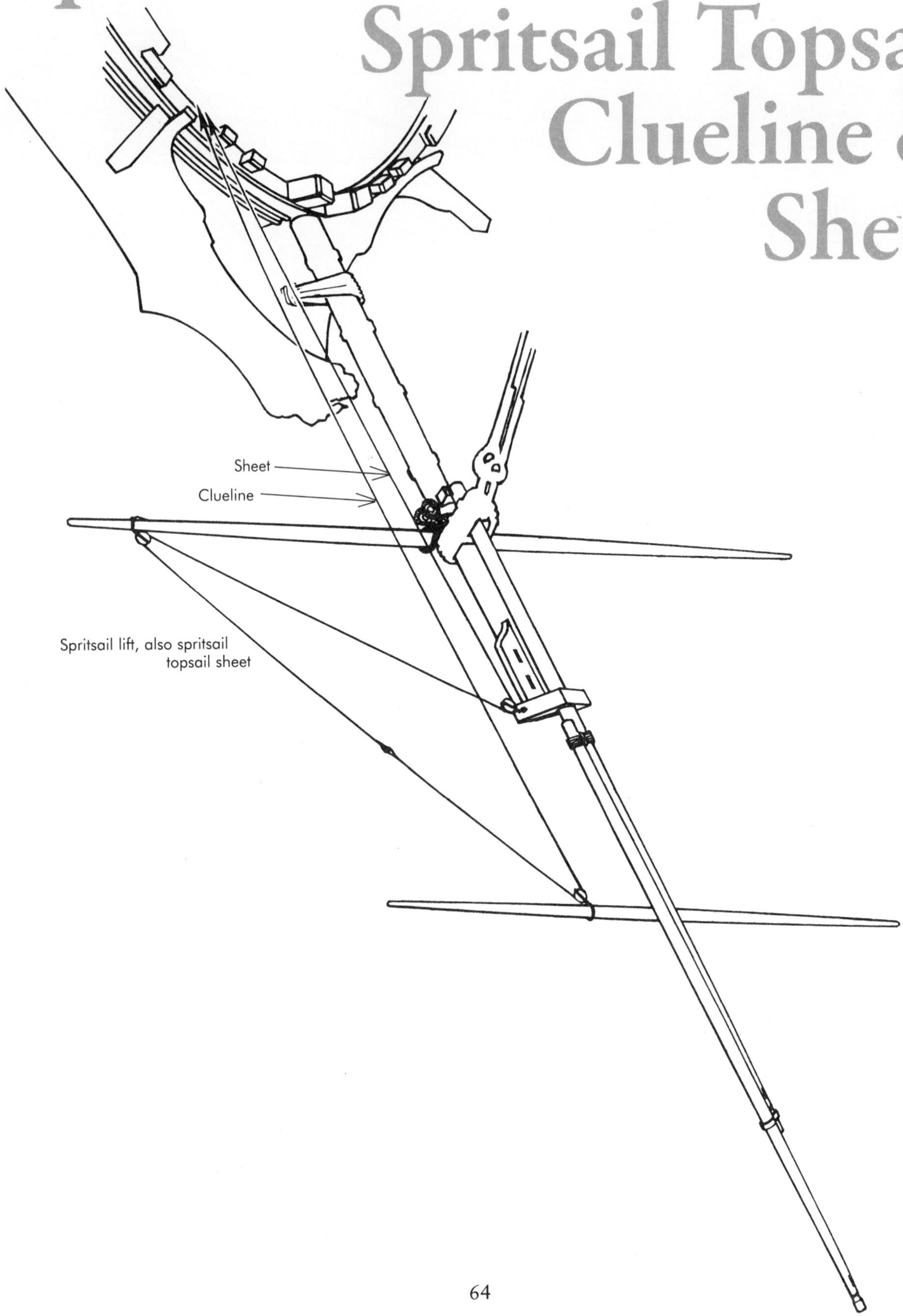

Sheet

Clueline

Spritsail lift, also spritsail topsail sheet

Spritsail Clueline & Sheet
Spritsail Topsail Lift

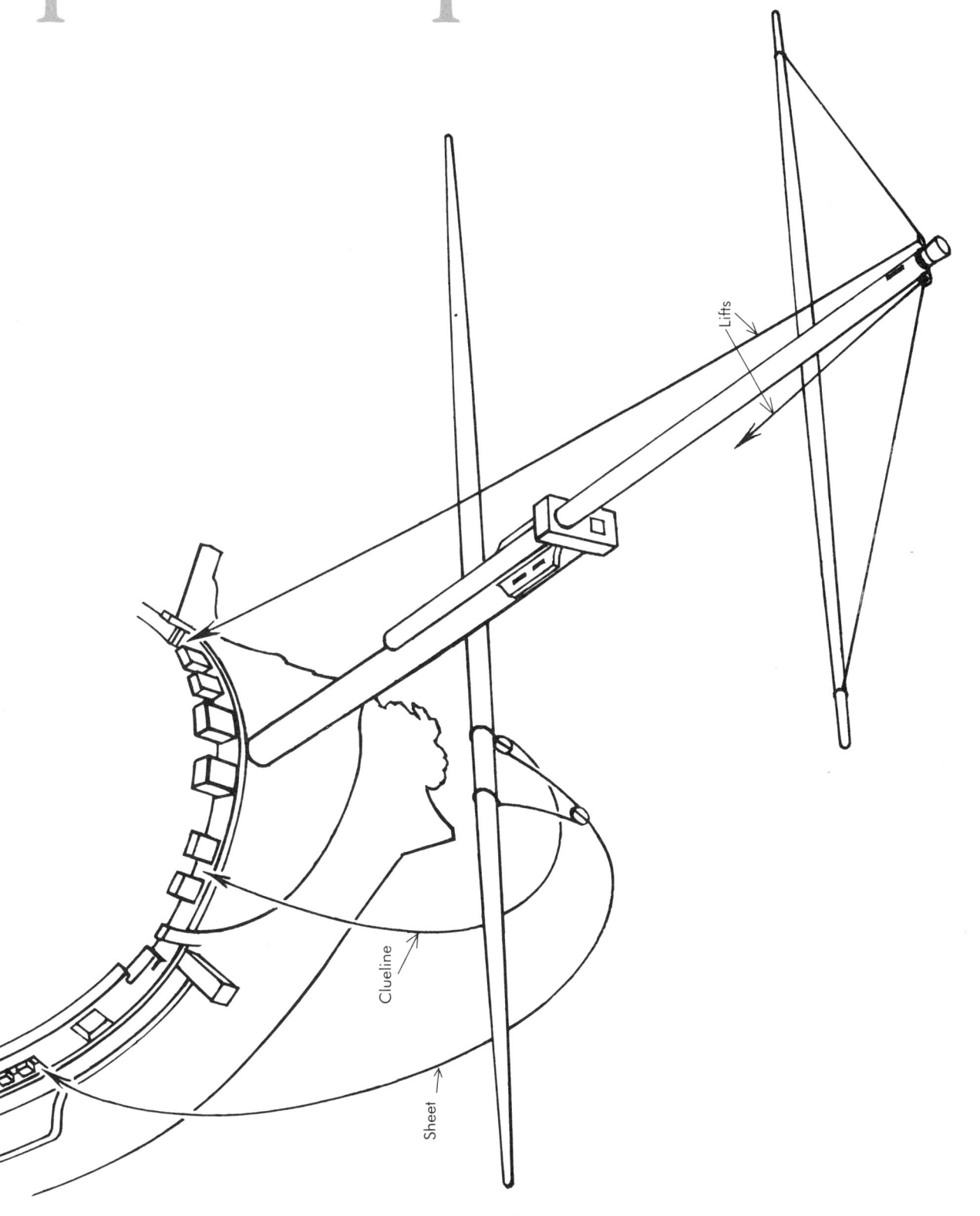

Fore Topsail Reef Tackle

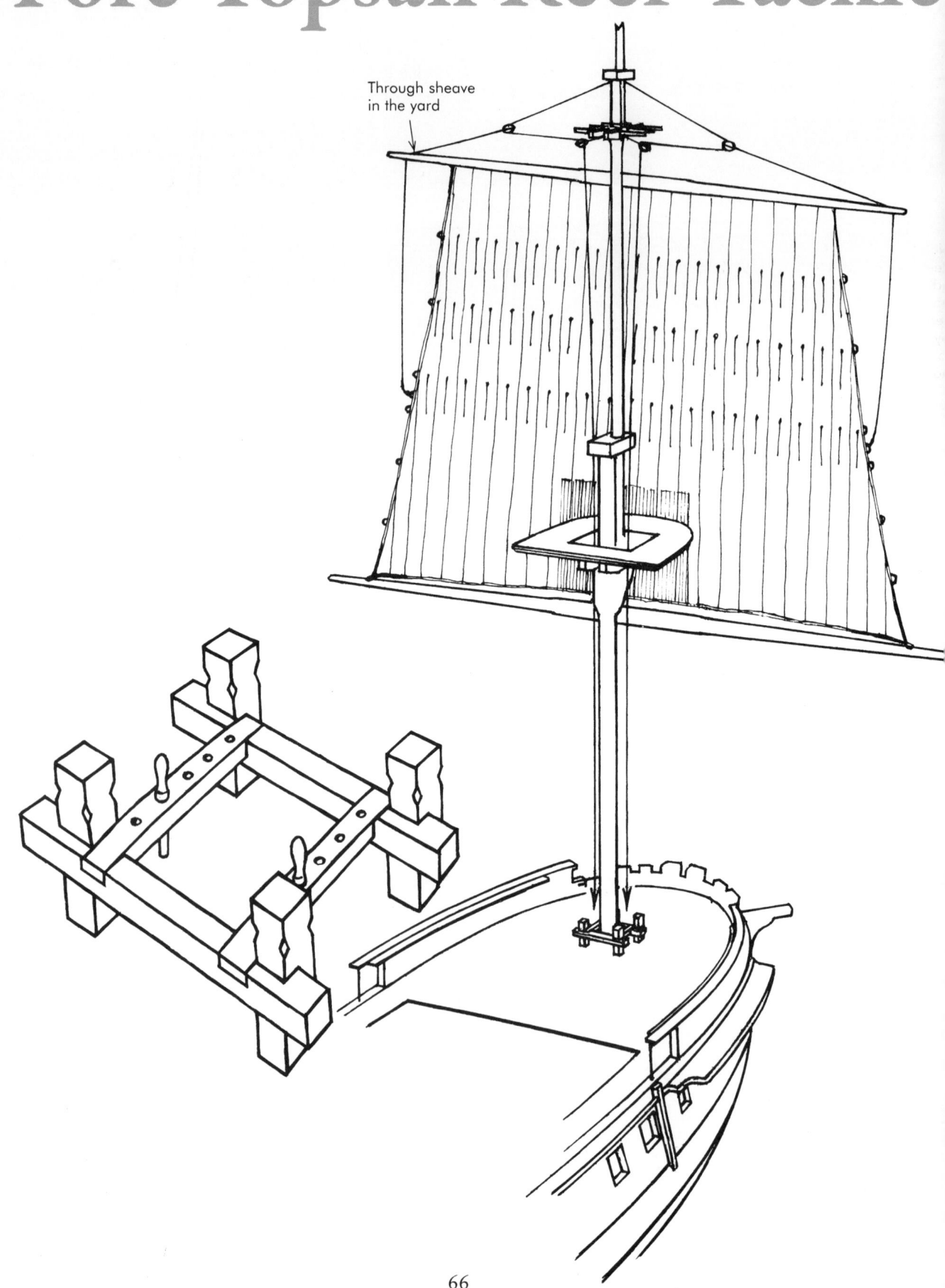

Through sheave in the yard

Main Topsail Reef Tackle

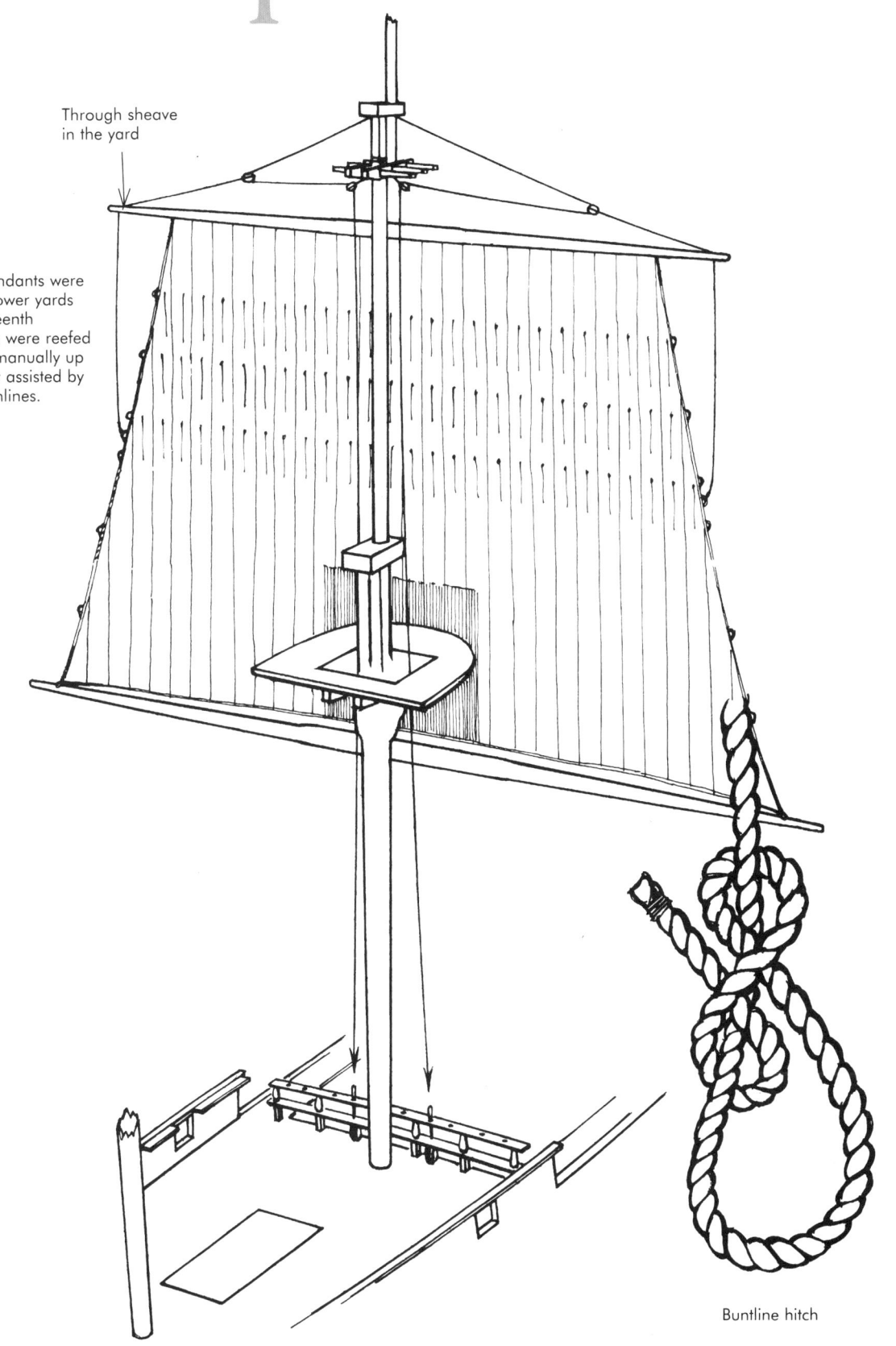

Through sheave in the yard

Note:
Reef tackles and pendants were not carried on the lower yards until the early nineteenth century. The courses were reefed by hauling the sail manually up to the yard, possibly assisted by hauling on the leechlines.

Buntline hitch

Mizzen Topsail Reef Tackle

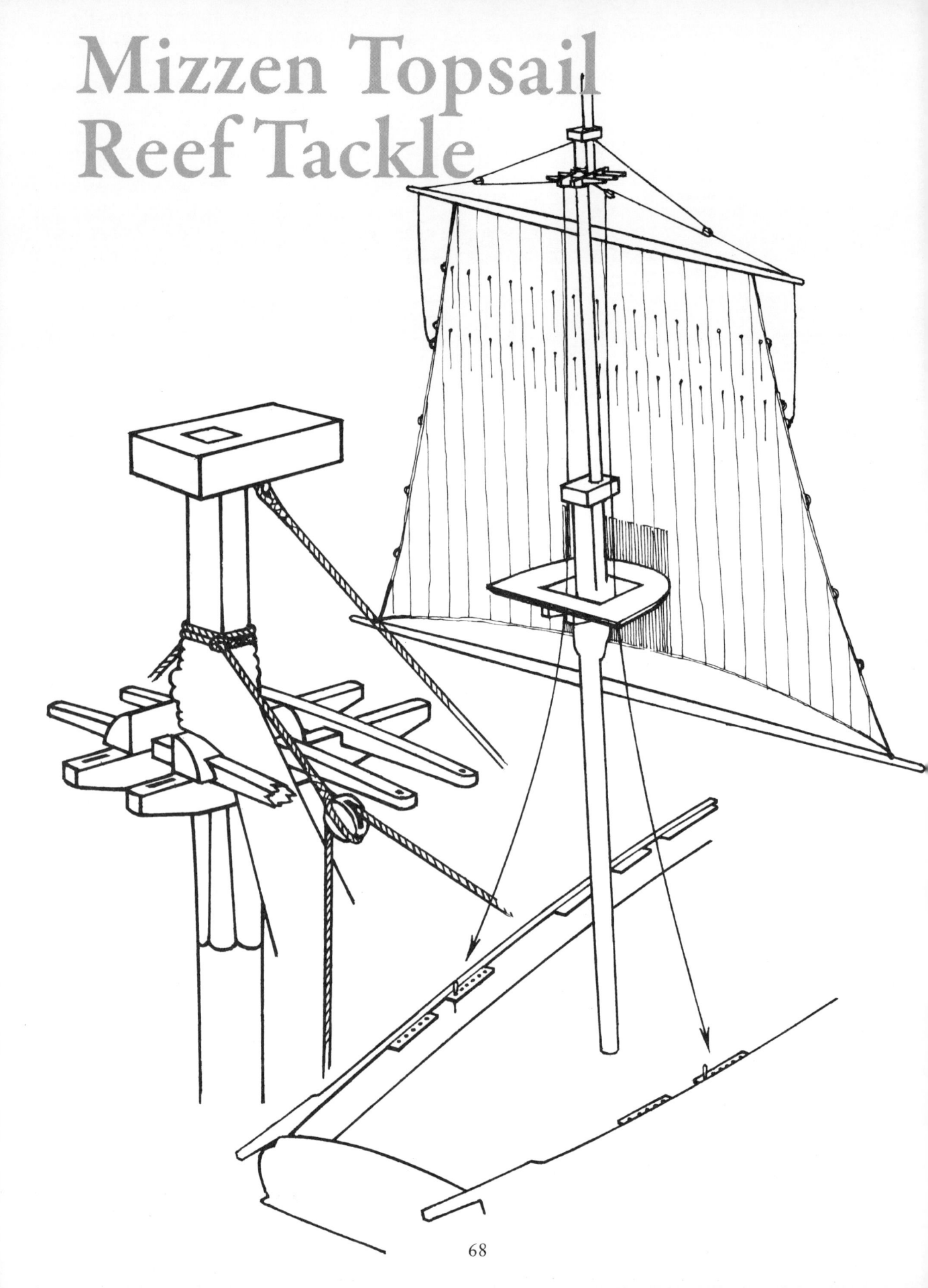

Spritsail Buntlines

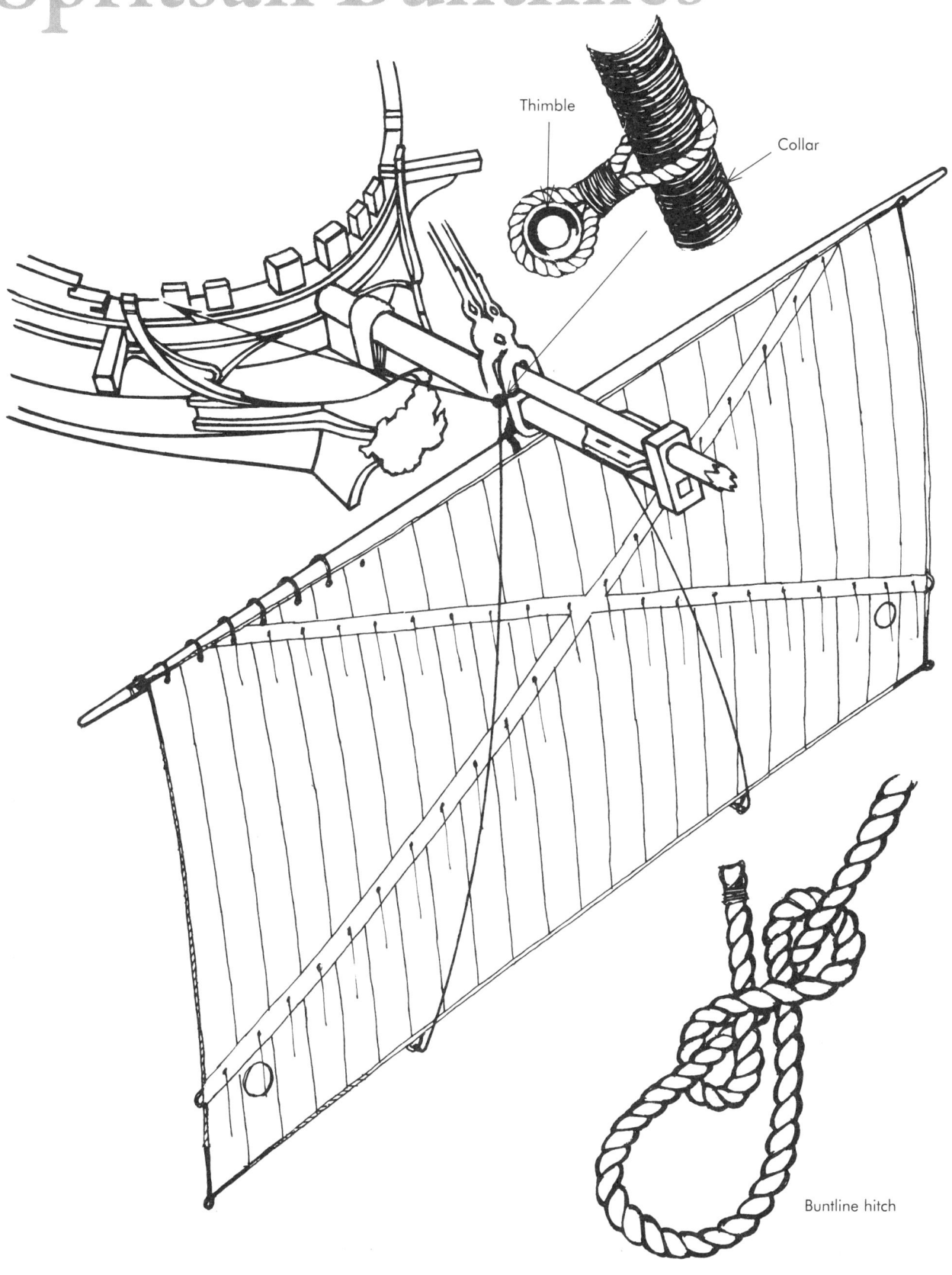

Fore Course Buntlines & Leechlines

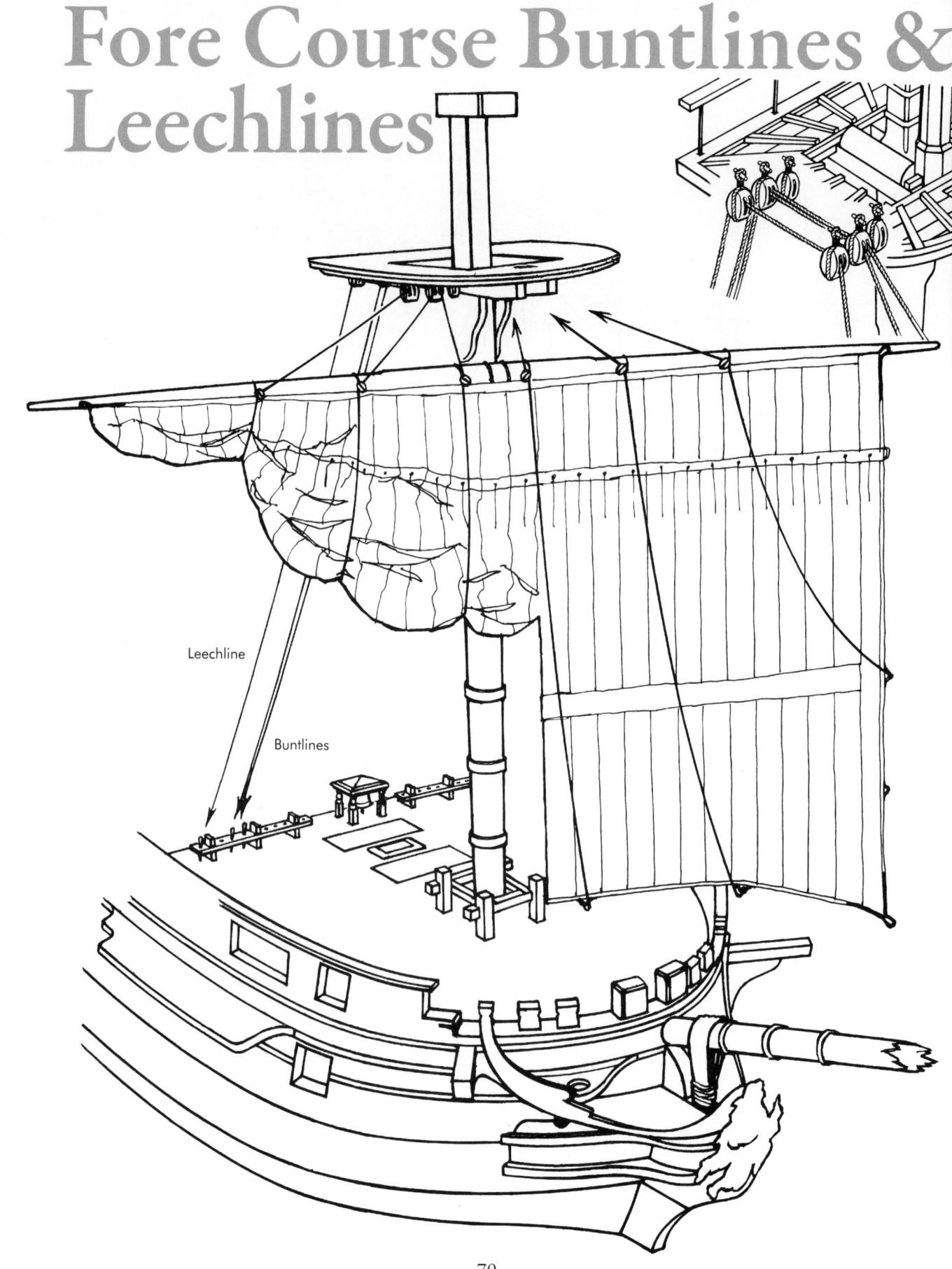

Fore Topsail
Buntlines

Main Course Buntlines & Leechlines

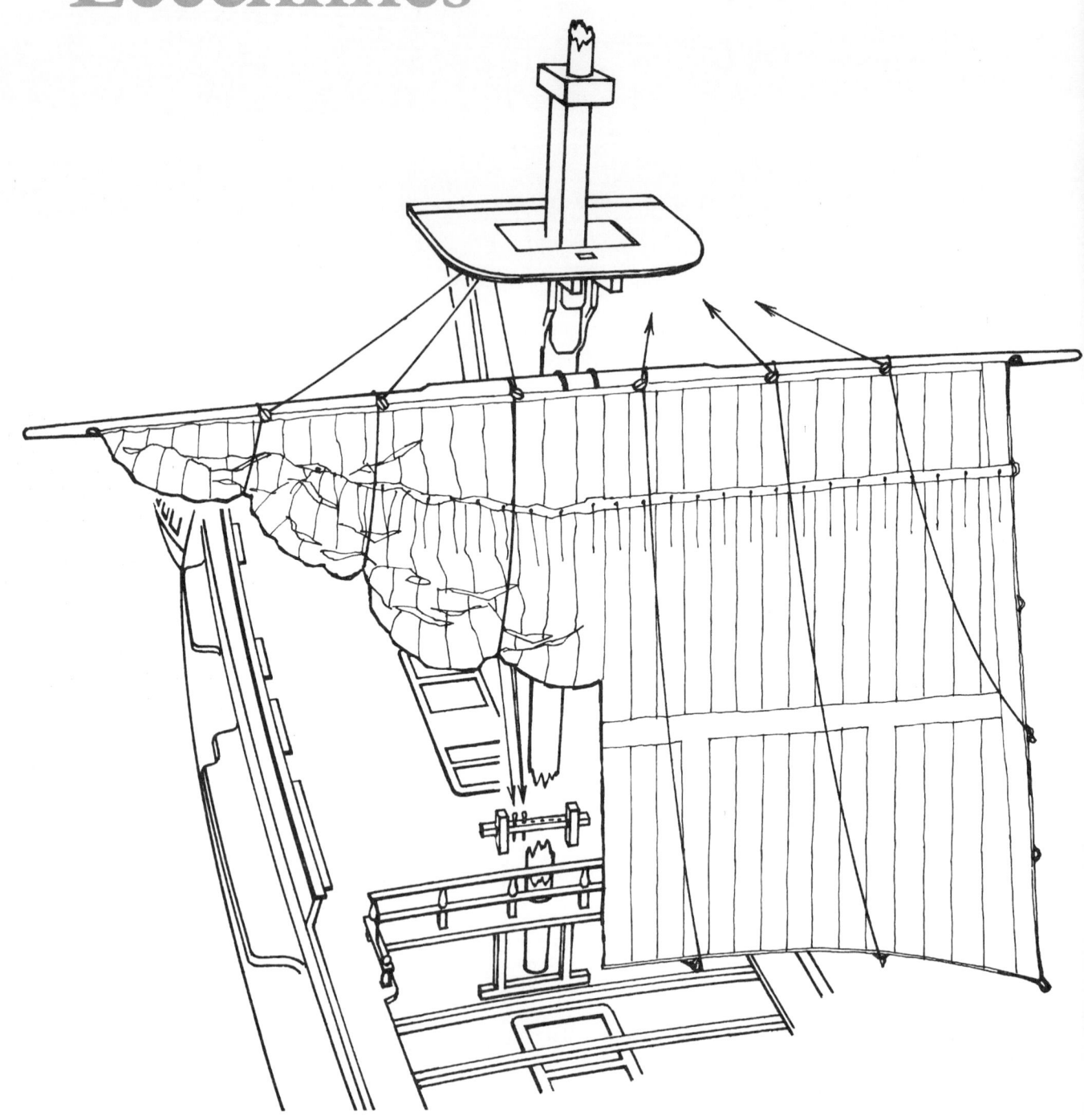

Main Topsail Buntlines

Mizzen Topsail Buntlines

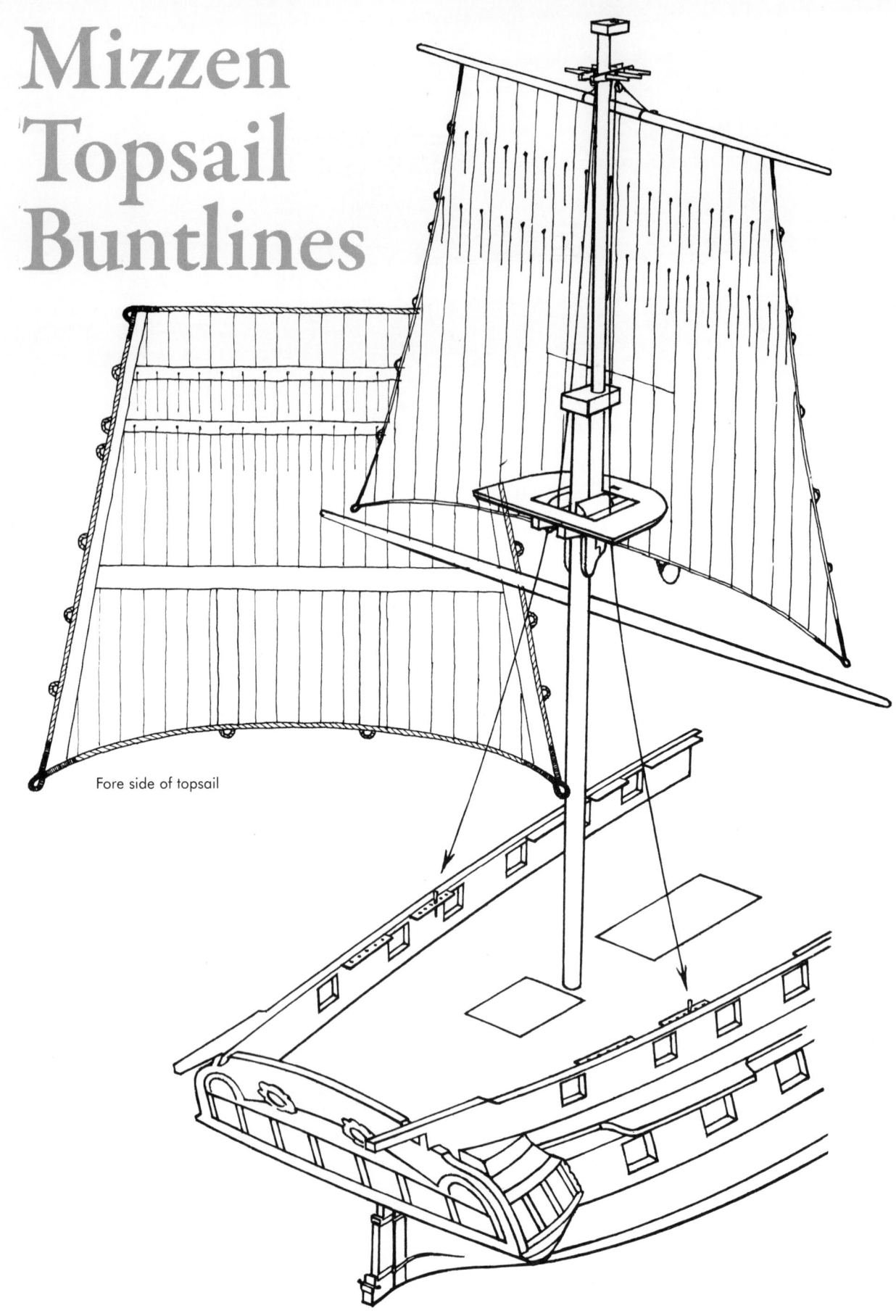

Fore side of topsail

Fore Course & Topsail Bowlines

Bowline knot or splice was used (see page 76)

Through single blocks lashed to the bowsprit a little aft of the fore stay hearts

Through single blocks on the bowsprit cap

Fore Topgallant Bowlines

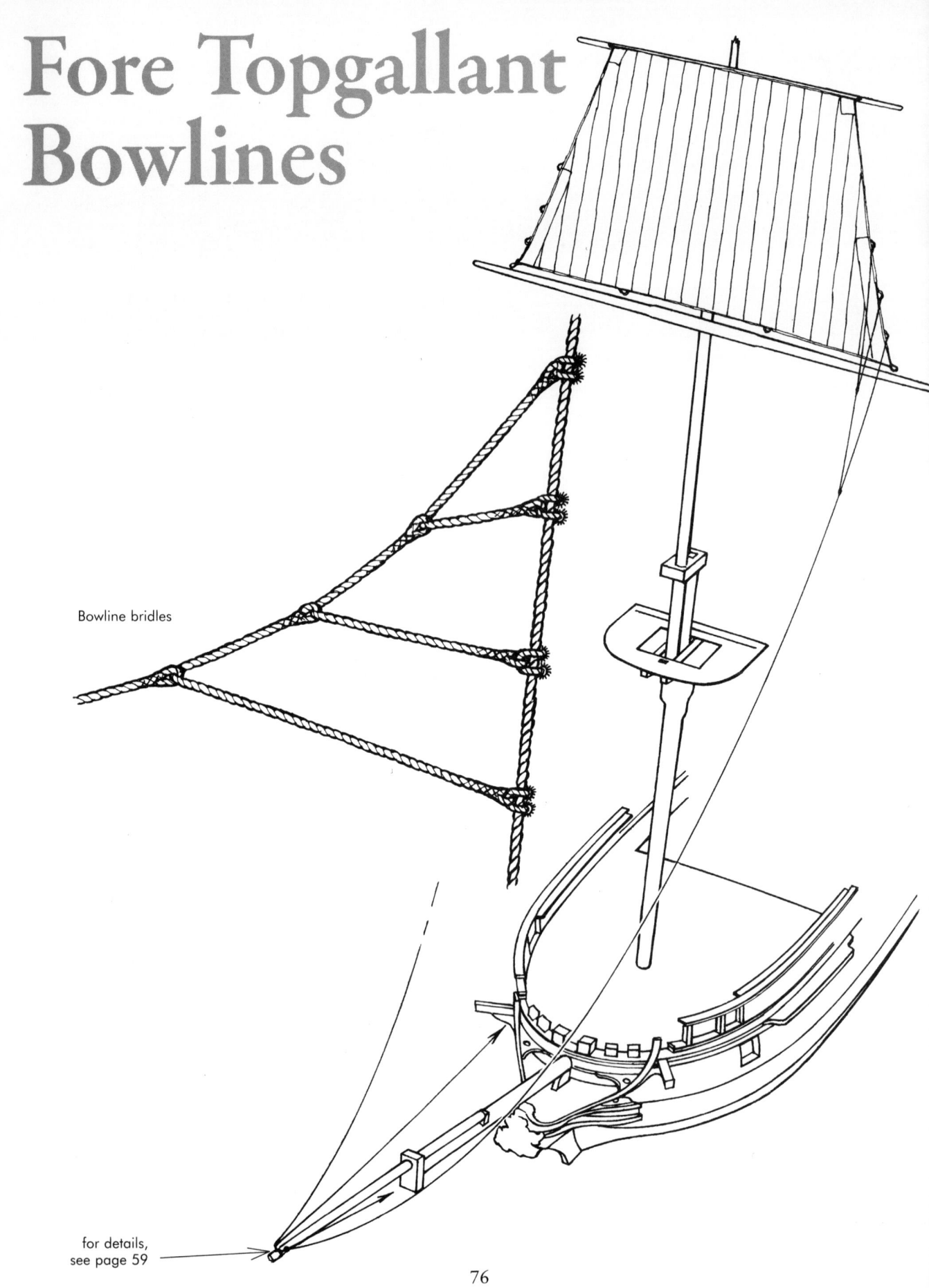

Bowline bridles

for details,
see page 59

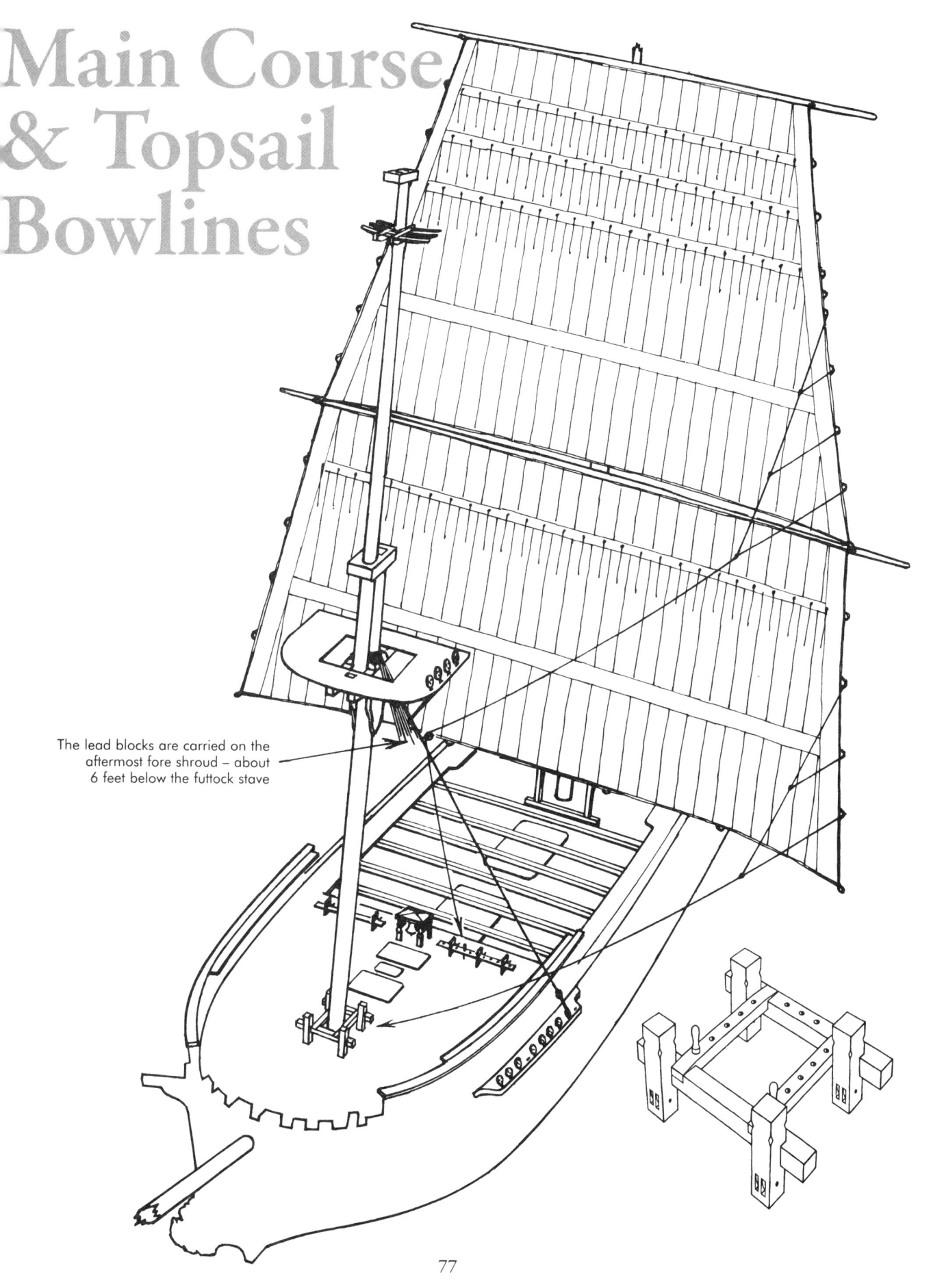

Main Course & Topsail Bowlines

The lead blocks are carried on the aftermost fore shroud – about 6 feet below the futtock stave

Main Topgallant Bowlines

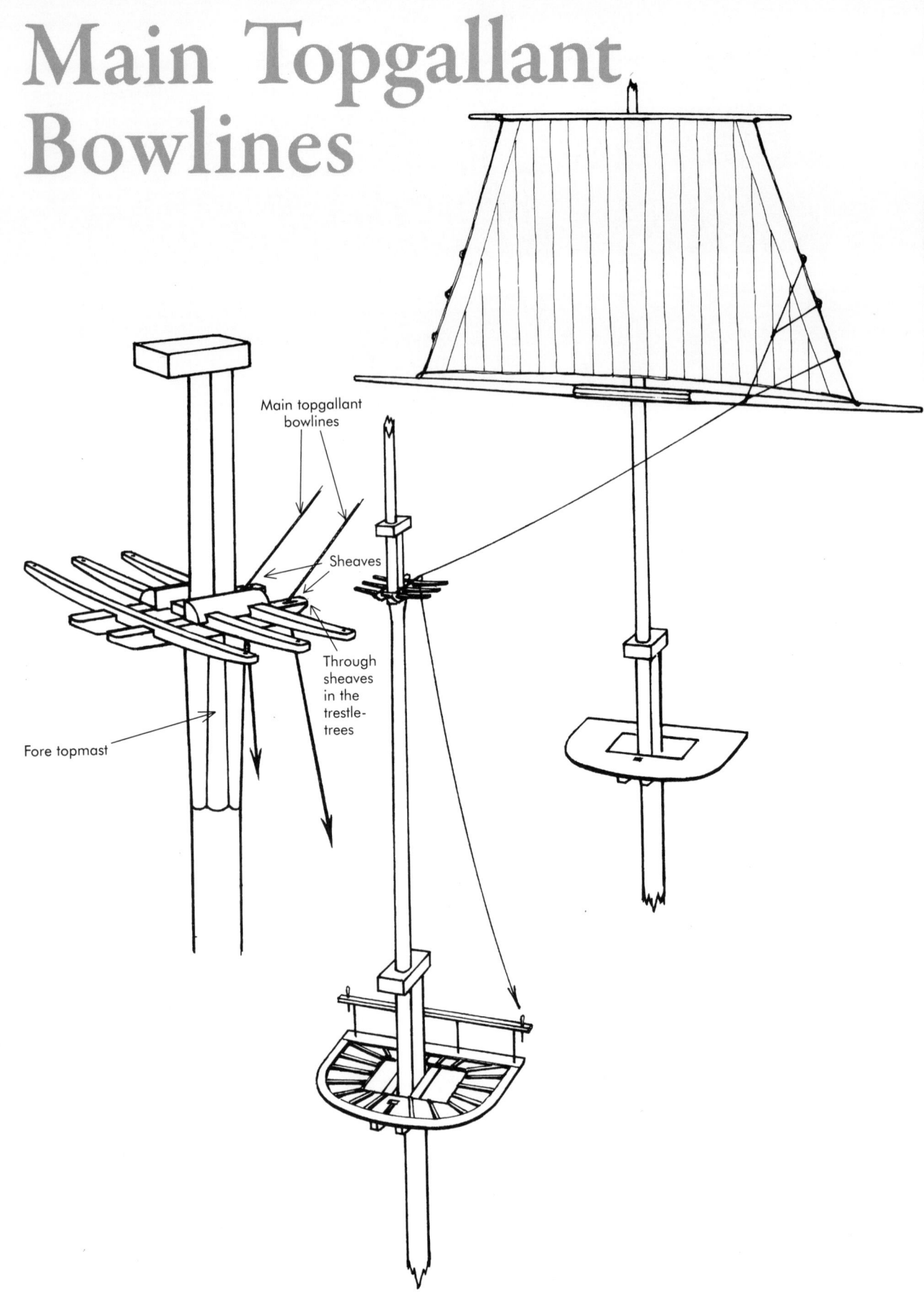

Mizzen Topsail & Topgallant Bowlines

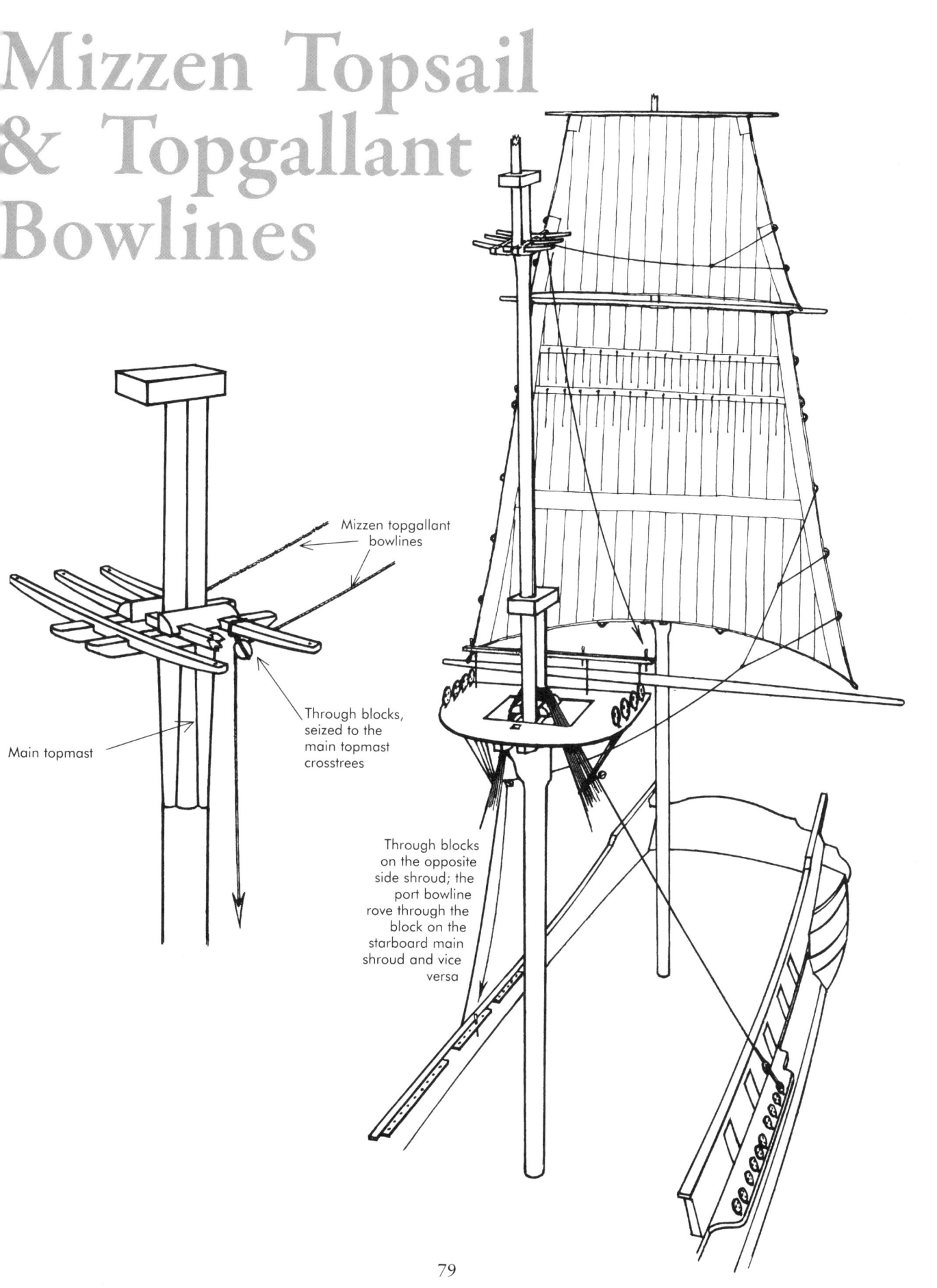

Mizzen Mast Square Sails

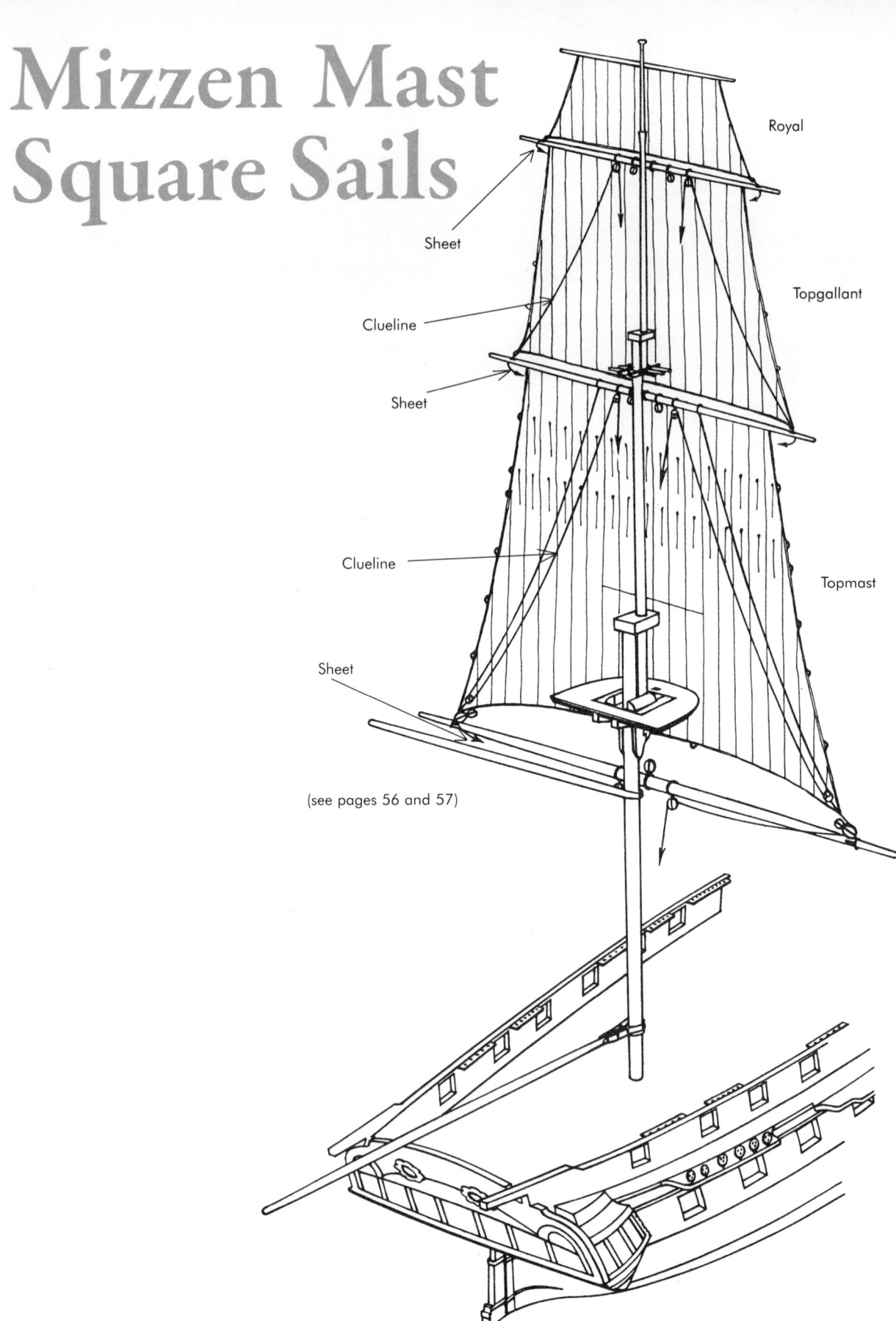

(see pages 56 and 57)

Spanker

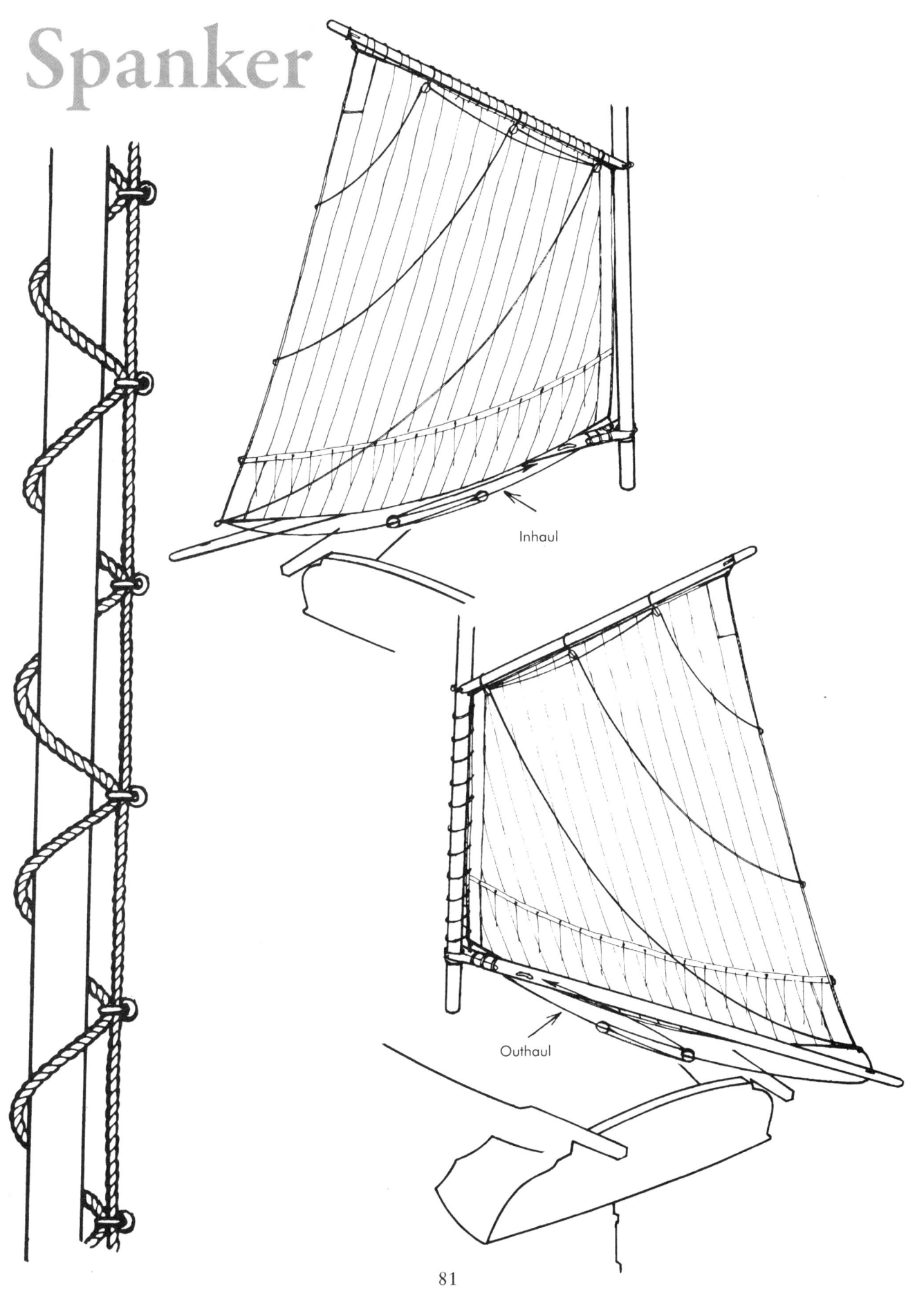

Mainmast Square Sails

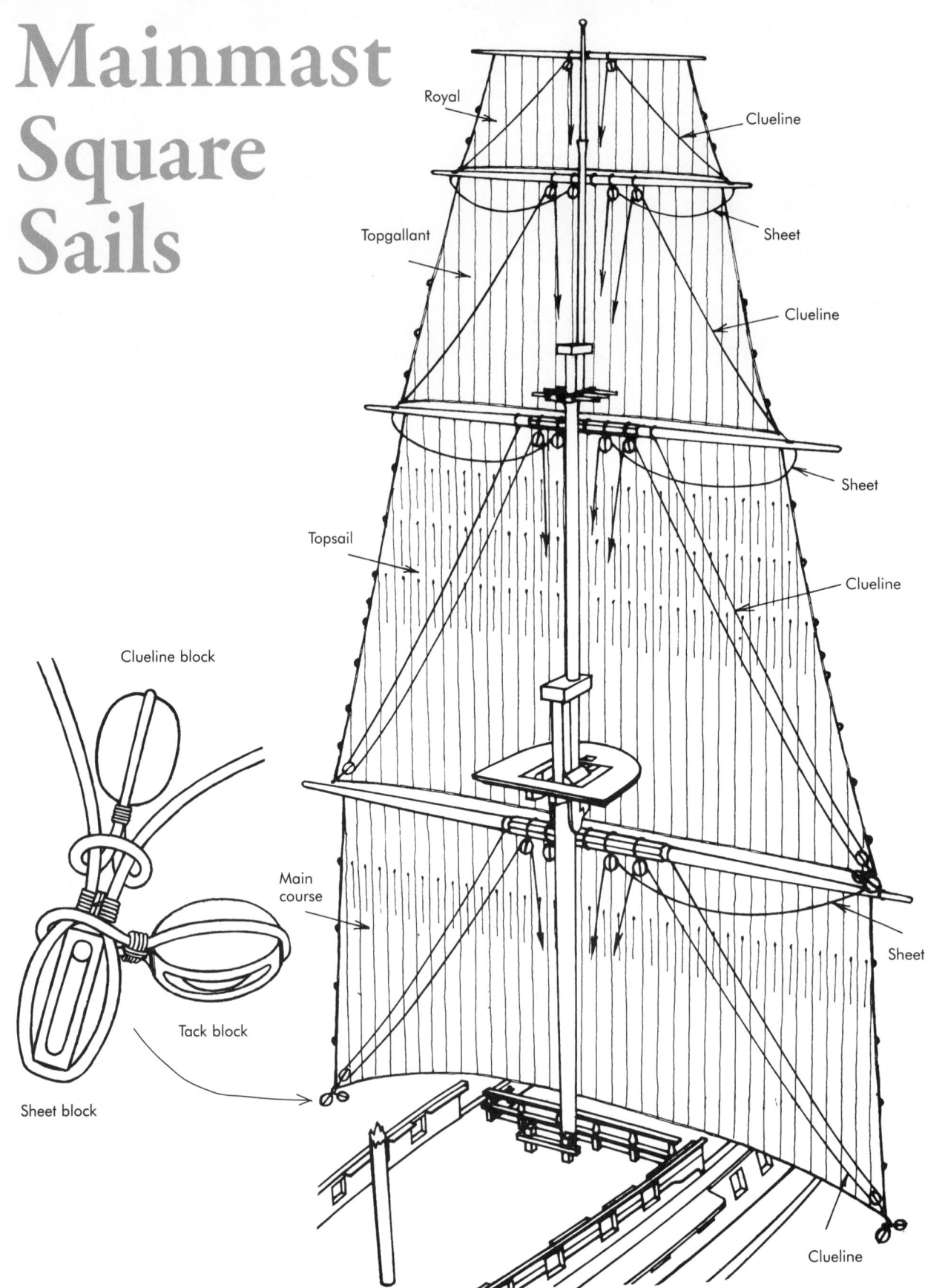

Fore Mast Square Sails

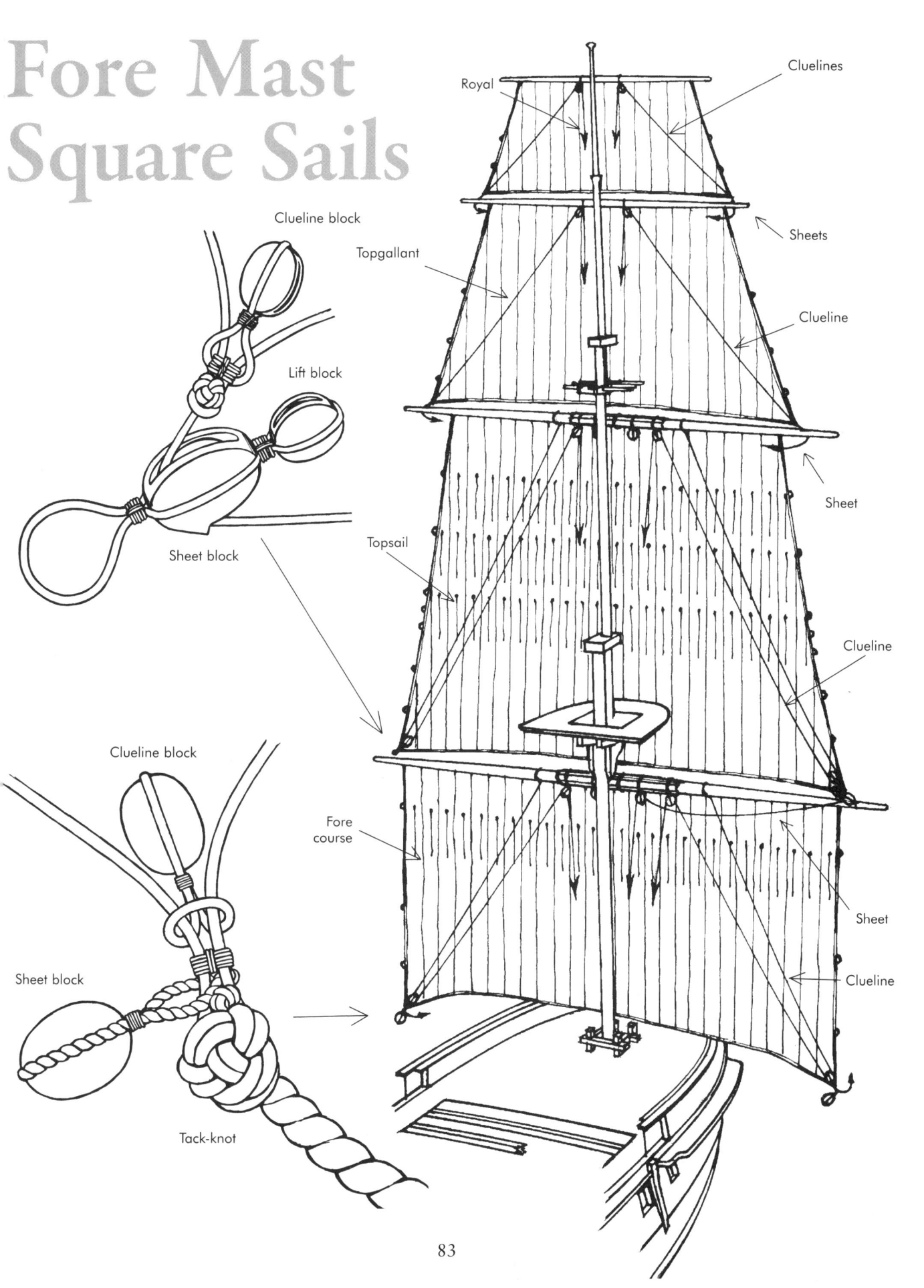

Yard Tackle & Tricing Lines

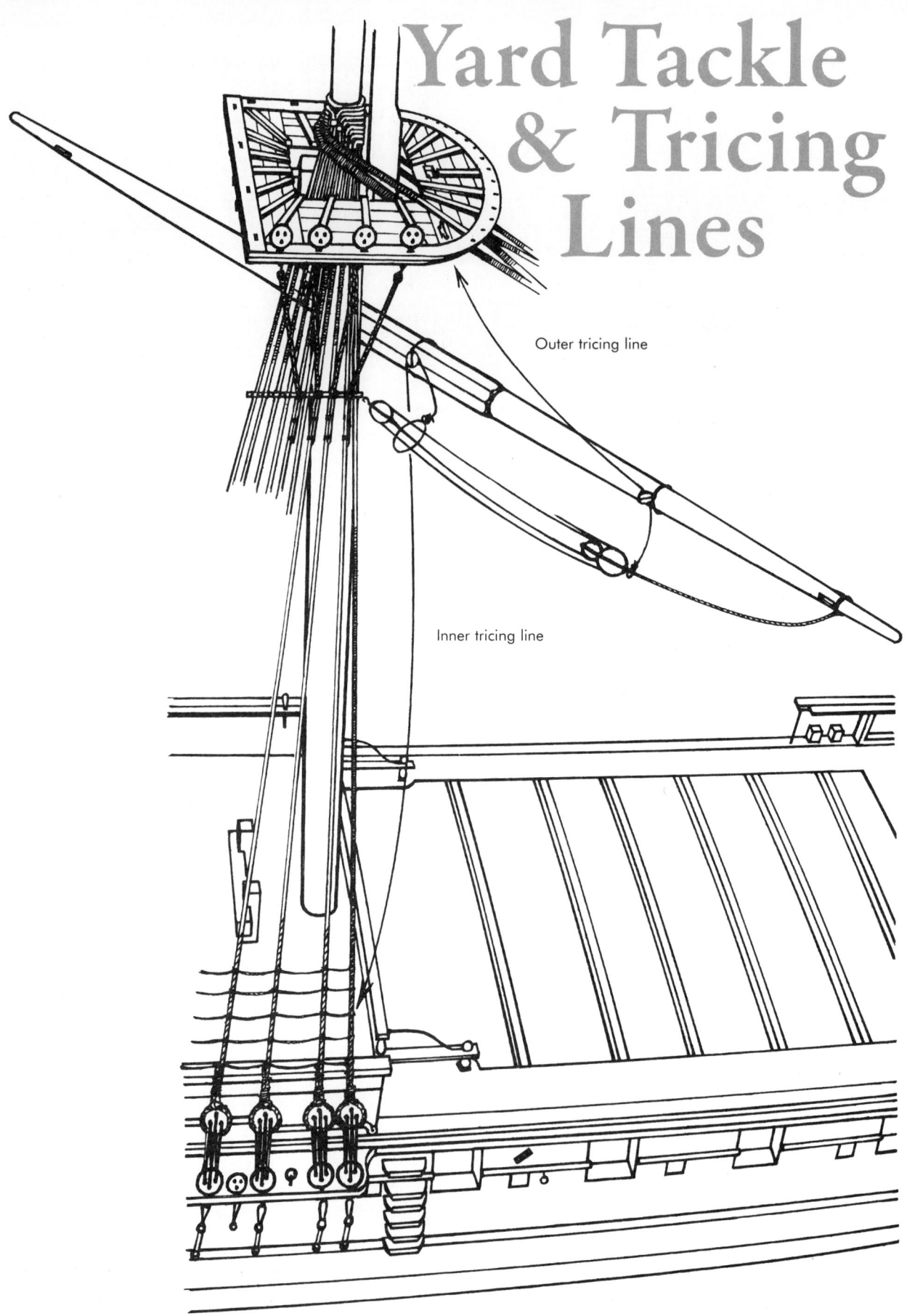

Outer tricing line

Inner tricing line

Yards

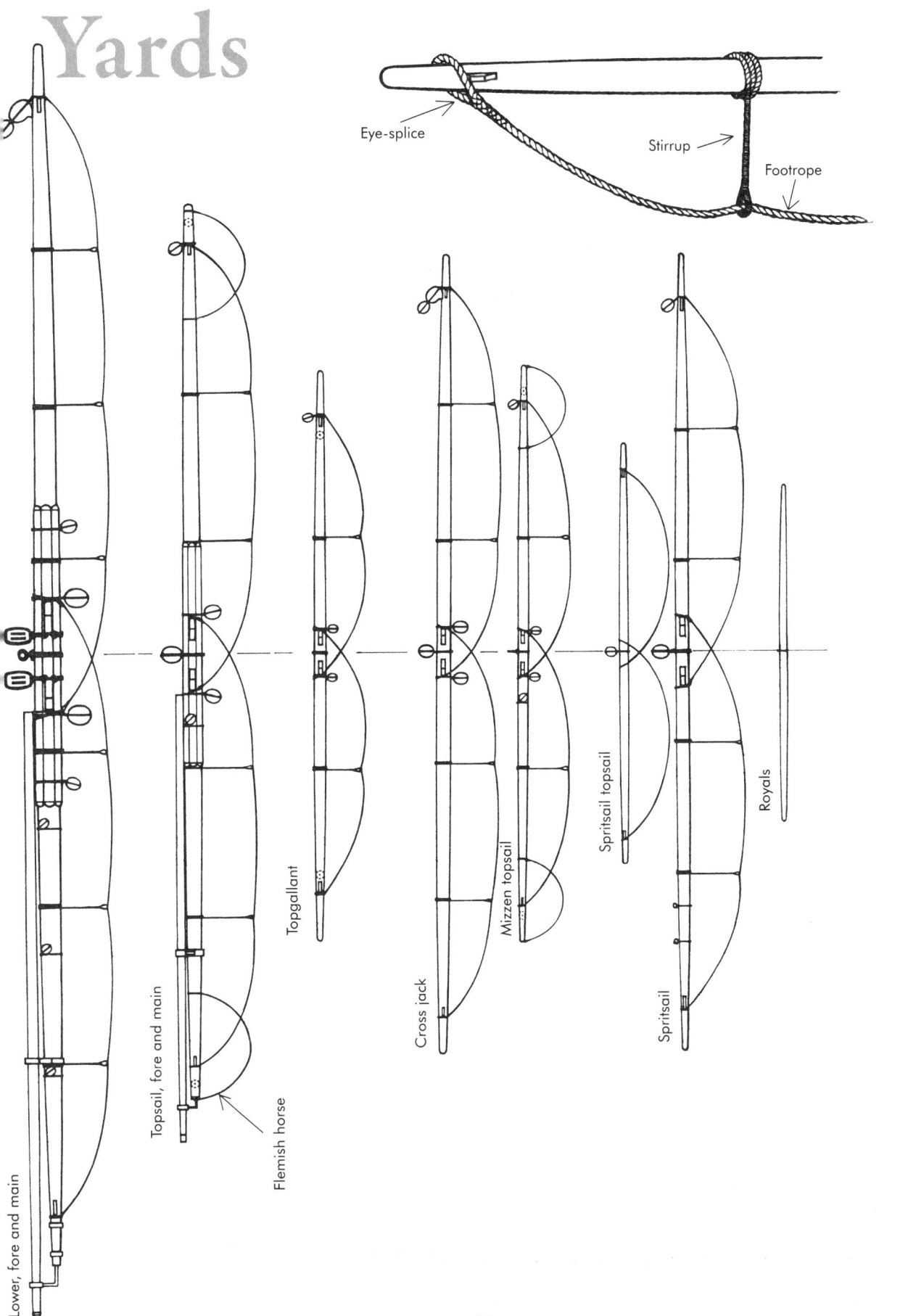

Main Yard with Stun-Sail Boom & Stunsail Boom Irons

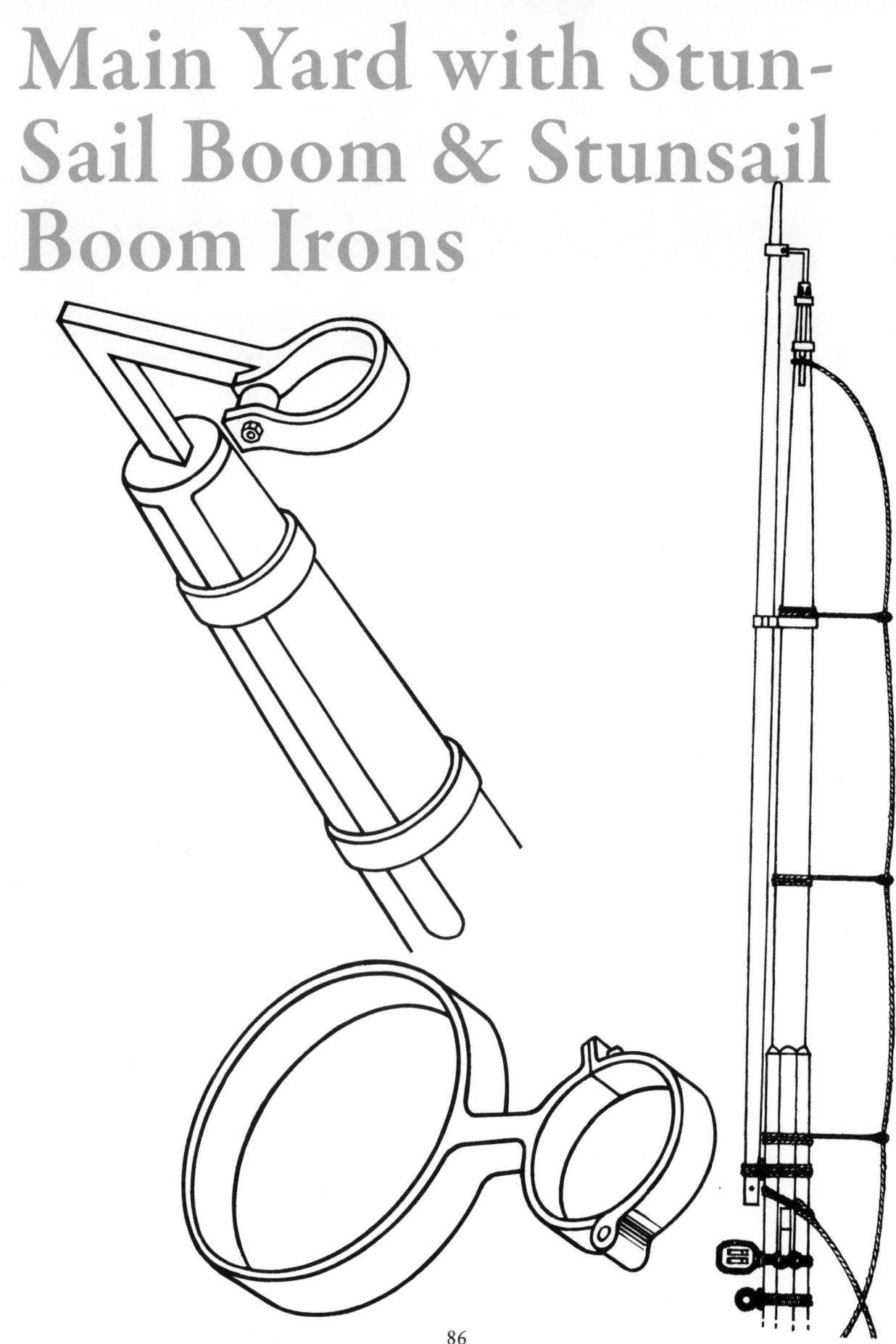

Fore Staysail

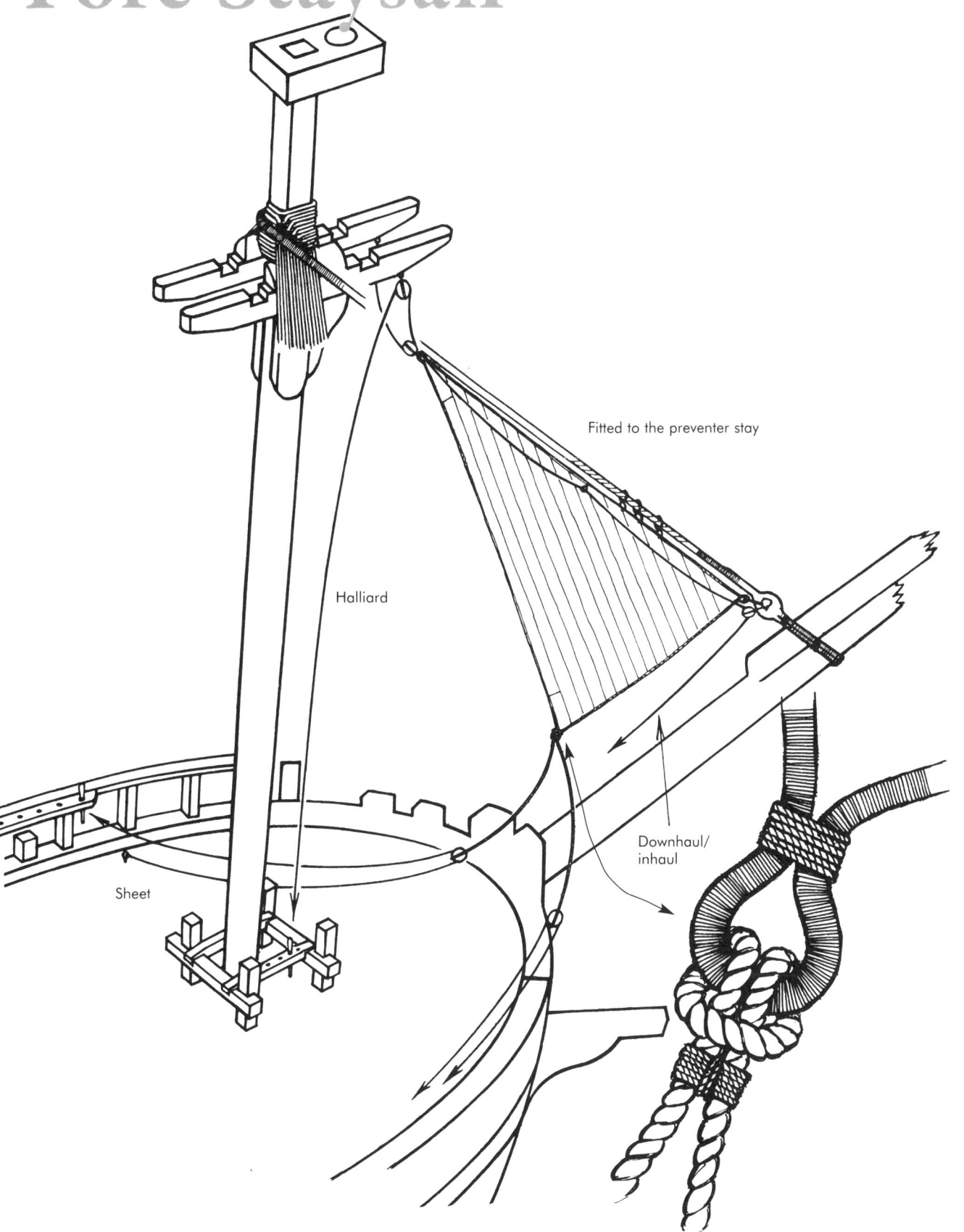

Main Staysail

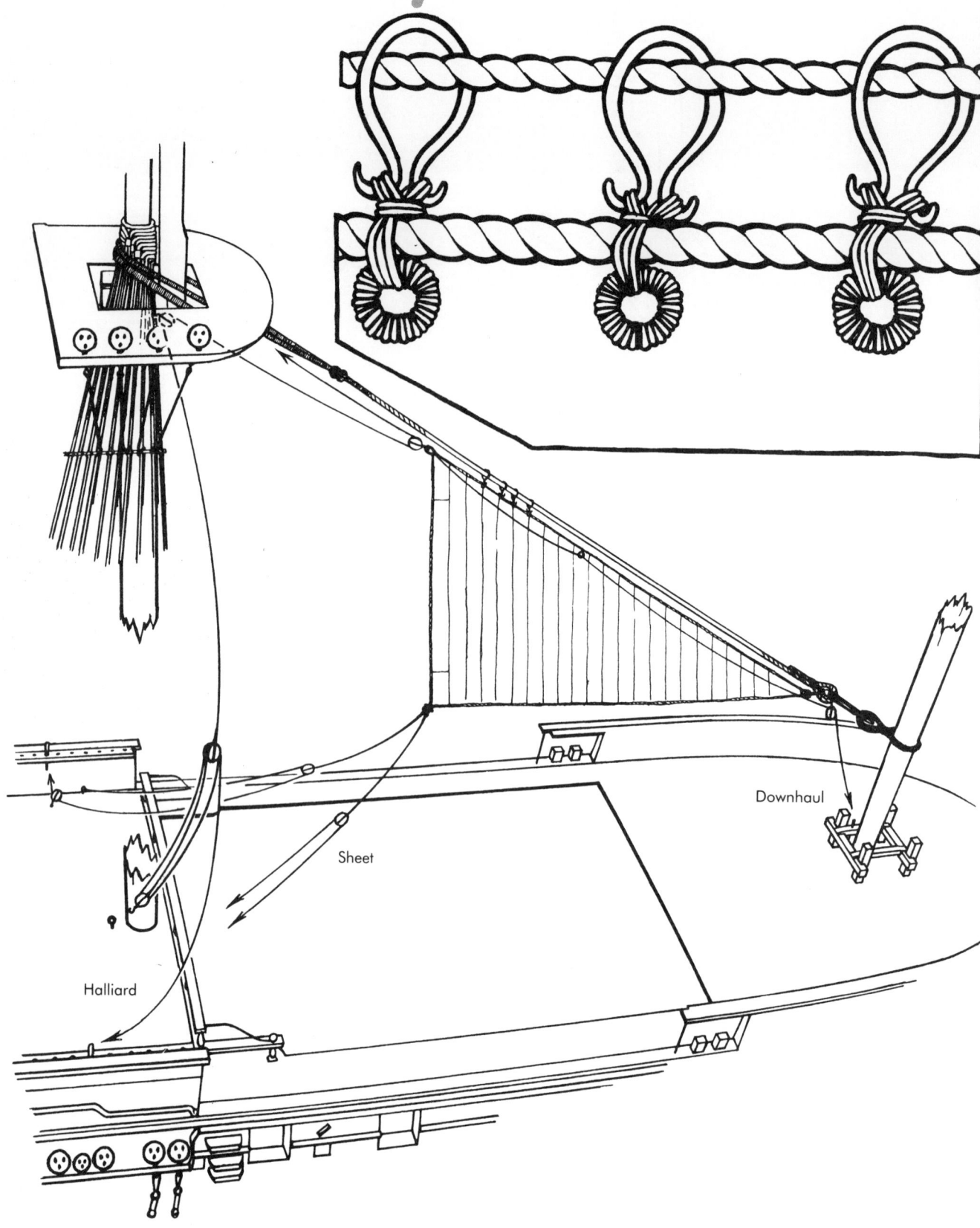

Mizzen Staysail

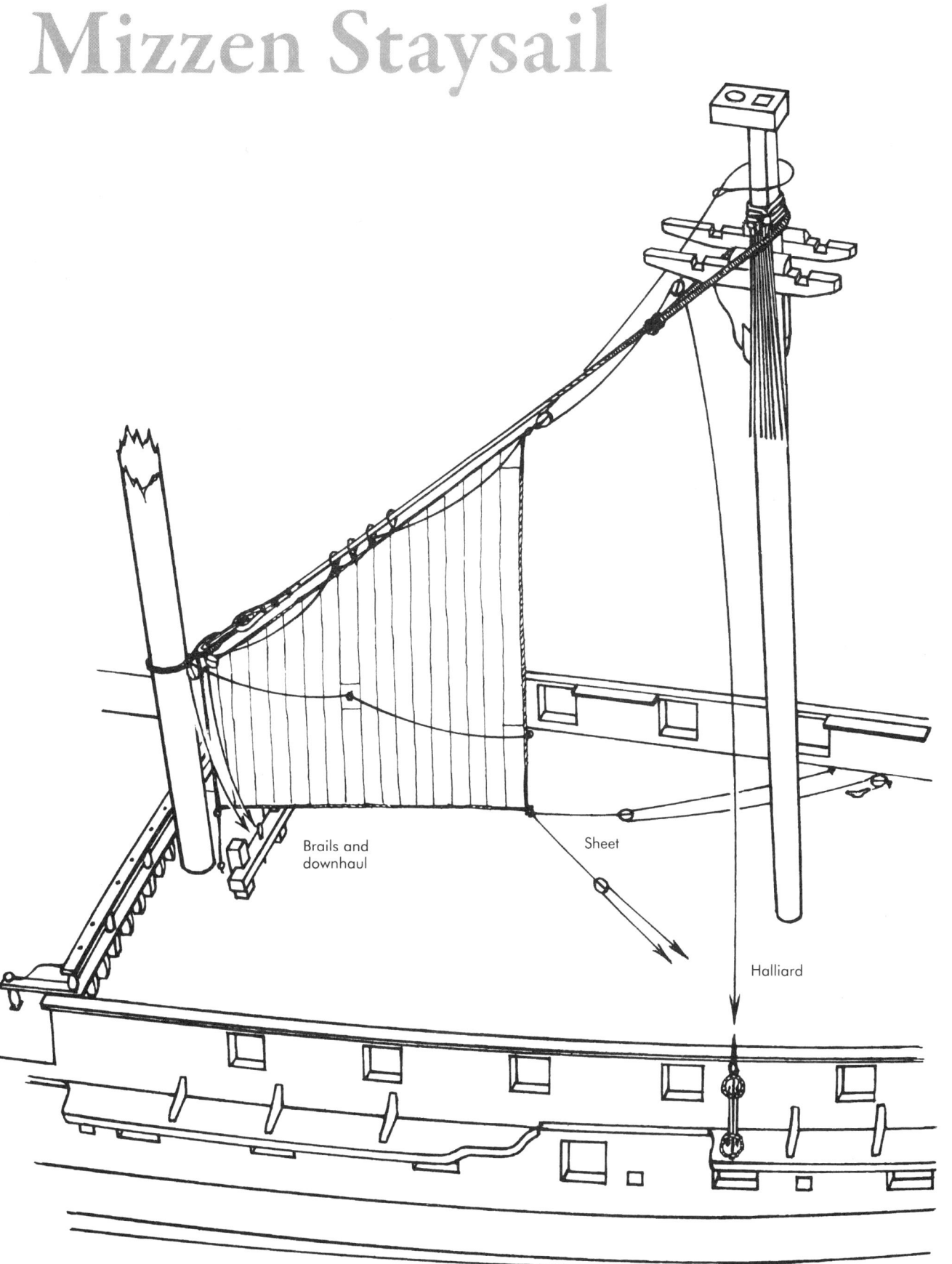

Fore Topmast Staysail Stay

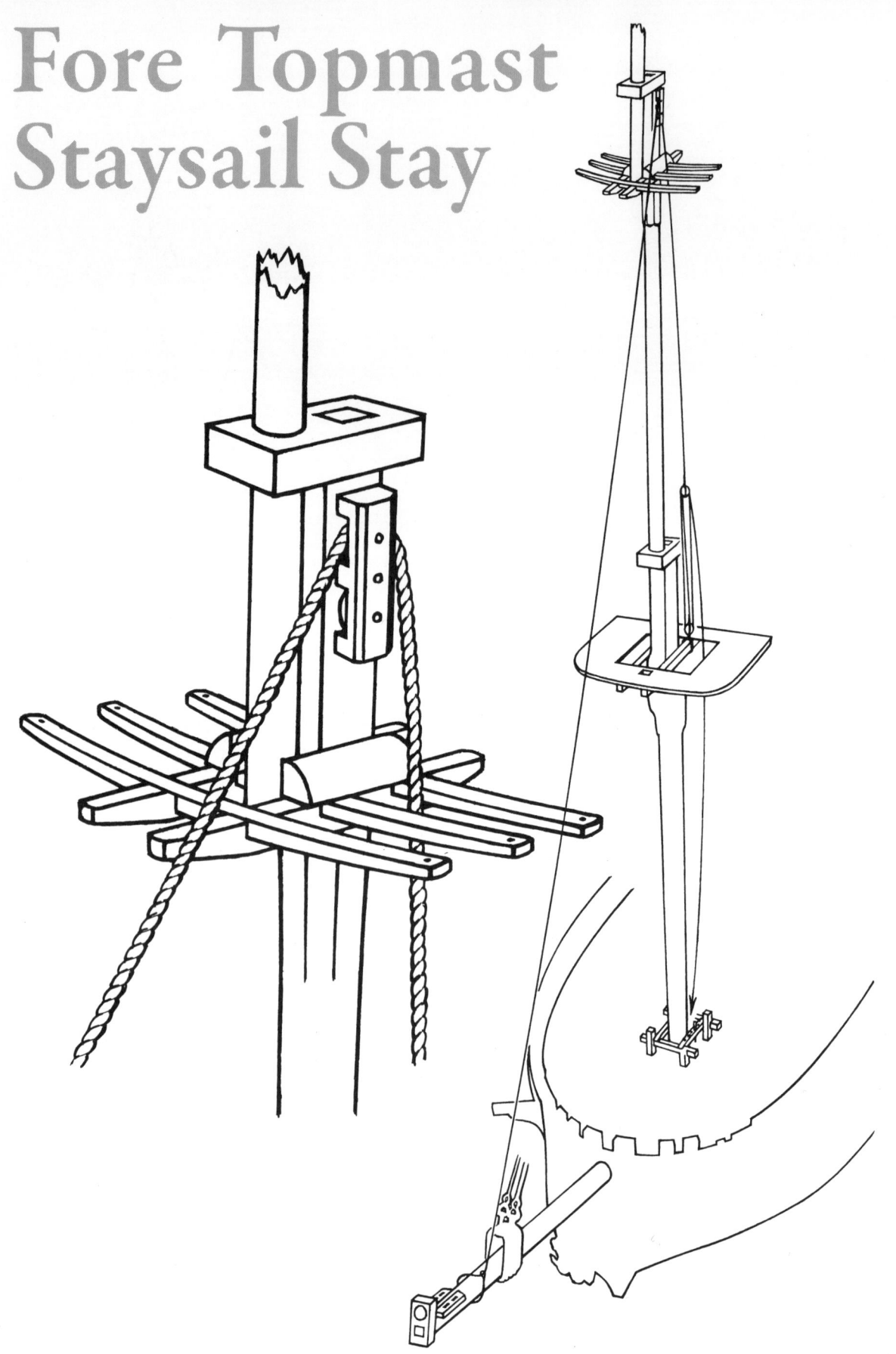

Fore Topmast Staysail

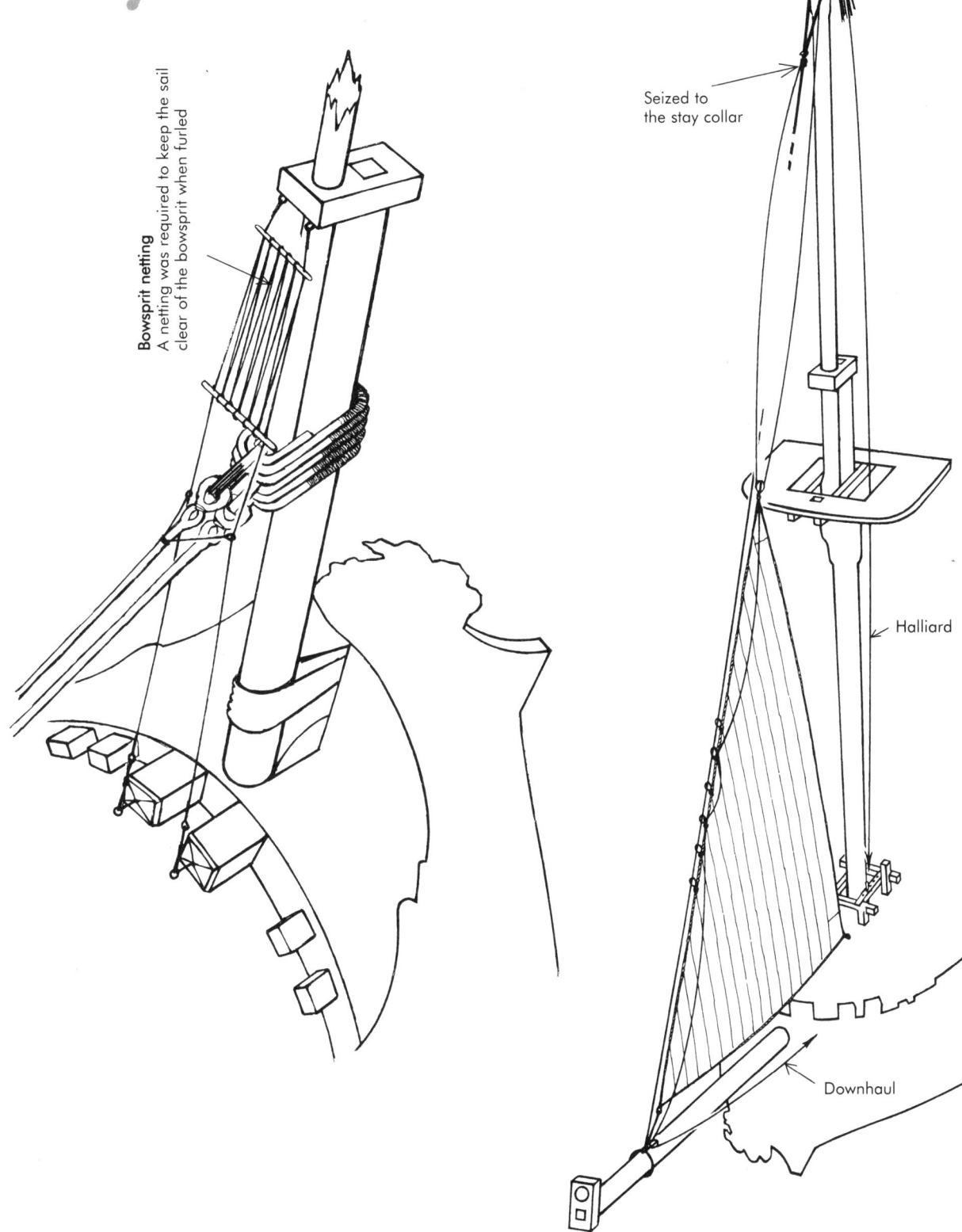

Bowsprit netting
A netting was required to keep the sail clear of the bowsprit when furled

Seized to the stay collar

Halliard

Downhaul

Fore Topmast Staysail

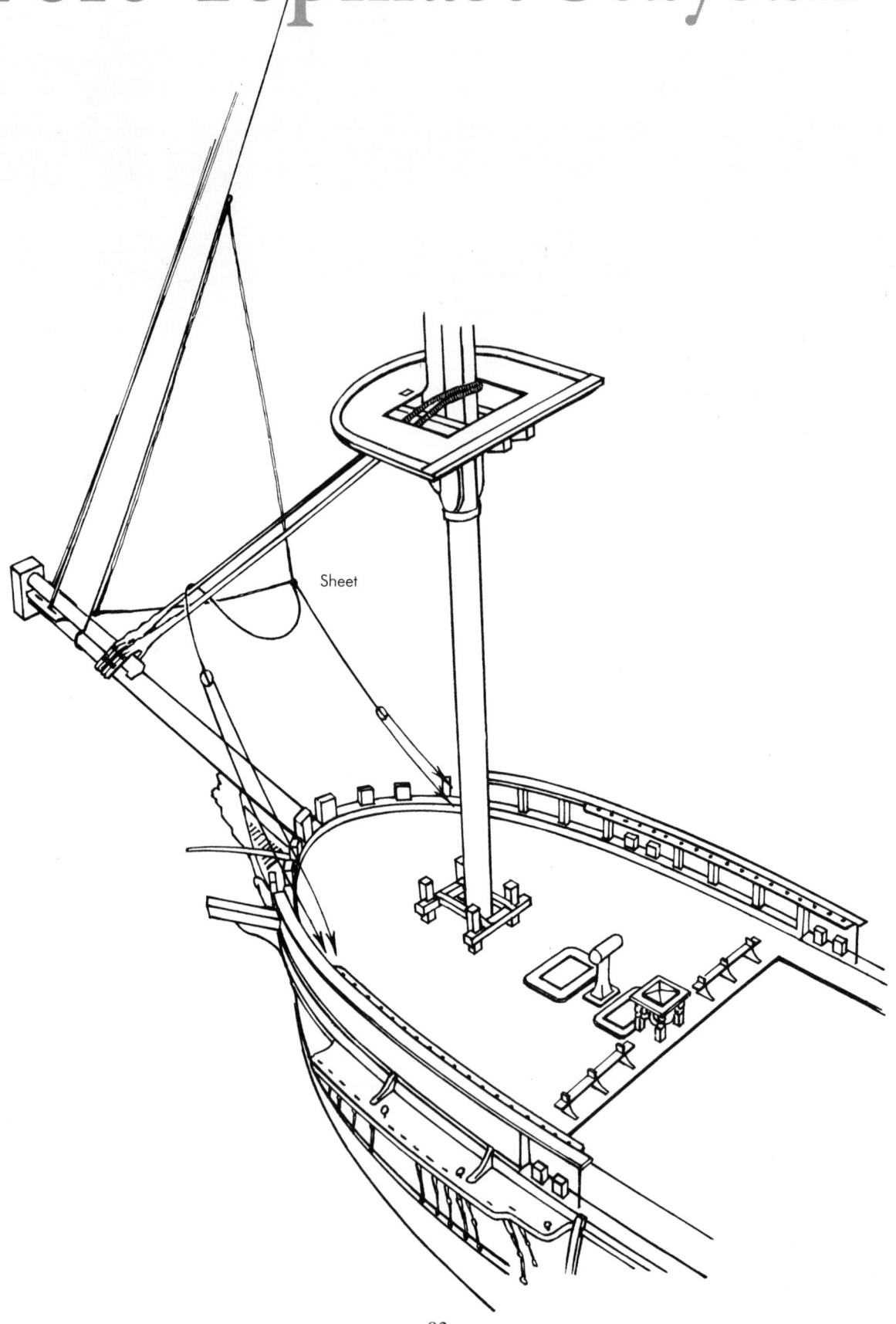

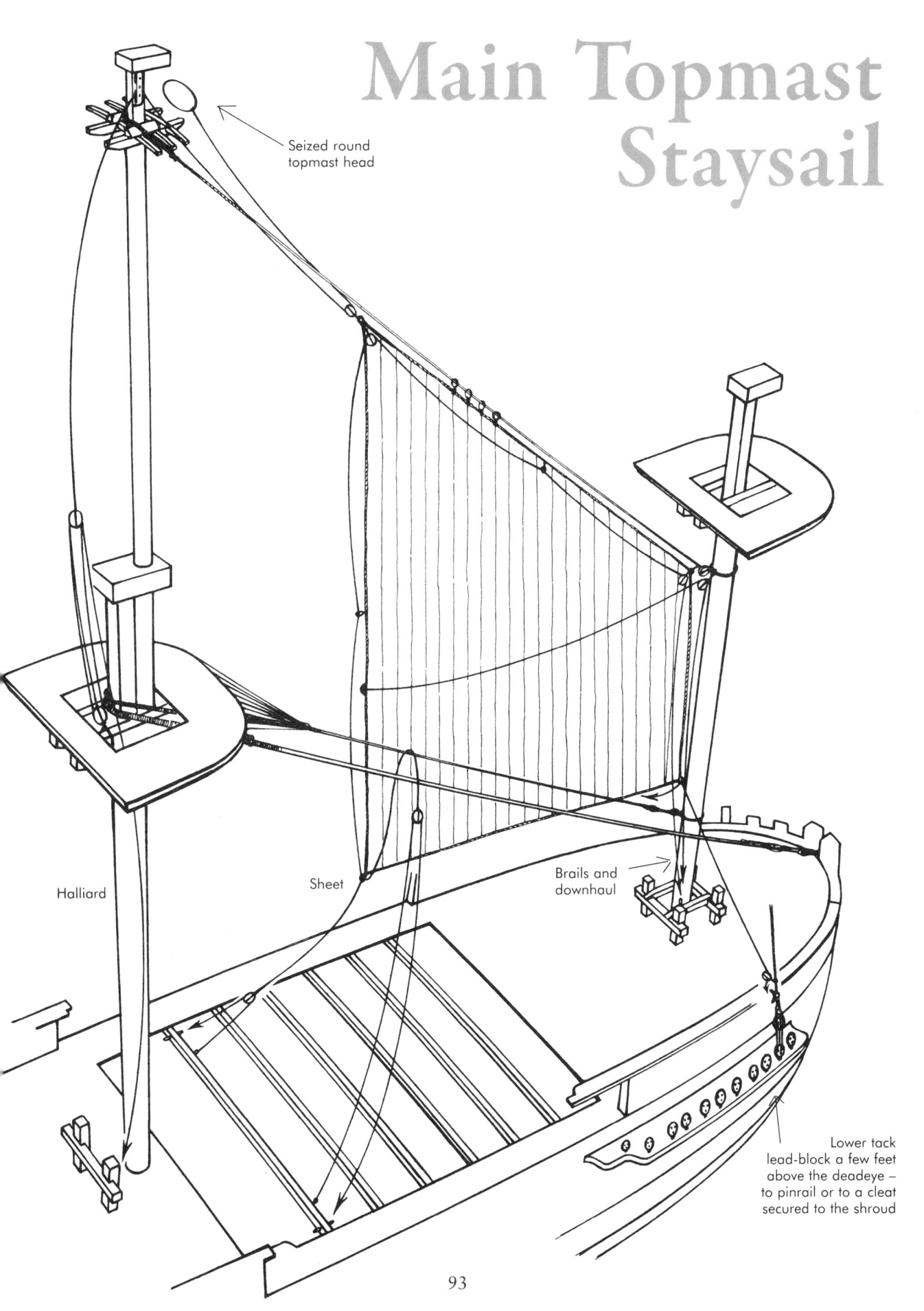

Mizzen Topmast Staysail

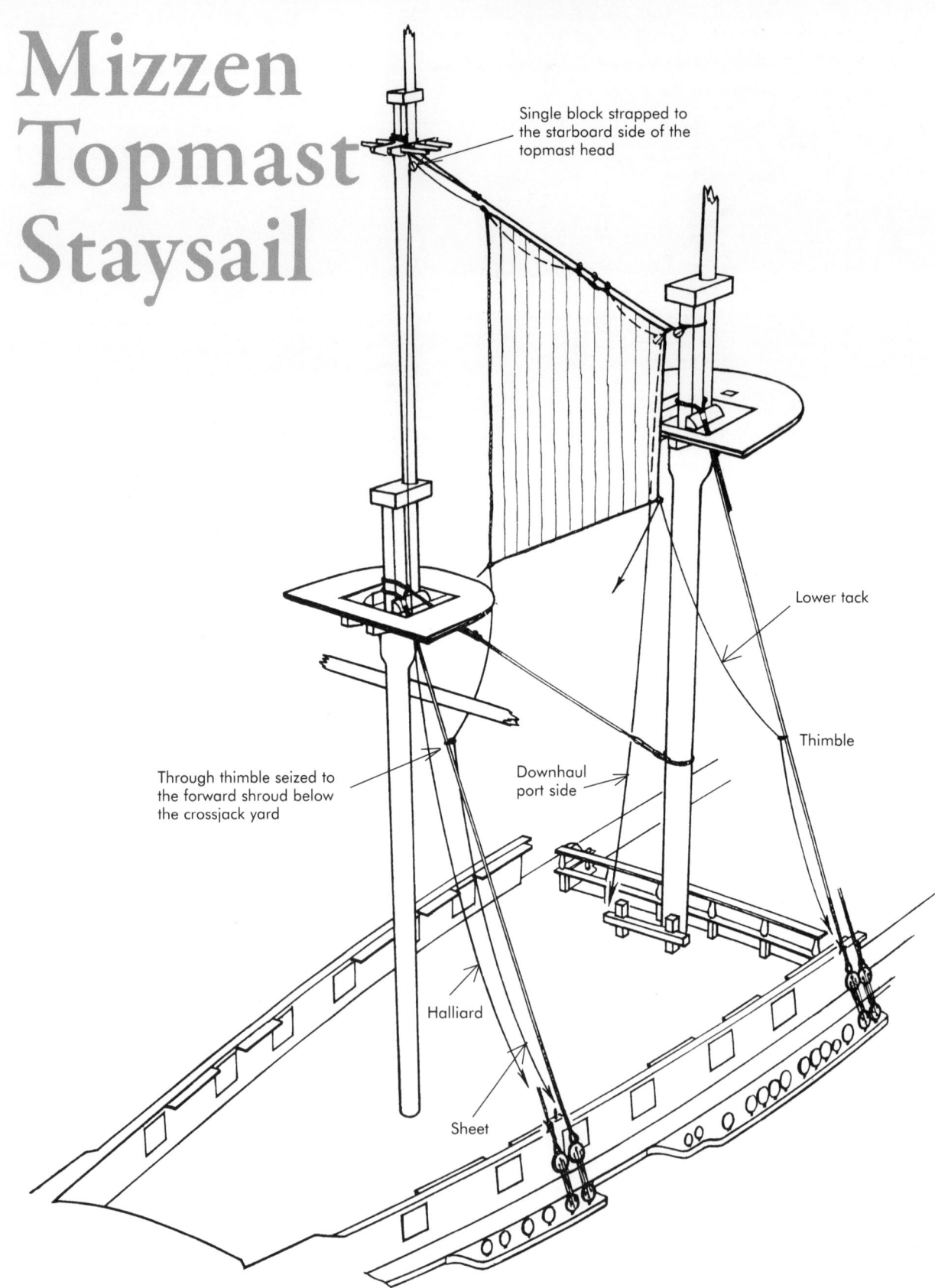

Main Topgallant Staysail

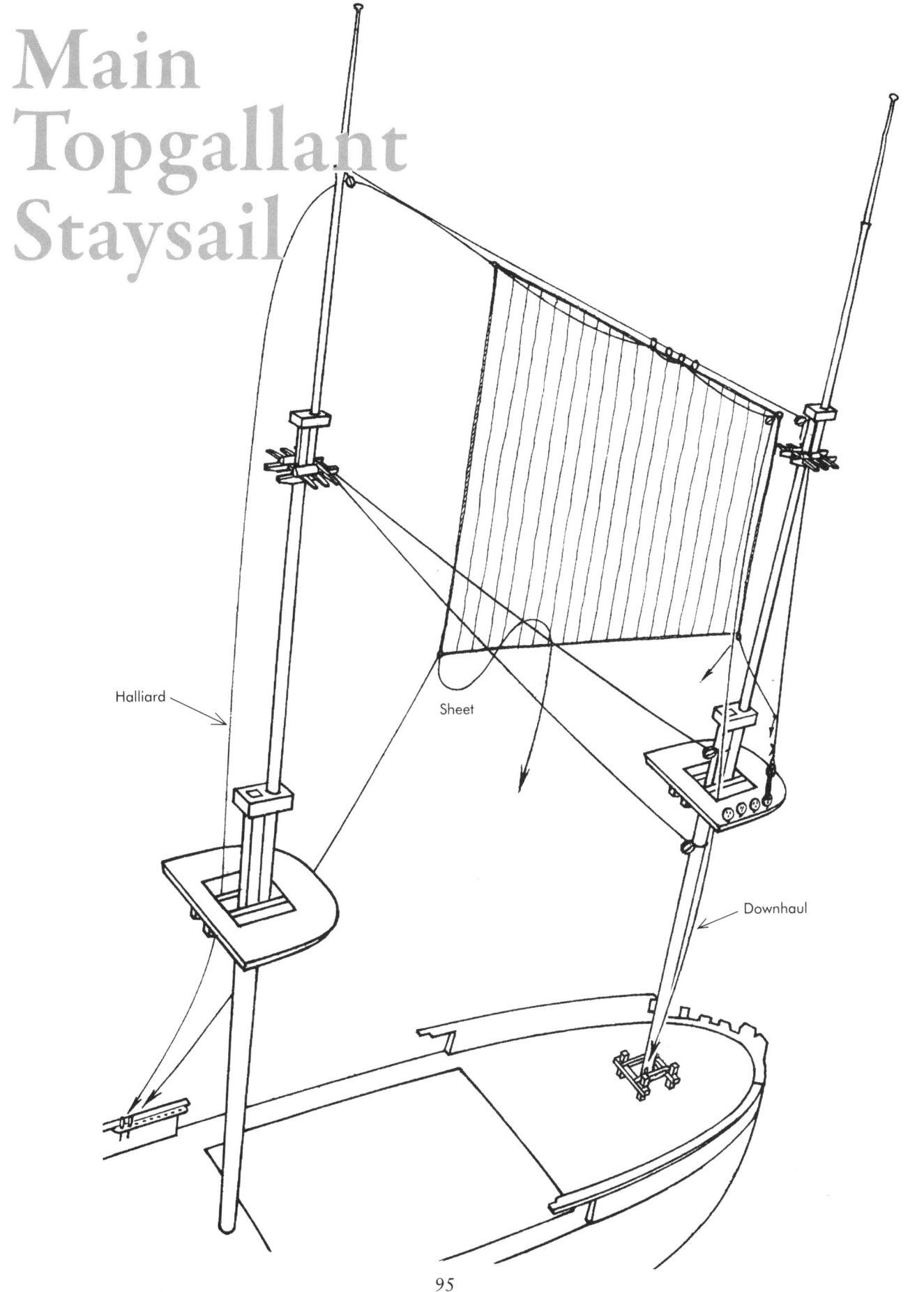

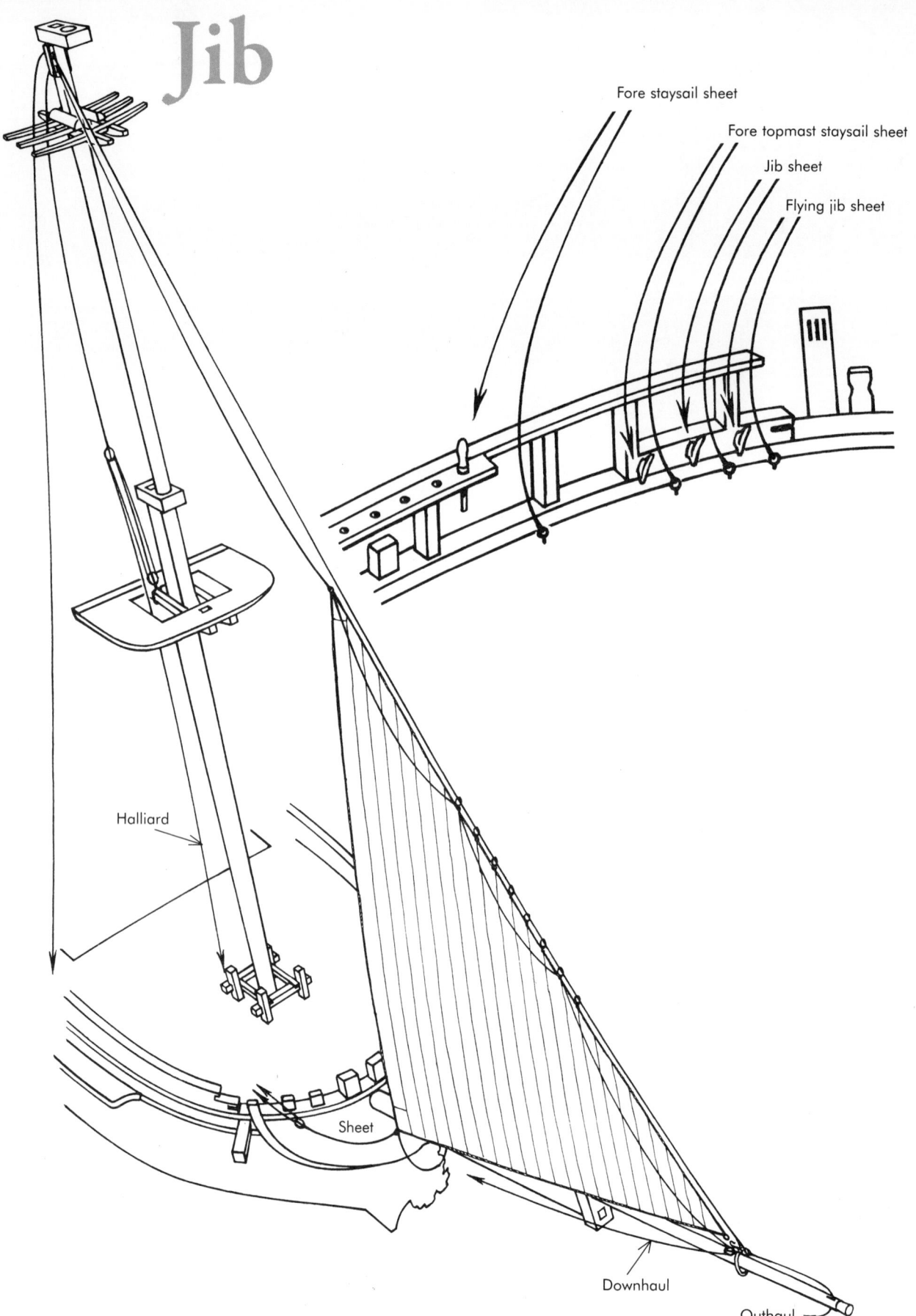

Flying Jib

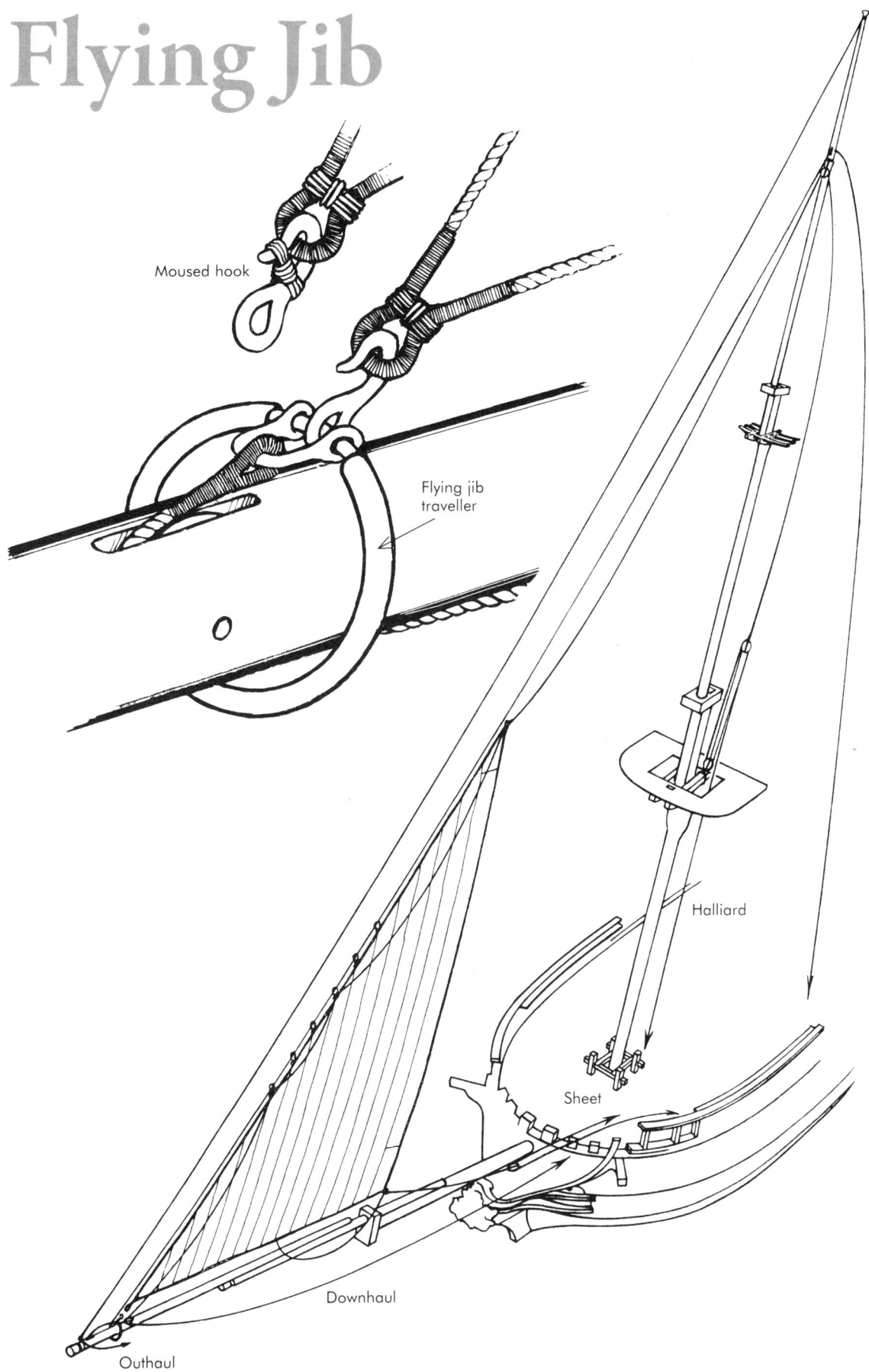

Moused hook

Flying jib traveller

Halliard

Sheet

Downhaul

Outhaul

Belaying Plan A

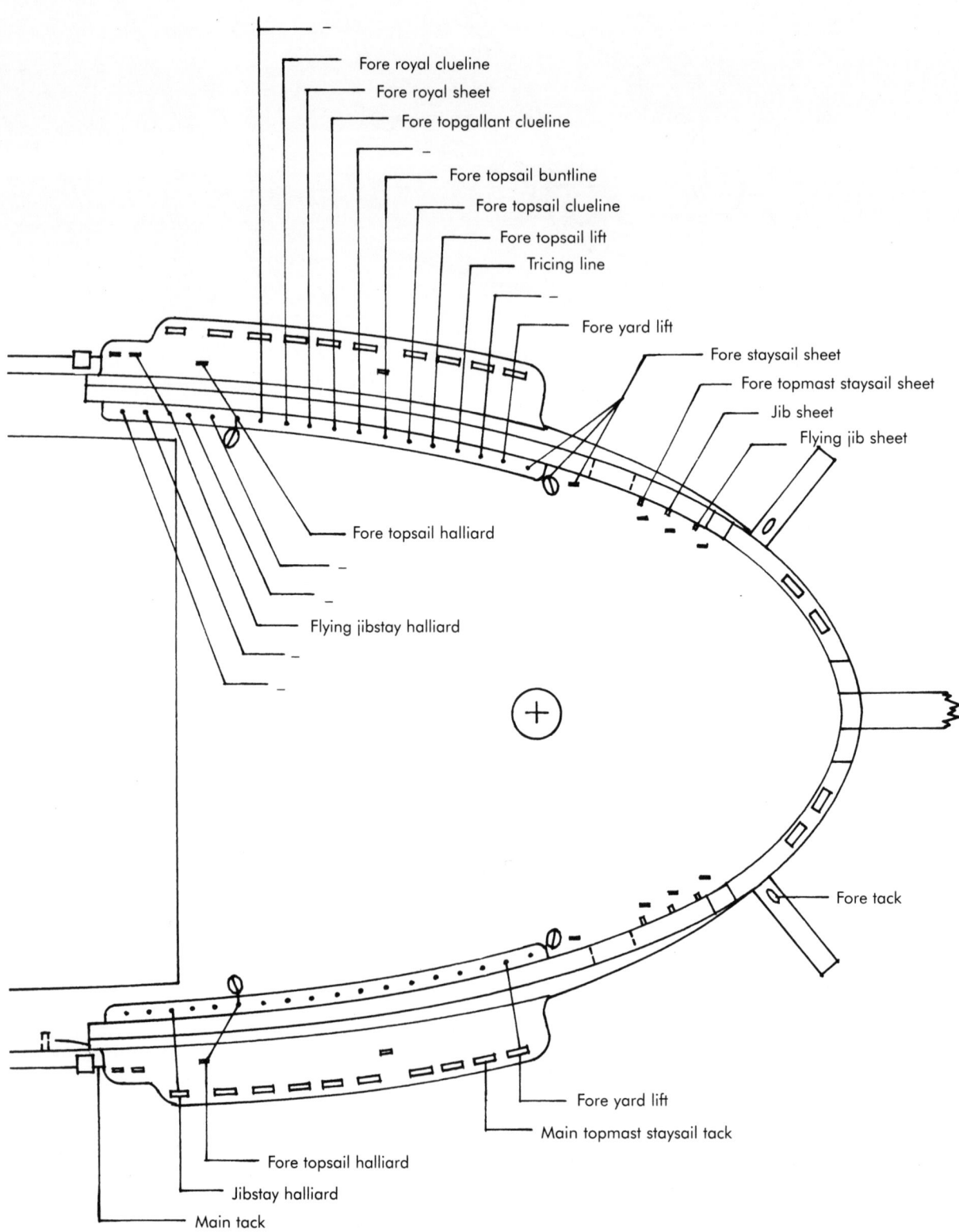

Belaying Plan B

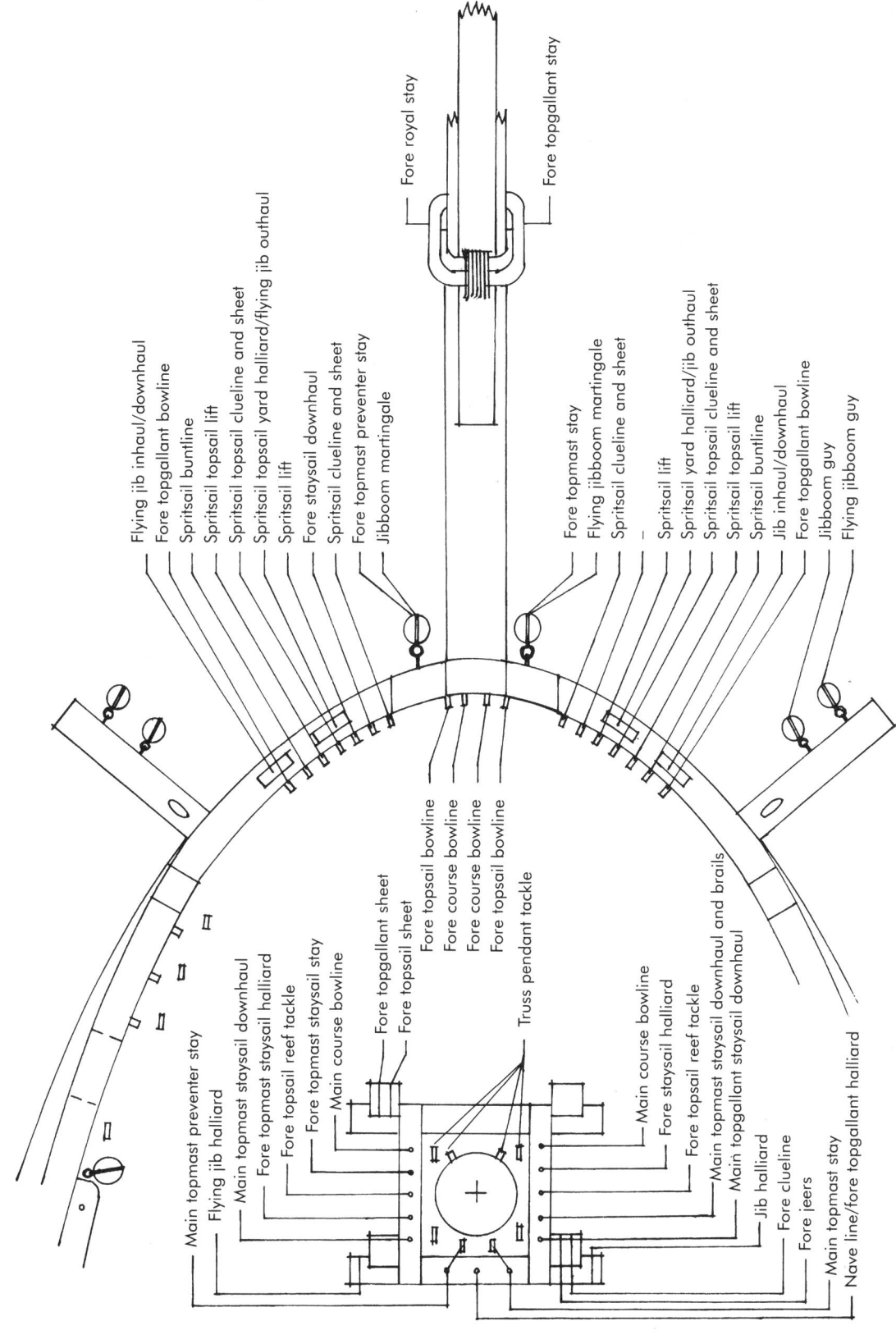

Belaying Plan C

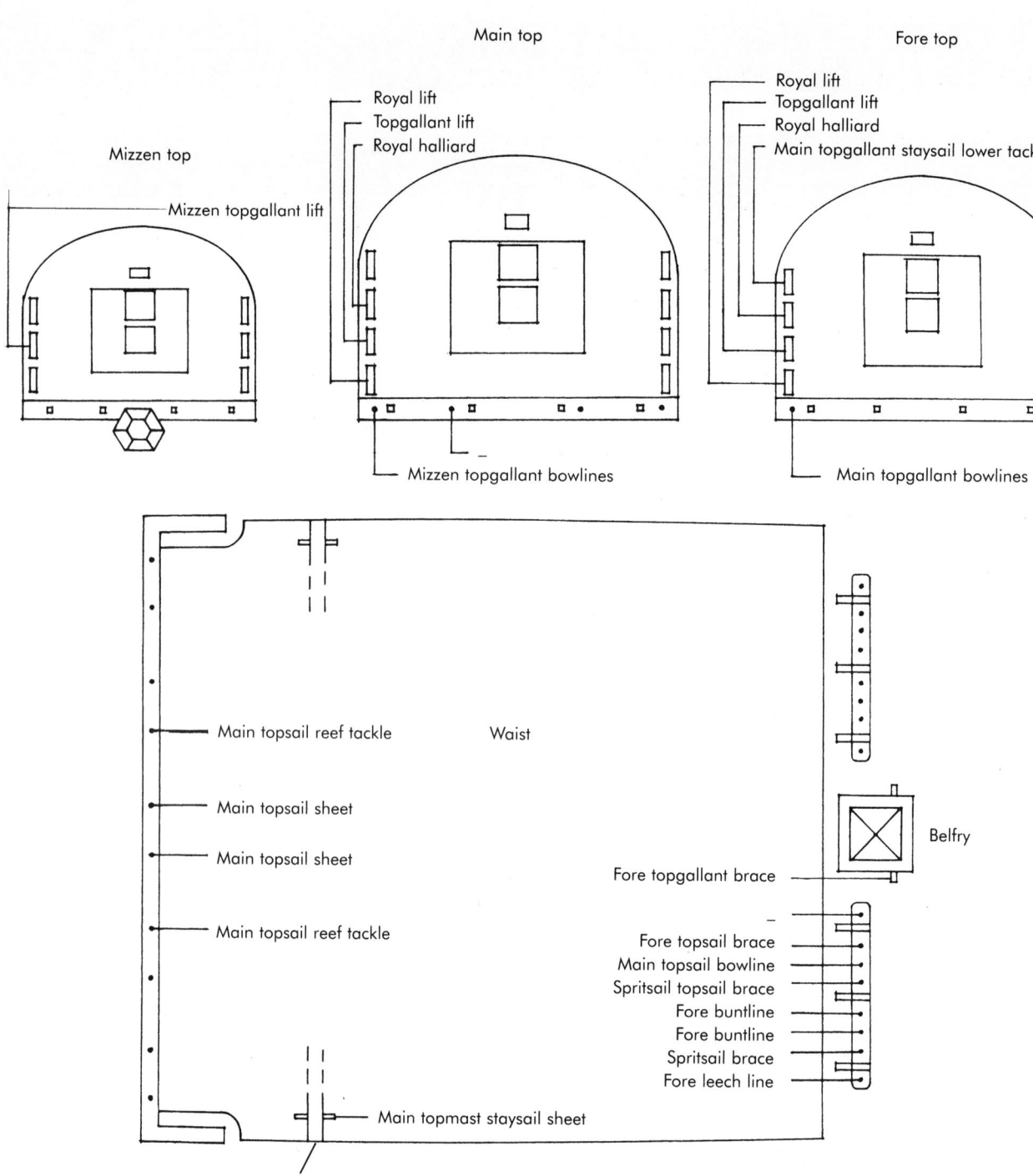

Belaying Plan D

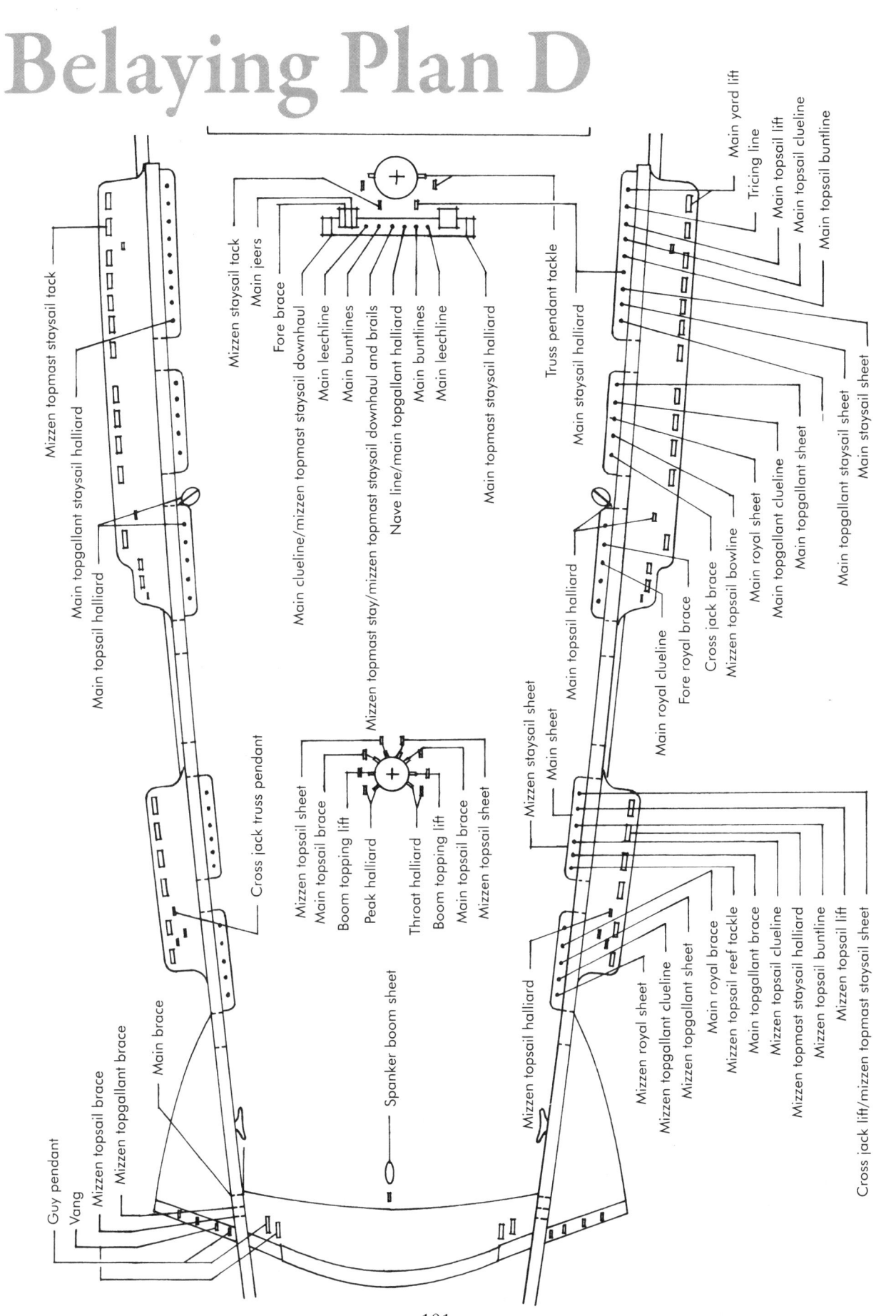

Cross-section

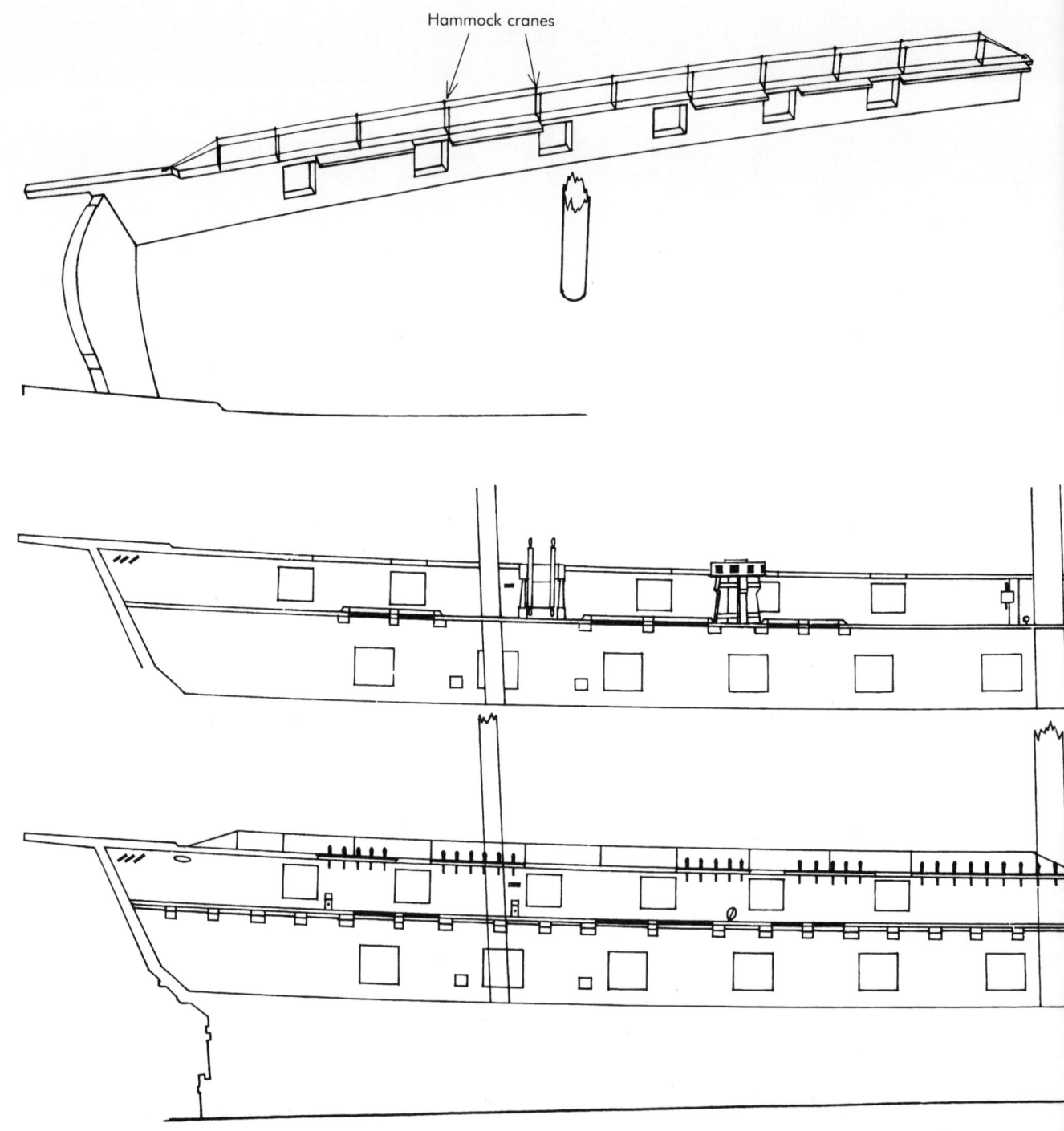

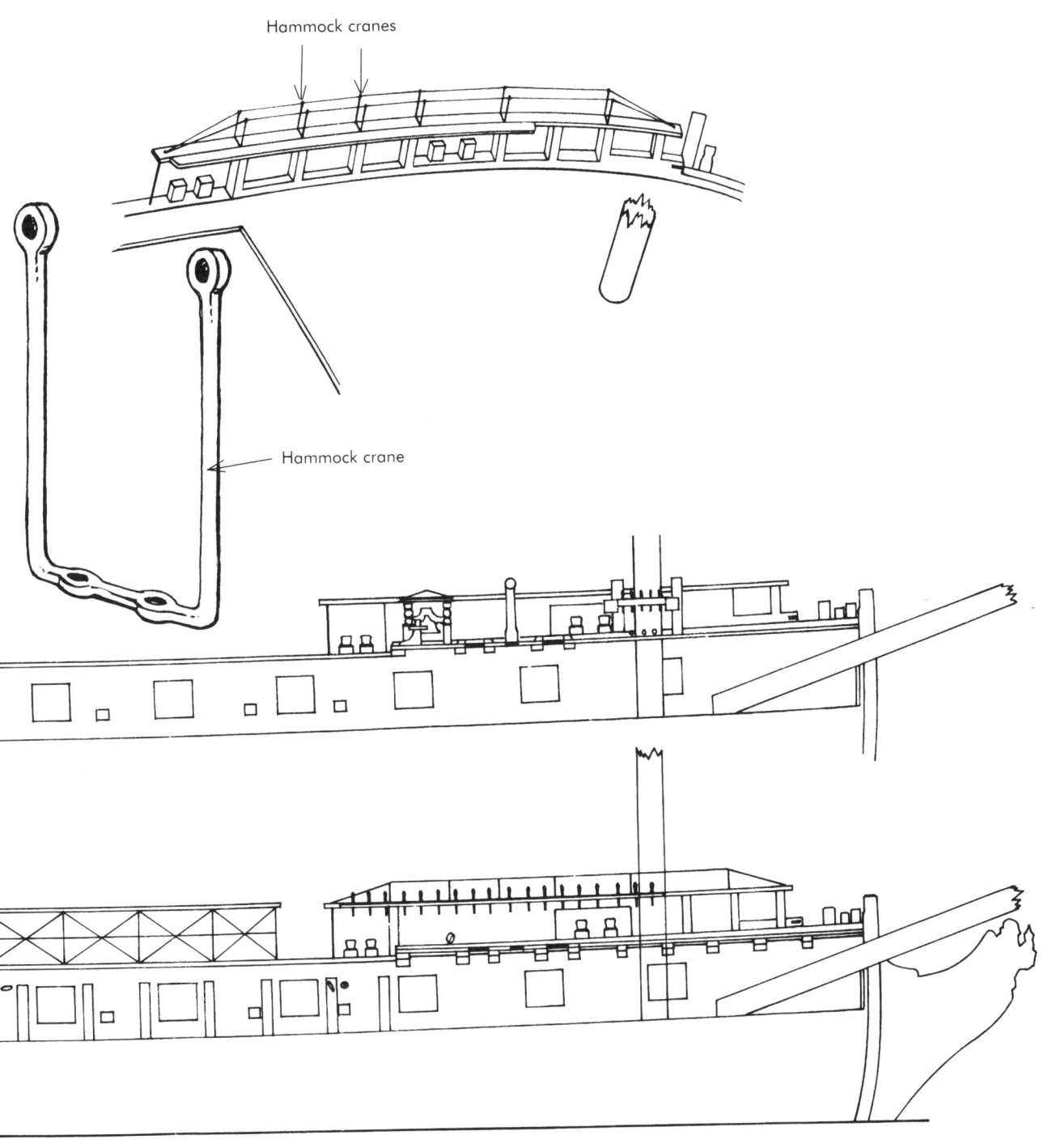

External Hull

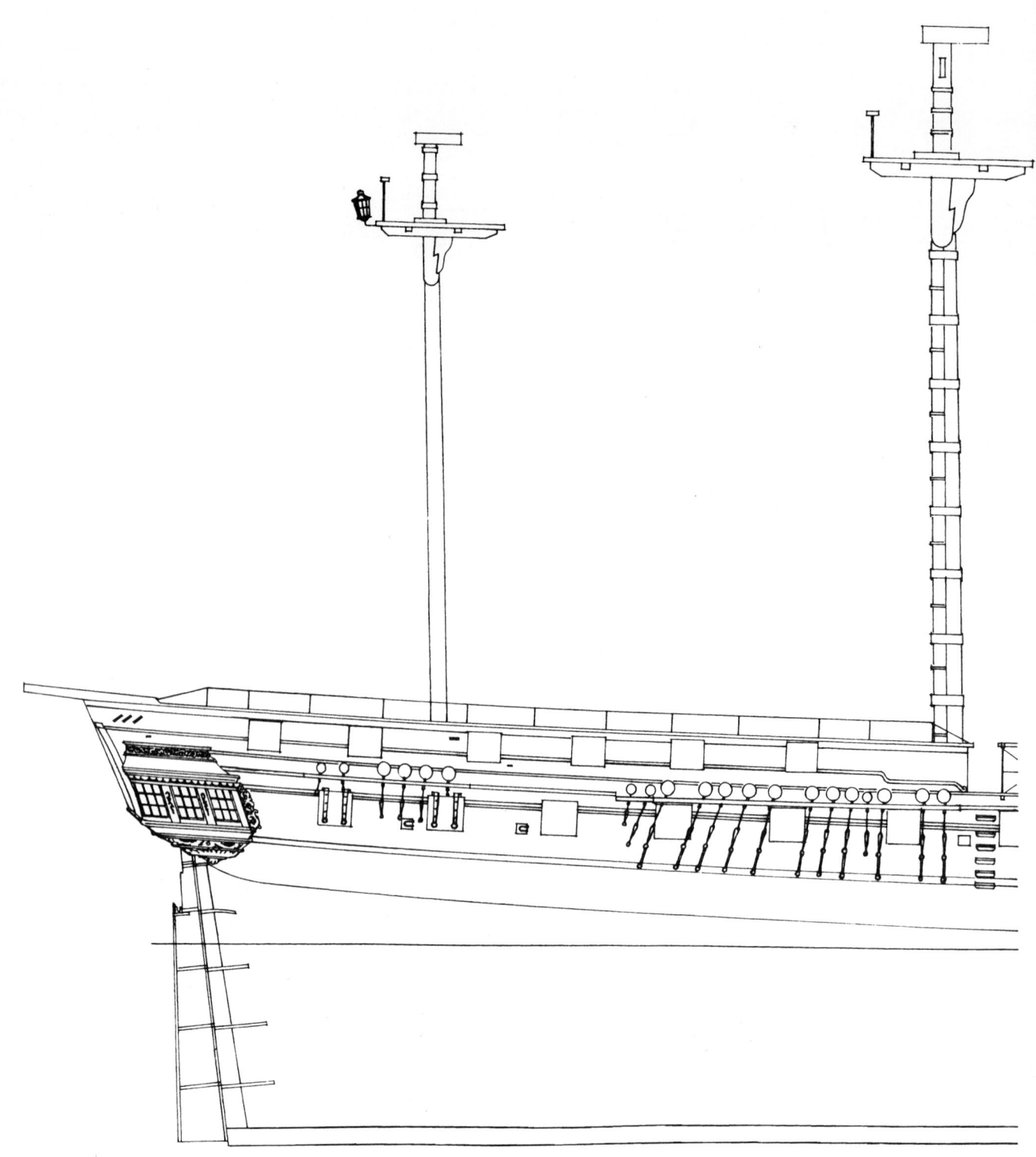

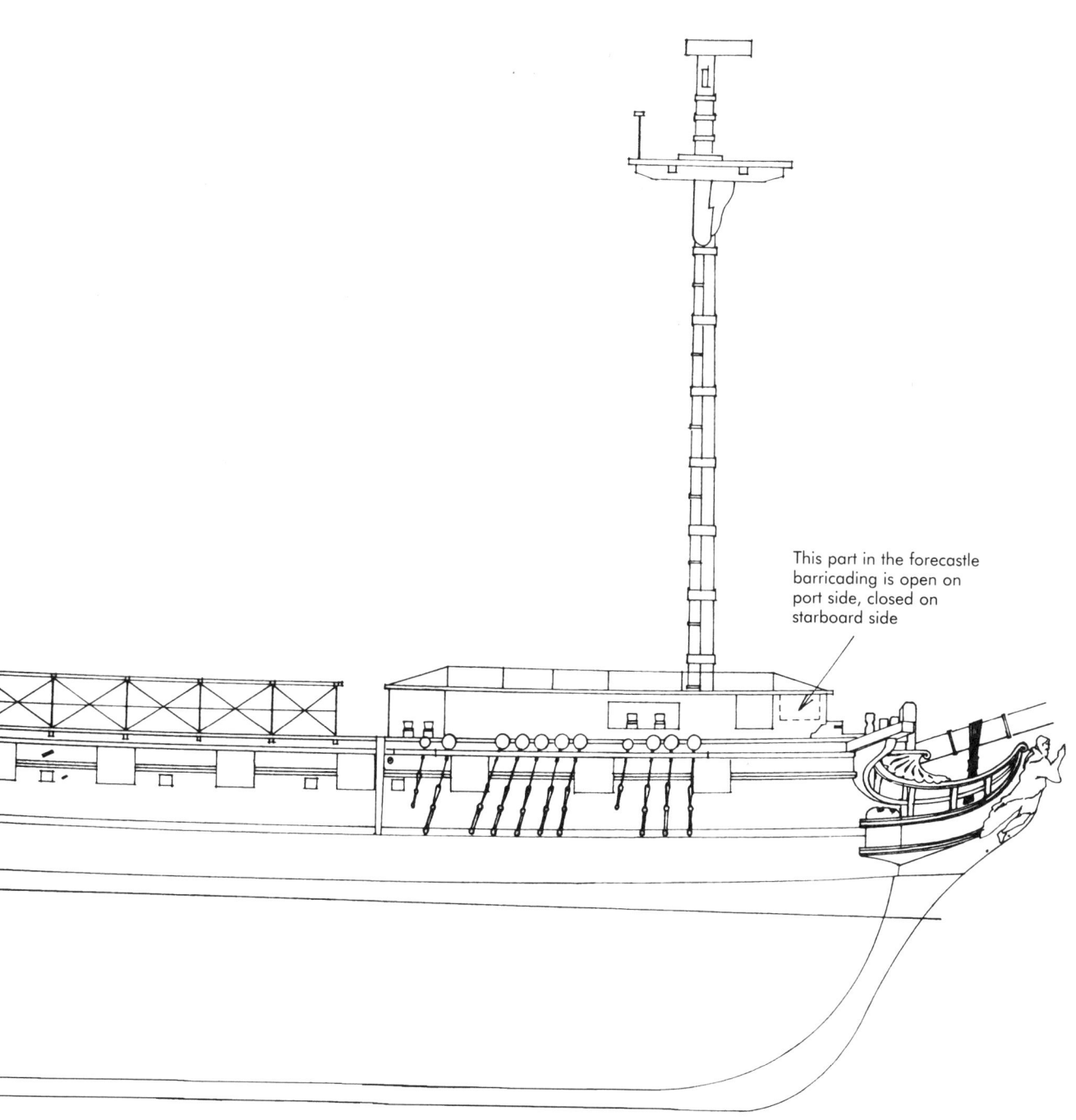

Square Sails

see studding sails page 108

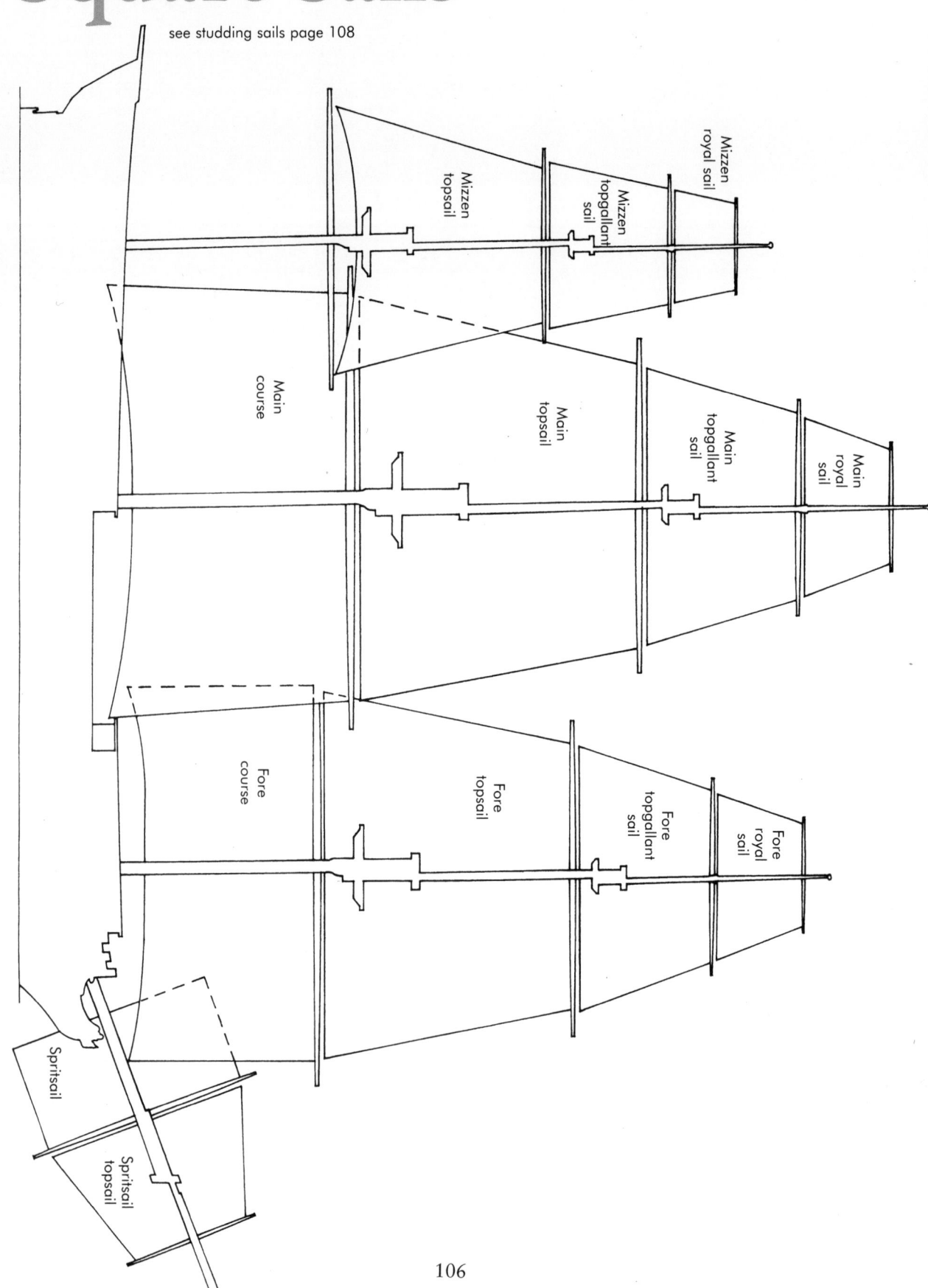

Fore and aft Sails

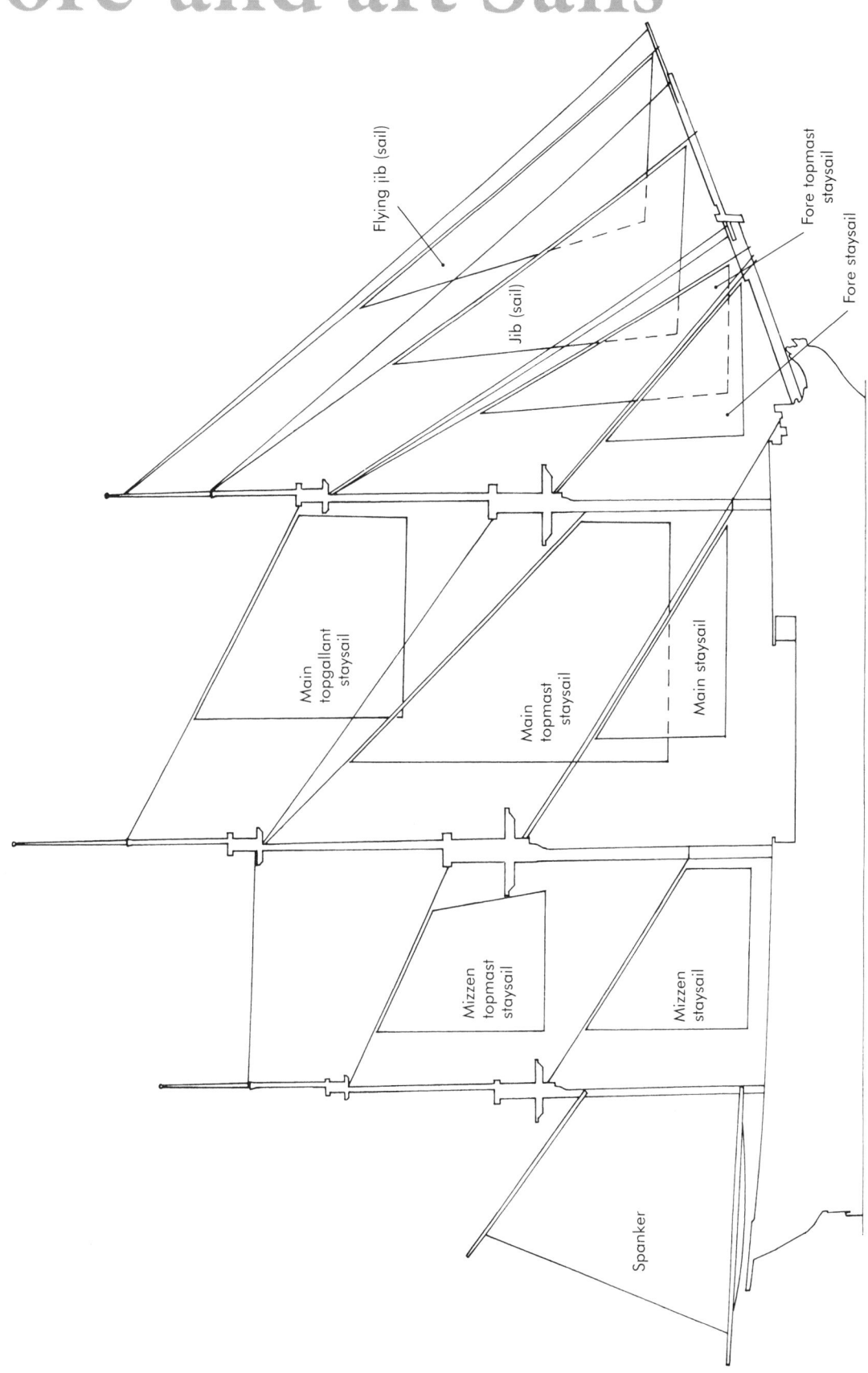

Studding Sails

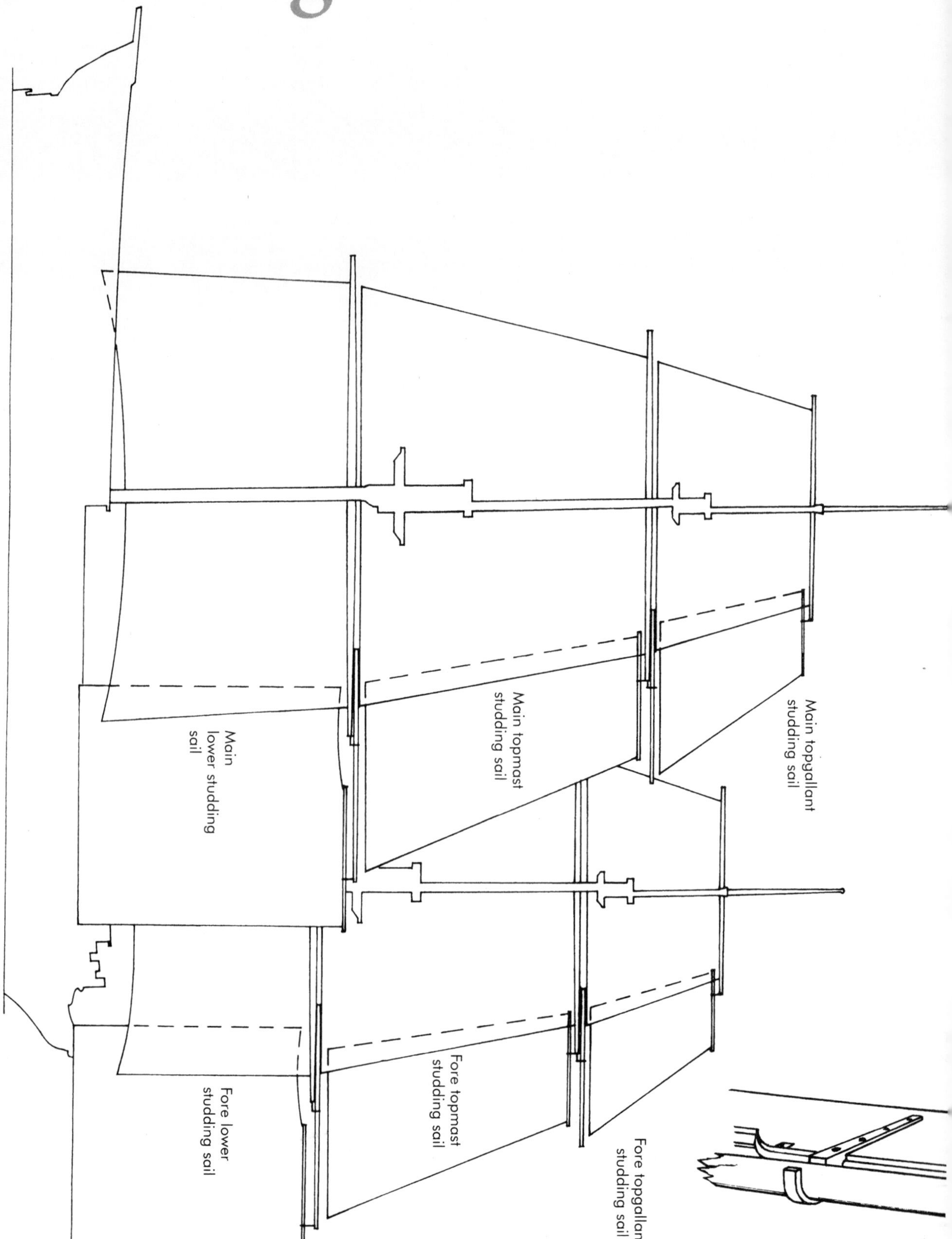

Main topgallant studding sail

Main topmast studding sail

Main lower studding sail

Fore topgallant studding sail

Fore topmast studding sail

Fore lower studding sail

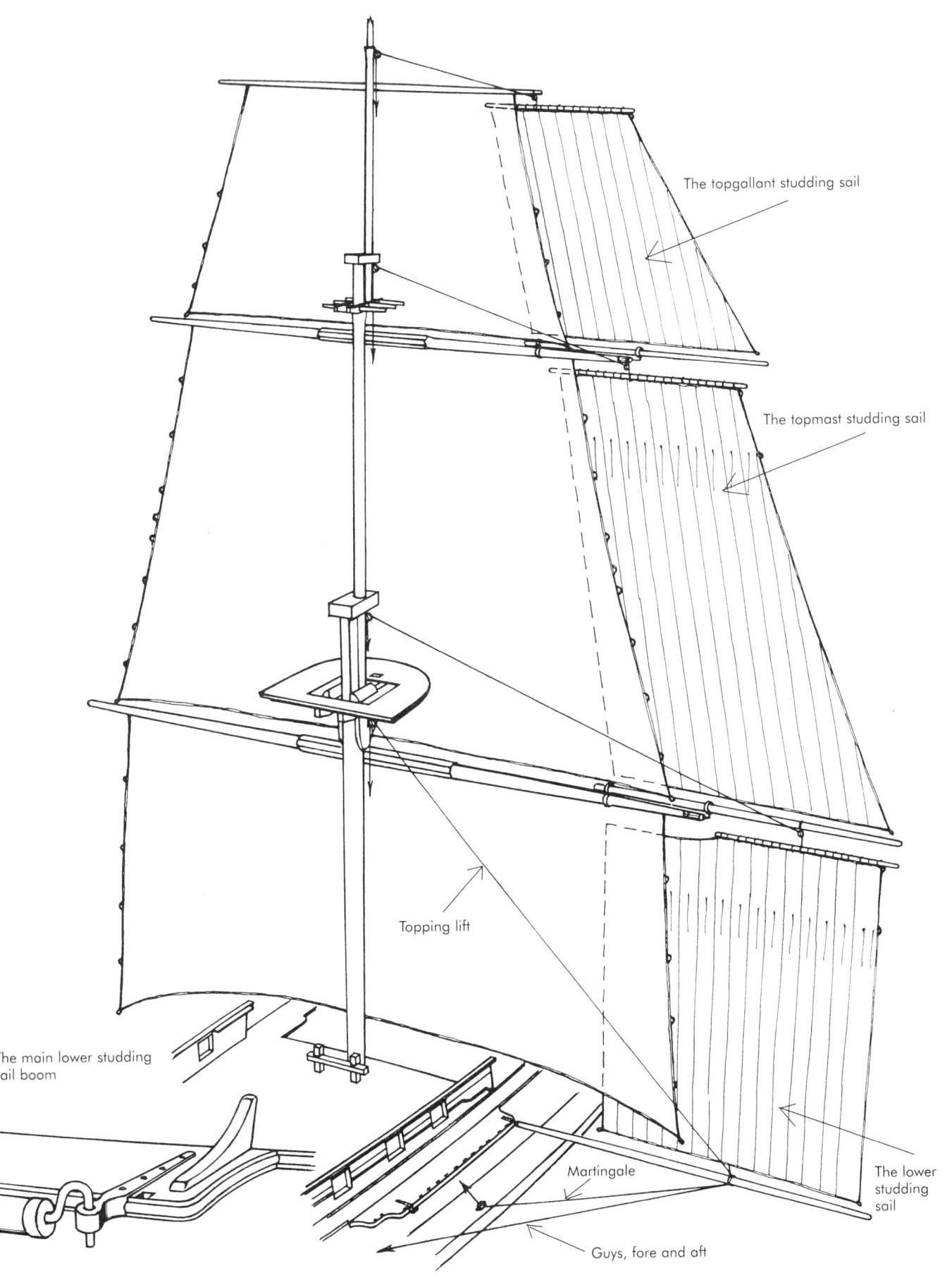

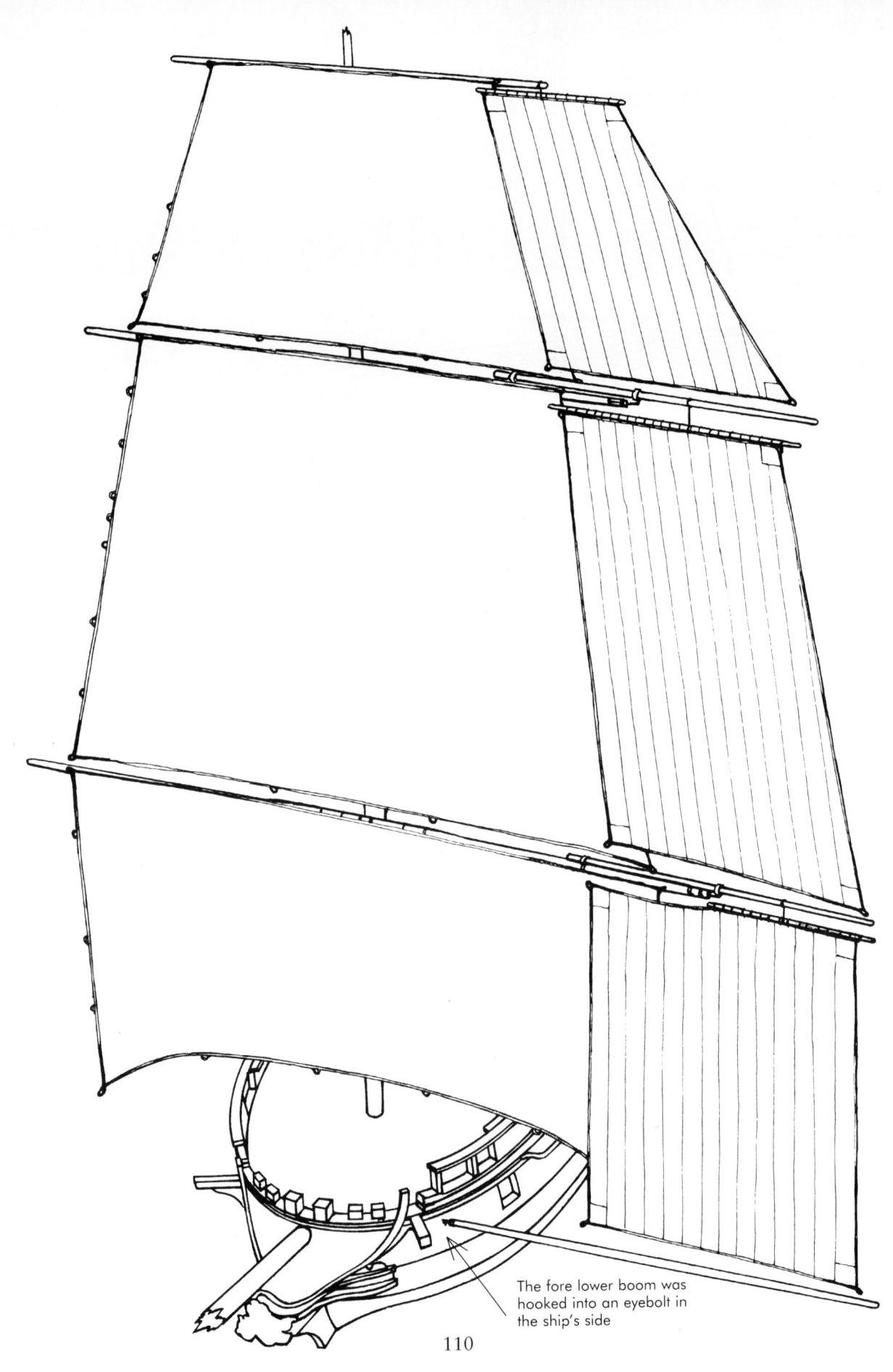
110

Quarter Deck

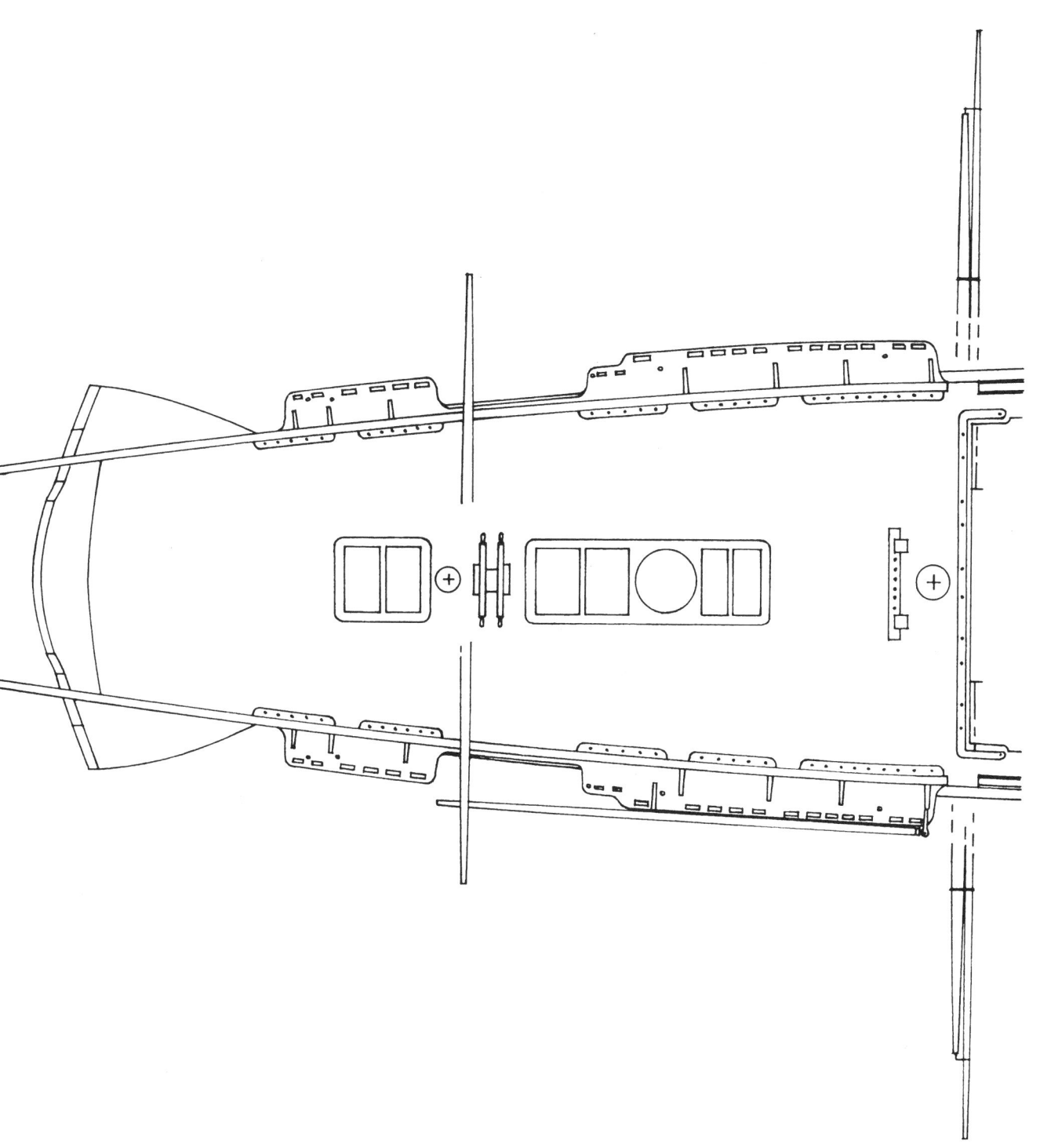

The Bow

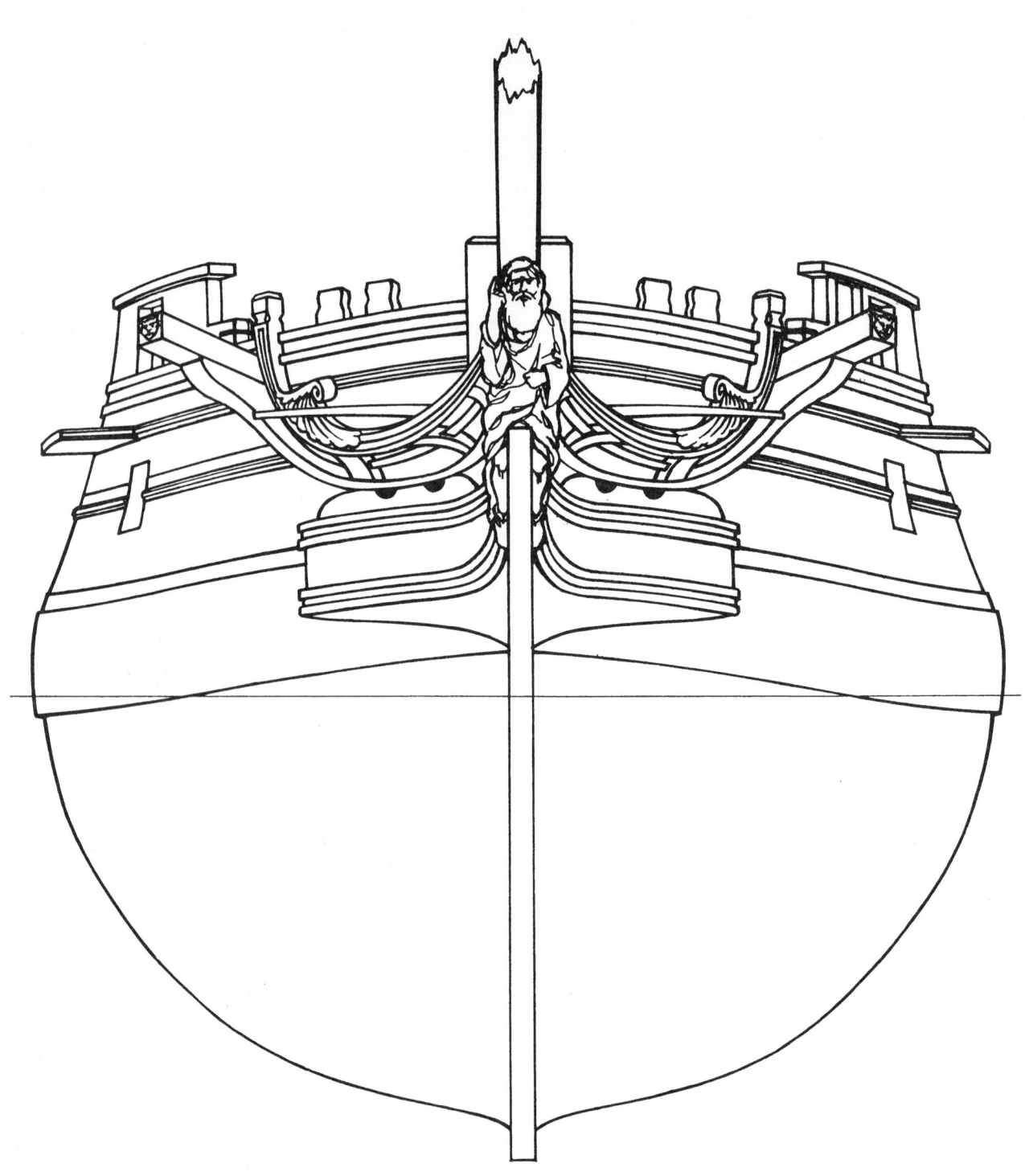

The Stern

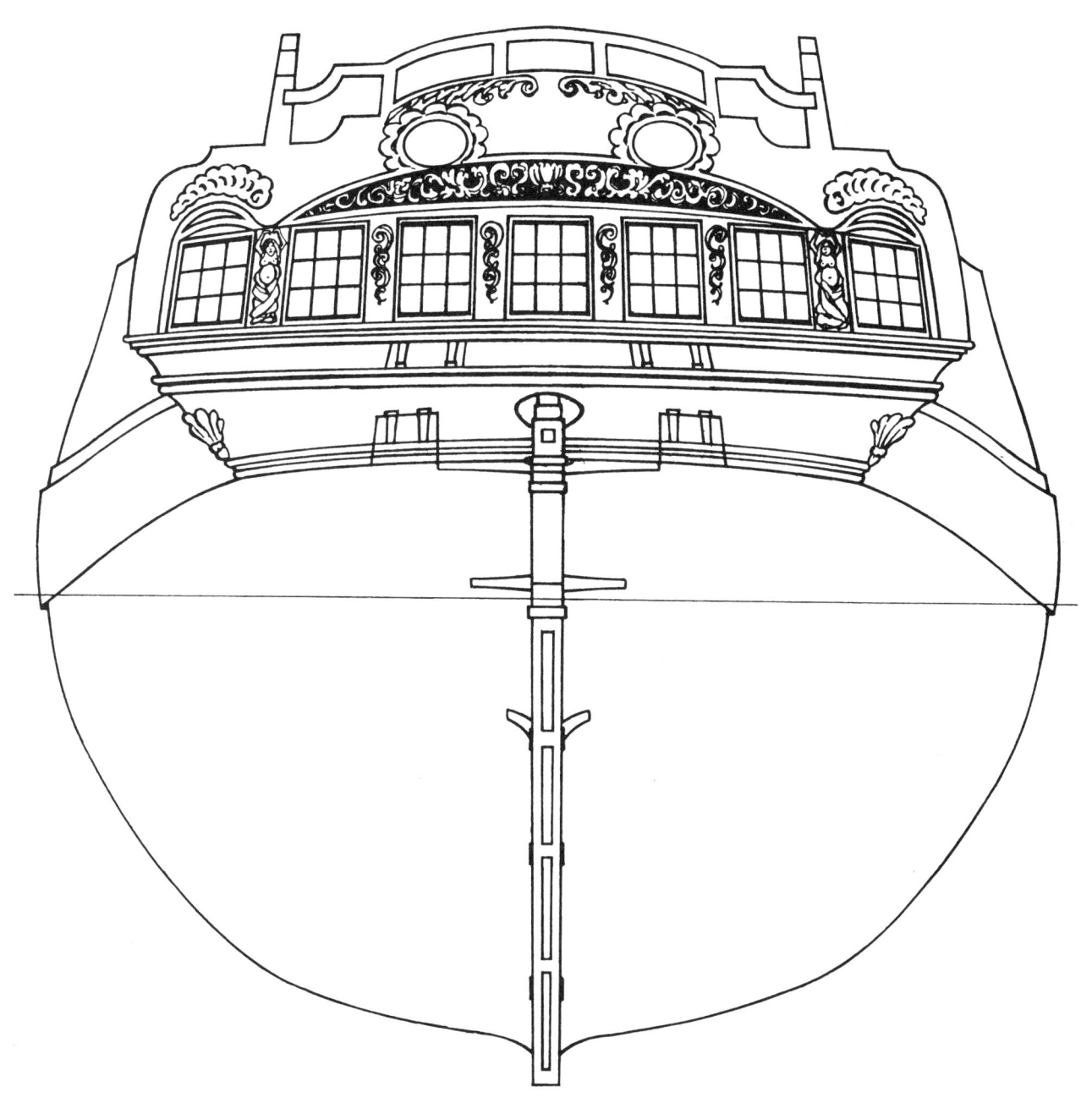

Waist & Forecastle

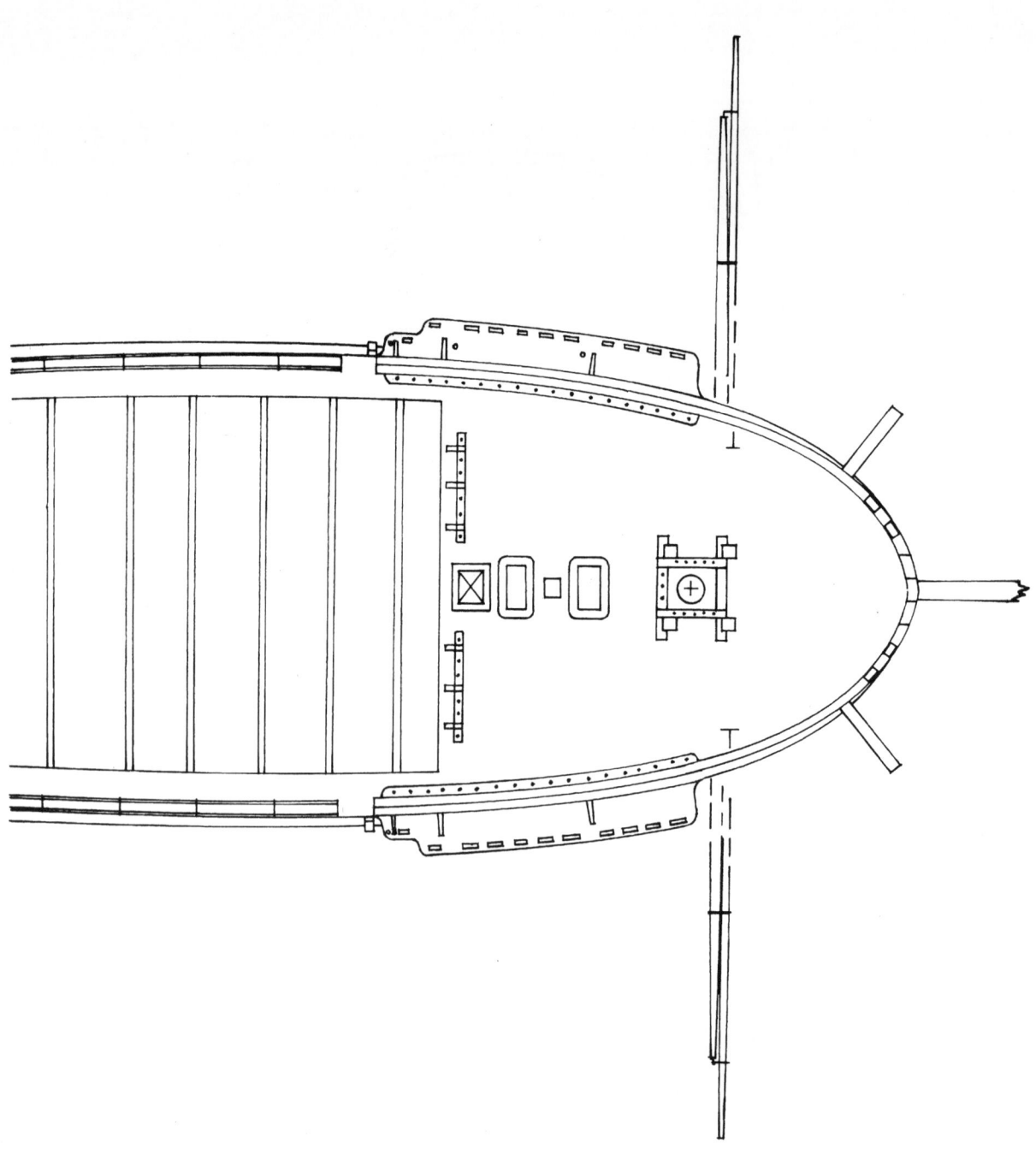

Index

	Page		Page
Backstays	8, 9, 10, 11	Cluelines, main topsail	54
Belaying points	98, 99, 100, 101	Cluelines, mizzen topgallant	57
Belfry	45	Cluelines, mizzen topsail	56
Blocks	37, 39, 43, 44, 48, 82, 83	Cluelines, spritsail	65
		Cluelines, spritsail topsail	64
Bobstay	20	Cranes, forecastle	103
Boom, spanker	25	Cranes, quarter deck	102
Boom, irons	86	Cranes, waist	44, 103
Boom, lower studding sail	108, 109, 110, 111	Crossjack yard	22, 23, 24, 85
Boom, topgallant studding sail	43, 108, 109, 110	Cross trees, fore mast	7, 10, 11
Boom, topmast studding sail	43, 108, 109, 110	Cross trees, fore topmast	11, 19, 78
Bowline bridles	76	Cross trees, main mast	13
Bowlines, fore course	75	Cross trees, main topmast	16, 17, 79
Bowlines, fore topgallant	76	Cross trees, mizzen mast	4, 8
Bowlines, fore topsail	75	Cross trees, mizzen topmast	28, 30
Bowlines, main course	77	Deadeyes	2
Bowlines, main topgallant	78	Deck, forecastle	103, 114
Bowlines, main topsail	77	Deck, quarter	102, 111
Bowlines, mizzen topgallant	79	Dolphin striker	20, 21
Bowlines, mizzen topsail	79	Downhaul, flying jib	97
Bowsprit, bees	20	Downhaul, fore staysail	87
Bowsprit, cap	20	Downhaul, fore topmast staysail	91
Bowsprit, shrouds	20	Downhaul, jib	96
Braces, crossjack	32	Downhaul, main staysail	88
Braces, fore royal	46	Downhaul, main topmast staysail	93
Braces, fore topgallant	45	Downhaul, main topgallant staysail	95
Braces, fore topsail	44	Downhaul, mizzen staysail	89
Braces, fore yard	44	Downhaul, mizzen topmast staysail	94
Braces, main royal	46	End seizing	2
Braces, main topgallant	45	Eye bolts	17, 36
Braces, main topsail	43	Eye seizing	2
Braces, mizzen topgallant	33	Eye splice	18, 85
Braces, mizzen topsail	33	Figurehead	112
Braces, spritsail topsail	47	Fittings of main yard	85, 86
Braces, spritsail yard	47	Flemish horses	85
Brails, spanker	81	Flying jibboom	21, 47, 63
Bumpkin shrouds	48, 61	Flying jibboom, guys	58
Buntlines, fore course	70	Flying jibboom, horses	60
Buntlines, fore topsail	71	Flying jibboom, purchase	59
Buntlines, main course	72	Flying jibboom, stay	19
Buntlines, main topsail	73	Flying jibboom, traveller	97
Buntlines, mizzen topsail	74	Forecastle deck	103, 114
Buntlines, spritsail	69	Fore course rigging	48, 70, 75, 83
Burton pendants	5, 6, 11, 13	Fore lower mast	5, 7, 15
Catharpins	7	Foremast crosstrees	7, 11, 18, 19
Channels, fore	2	Foremast trestletrees	7, 11, 18, 19
Channels, main	3	Foremast preventer stay	15
Channels, mizzen	4	Fore royal mast	19
Cleat, shroud	31, 42, 94	Fore royal stay	19
Cluelines, fore topgallant	50	Fore stay	15
Cluelines, fore topsail	49	Fore topgallant mast	17, 19
Cluelines, main topgallant	55	Fore topgallant stay	19

	Page		Page
Fore topgallant yard	50, 85	Jib traveller	21
Fore topmast	7, 11	Lanyards, lower deadeye	2
Fore topmast crosstrees	11, 18, 19	Lantern, stern	28, 104
Fore topmast preventer stay	18, 20	Lashing	3, 11, 15, 23
Fore topmast stay	18, 20	Leech lines, fore course	70
Fore topmast trestletrees	11, 18, 19	Leech lines, main course	72
Fore topsail yard	85	Lifts, crossjack yard	24
Fore yard	35, 36, 38, 44, 48, 49, 85	Lifts, fore topgallant yard	42
		Lifts, fore topsail yard	42
Futtock shrouds	7	Lifts, fore yard	38
Futtock staves	7	Lifts, main yard	37
Gaff, spanker	26, 27, 28, 29, 33	Lifts, main topgallant yard (same as fore topgallant yard)	42
Grommet, mast	31		
Guys, jibboom	58	Lifts, main topsail yard (same as fore topsail yard)	42
Guy pendants, spanker boom	25		
Guys, studding sails	109	Lifts, mizzen topgallant yard	31
Halliard, flying jib	97	Lifts, mizzen topsail yard	31
Halliard, jib	96	Lifts, royal yard	42
Halliard, spritsail yard	59	Lifts, spritsail topsail yard	65
Halliard, sprit topsail yard	59	Lifts, spritsail yard	64
Halliard, staysail fore	87	Lower studding sails	108, 109, 110
Halliard, staysail fore topmast	91	Main brace	43
Halliard, staysail main	88	Main jeers	35
Halliard, staysail main topmast	93	Main mast	12, 13, 14
Halliard, staysail main topgallant	95	Main preventer stay	14
Halliard, staysail mizzen	89	Main royal mast	9, 12
Halliard, staysail mizzen topmast	94	Main royal stay	12, 17
Hammock cranes	44, 102, 103	Main sheet	51
Hawse holes	112	Main stay	12, 14
Hearts	14, 15	Main top	34, 35, 43, 44, 52, 100
Horse, boom	26	Main topgallant mast	12, 17
Horse, crossjack	85	Main topgallant stay	12, 17
Horse, flemish	85	Main topgallant yard	45, 55, 82, 85,
Horse, flying jibboom	60	Main topmast preventer stay	12, 17
Horse, fore topgallant	85	Main topsail yard	39, 43, 52, 53, 54, 67, 85
Horse, fore topsail	85		
Horse, fore yard	85	Main yard	43, 51, 52, 84, 85,
Horse, main topgallant	85	Martingales	21, 109
Horse, main topsail	85	Middle seizing	2
Horse, main yard	85	Mizzen mast	4, 6, 8
Horse, mizzen topgallant	85	Mizzen mast, crosstrees	4, 13
Horse, mizzen topsail	85	Mizzen mast, top	23, 24, 26, 27, 43
Horse, spritsail topsail	85	Mizzen mast, trestle trees	4, 13
Horse, spritsail yard	85	Mizzen royal mast	8, 12
Inner martingale	21	Mizzen topgallant mast	8, 12
Inner tricing line, fore	98	Mizzen topgallant stay	12, 16
Jaws, spanker boom	81	Mizzen topgallant yard	85
Jaws, spanker gaff	29	Mizzen topmast crosstrees	30
Jeer blocks, fore yard	35	Mizzen topmast stay	12, 16
Jeer blocks, main yard	35	Mizzen topmast trestle trees	30
Jibboom guys	58	Mizzen topmast yard	30, 37, 56, 85
Jibstay	19, 21	Nave line, fore	36

	Page		Page
Nave line, main	36	Spritsail, yard	85
Open hearts	15	Spritsail topsail, braces	47
Outer martingale	21	Spritsail topsail, cluelines	64
Outer tricing line	84	Spritsail topsail, halliard	59
Outhauler, flying jib	63, 97	Spritsail topsail, lifts	65
Outhauler, jib	62, 96	Spritsail topsail, yard	65, 85
Parcelling	15	Staves, futtock	7
Parral	40	Stay, jib	12, 19, 21
Peak, spanker gaff	27, 28	Stays, overall view	12
Peak halliard	28	Staysails	107
Pendants, burton	5, 6, 11, 13	Stern	113
Quarter deck	102, 111	Stirrups	85, 86
Ratlines	3	Studding sail boom irons	86
Reef tackle purchase, fore topsail	66	Studding sail booms	108, 109, 110, 111, 114
Reef tackle purchase, main topsail	67		
Reef tackle purchase, mizzen topsail	68	Studding sail yards	108, 109, 110
Ringbolts	17, 36	Tack, fore course	48
Royal backstays	8, 9, 10	Tack, main course	51
Royal stay, fore	12, 19, 60	Throat halliard, spanker gaff	29
Royal stay, main	12, 17	Topgallant mast, mizzen	8, 16
Saddle, bowsprit	20, 59, 61	Topgallant mast, shrouds	11
Serving	15	Topgallant mast, stays	12, 16, 17, 19
Sheet blocks, spanker	25	Topmast, backstays	8, 9, 11
Sheets, fore course	48	Topmast, shrouds	7, 11
Sheets, fore topgallant	50	Topmast, stays	12, 16, 17, 18, 20
Sheets, fore topsail	49	Topping lift, spanker boom	26
Sheets, fore royal	50	Topsail sheet, fore	49
Sheets, main course	51	Topsail sheet, main	52
Sheets, main topgallant	55	Topsail sheet, mizzen	56
Sheets, main topsail	52	Traveller, flying jib	97
Sheets, main royal	55	Traveller, jib	21
Sheets, mizzen topgallant	57	Tricing line	84
Sheets, mizzen topsail	56	Trestle trees, fore topmast	19, 78
Sheets, mizzen royal	57	Truss pendants, crossjack	22
Sheets, spritsail	65	Truss pendants, fore yard	36
Sheets, spritsail topsail	64	Tye, fore topgallant	41
Shroud cleats	31, 42, 94	Tye, fore topsail	40
Shrouds, bowsprit	20	Tye, fore royal	41
Shrouds, bumpkin	61	Tye, main topgallant	41
Shrouds, futtock	7	Tye, main topsail	39
Shrouds, lower	2, 3, 4, 5, 6, 7, 10	Tye, main royal	41
Shrouds, topgallant	11	Tye, mizzen topgallant	30
Shrouds, topmast	7, 11	Tye, mizzen topsail	30
Slings	20, 23, 34, 59	Tye, mizzen royal	30
Spars	85, 86	Vangs	27
Spritsail, braces	47	Waist	103, 114
Spritsail, buntlines	69	Windows, quarter gallery	6
Spritsail, cluelines	65	Windows, stern	113
Spritsail, halliard	59	Worming	15
Spritsail, sheets	65	Yards	85, 86